PROFILES

AMERICAN HISTORY

Significant Events and the People

Who Shaped Them

PROFILES IN
AMERICAN HISTORY

Exploration to Revolution

c. 30,000 B.C.
▼
Asians cross Bering Strait to North America.

c. 1000
▼
Leif Eriksson lands in North America.

1492
▼
Christopher Columbus sails to "the Indies" for Spain.

1585
▼
Walter Raleigh founds Roanoke Colony for England.

1622-1675
▼
Indians try to dislodge colonists in Powhatan's War, the Pequot War, and King Philip's War.

1692-1695
▼
Twenty "witches" are executed during the Salem Witch Trials.

1755-1763
▼
The French and Indian War fought between the English and the French and their Indian allies.

1775-1781
▼
The Revolutionary War fought between the English and the colonists.

1776
▼
The United States declares independence from England.

1783
▼
The Treaty of Paris officially ends the Revolutionary War.

$\mathscr{P}$ROFILES IN AMERICAN HISTORY

Significant Events and the People

Who Shaped Them

Exploration to Revolution

JOYCE MOSS

and

GEORGE WILSON

29.95

AN IMPRINT OF GALE RESEARCH INC.

PROFILES IN AMERICAN HISTORY:
Significant Events and the People Who Shaped Them

VOLUME 1: EXPLORATION TO REVOLUTION

Joyce Moss and George Wilson

Staff

Carol DeKane Nagel, *U•X•L Developmental Editor*
Thomas L. Romig, *U•X•L Publisher*

Christine Nasso, *Acquisitions Editor*

Shanna P. Heilveil, *Production Assistant*
Evi Seoud, *Assistant Production Manager*
Mary Beth Trimper, *Production Director*

Mary Krzewinski, *Cover and Page Designer*
Cynthia Baldwin, *Art Director*
Arthur Chartow, *Technical Design Services Manager*
Barbara J. Yarrow, *Graphic Services Supervisor*

The Graphix Group, *Typesetting*

∞ ™ This book is printed on acid-free paper that meets the minimum requirements of American National Standard for Information Sciences—Permanence Paper for Printed Library Materials, ANSI Z39.48-1984.

ISBN 0-8103-9207-0 (Set)
ISBN 0-8103-9208-9 (Volume 1)

Printed in the United States of America

Published simultaneously in the United Kingdom
by Gale Research International Limited
(An affiliated company of Gale Research Inc.)

I(T)P™

The trademark ITP is used under license.

Contents

Reader's Guide

The many noteworthy individuals who shaped U.S. history from the exploration of the continent to the present day cannot all be profiled in one eight-volume work. But those whose stories are told in *Profiles in American History* meet one or more of the following criteria. The individuals:

- Directly affected the outcome of a major event in U.S. history
- Represent viewpoints or groups involved in that event
- Exemplify a role played by common citizens in that event
- Highlight an aspect of that event not covered in other entries

Format

Volumes of *Profiles in American History* are arranged by chapter. Each chapter focuses on one particular event and opens with an overview and detailed time line of the event that places it in historical context. Following are biographical profiles of two to seven diverse individuals who played active roles in the event.

Each biographical profile is divided into four sections:

- **Personal Background** provides details that predate and anticipate the individual's involvement in the event
- **Participation** describes the role played by the individual in the event and its impact on his or her life
- **Aftermath** discusses effects of the individual's actions and subsequent relevant events in his or her life
- **For More Information** provides sources for further reading on the individual

Additionally, sidebars containing interesting details about the events and individuals profiled, ranging from numbers of war casualties to famous quotes to family trees, are sprinkled throughout the text.

Additional Features

Maps are provided to assist readers in traveling back through time to an America arranged differently from today. Portraits and illustrations of individuals and events as well as excerpts from primary source materials are also included to help bring history to life. Sources of all quoted material are cited parenthetically within the text, and complete bibliographic information is listed at the end of the entry. A full bibliography of scholarly sources consulted in preparing the volume appear in the book's back matter.

Cross references are made in the entries, directing readers to other entries in the volume that elaborate on individuals connected in some way to the person under scrutiny. In addition, a comprehensive subject index provides easy access to people and events mentioned throughout the volume.

Comments and Suggestions

We welcome your comments on this work as well as your suggestions for individuals to be featured in future editions of *Profiles in American History*. Please write: Editors, *Profiles in American History,* U·X·L, 835 Penobscot Bldg., Detroit, Michigan 48226-4094; or call toll-free: 1-800-877-4253.

Preface

"There is properly no History; only Biography," wrote great American poet and scholar Ralph Waldo Emerson. *Profiles in American History* explores U.S. history through biography. Beginning with the first contact between Native Americans and the Vikings and continuing to the present day, this series offers a unique alternative to traditional texts by emphasizing the roles played by significant individuals, including many women and minorities, in historical events.

Profiles in American History presents the human story of American events, not the exclusively European or African or Indian or Asian story. But the guiding principle in compiling this series has been to achieve balance not only in gender and ethnic background but in viewpoint. Thus the circumstances surrounding an historical event are told from individuals holding opposing views, and even opposing positions. Slaves and slaveowners, business tycoons and workers, advocates of peace and proponents of war all are heard. American authors whose works reflect the times—from Thomas Paine to John Steinbeck—are also featured.

The biographical profiles are arranged in groups, clustered around one major event in American history, though each individual profile is complete in itself. But it is the interplay of these profiles—the juxtaposition of alternative views and experiences within a grouping—that broadens the readers' perspective on the event as a whole and on the participants' roles in particular. It is what makes it possible for *Profiles in American History* to impart a larger, human understanding of events in American history.

Acknowledgments

For their guidance on the choice of events and personalities and for their review of selected entries, the editors are grateful to:

Jonathan Betz-Zall, Children's Librarian, Sno-Isle Regional Library System, Washington

Janet Sarratt, Library Media Specialist, John E. Ewing Junior High School, Gaffney, South Carolina

Michael Salman, Assistant Professor of American History, University of California at Los Angeles

Appreciation is extended to Professor Salman for his careful review of chapter overviews and his guidance on key sources of information about the personalities and events.

For insights into specific personalities, the editors are grateful to Robert Sumpter, History Department Chairman at Mira Costa High School, Manhatten Beach, California.

Deep appreciation is extended to the writers who compiled data and contributed the biographical profiles for this volume of *Profiles in American History:*

Diane Ahrens
Erica Heet
Dana Huebler
Lawrence K. Orr
Robert Sumpter
Colin Wells

The editors also thank artist Robert Bates for his research and rendering of maps and Carol Nagel of U·X·L at Gale Research for her careful copy editing.

Introduction

The peoples now called Native Americans inhabited North America for 36,000 years before any Europeans arrived. Over the centuries the original immigrants, probably coming from Asia across the Bering Strait, spread across the continent. Societies developed, some of them building large settlements. By 1500 A.D. there was a town in the Great Lakes region that boasted a population of 5,000. It was larger than many European villages of the time.

The next hundred years brought a rush of European explorers to the North American continent: the French to Nova Scotia, the Spanish to Florida, the English to Virginia. They came not to an empty wilderness but to a land peopled by assorted native groups with established cultures. The earliest Europeans to come were the Vikings, led by Leif Eriksson, but their settlement was only temporary. The Spanish were the first to arrive for a lasting stay. In 1565 they built St. Augustine, Florida, the oldest occupied town on the continent.

Contact Among Societies

The next two centuries saw conflict and cooperation among the groups that populated the Americas. Into the mix of native peoples came several European powers—English, Dutch, French, and Spanish—who vied for control of territory. They competed among themselves and with the Native Americans.

Christopher Columbus, believing he had reached India rather than the Americas, had mistakenly named the native peoples *Indians,* grouping them all together. They were not, however, one nation, but hundreds of nations, and they were already named, for the most part after the 2,000 different languages they spoke— Cherokee, Shawnee, and Creek, for example. Thousands of African slaves were brought to the Americas after the arrival of Columbus, and they came from a similar mix of Yoruba, Ibo, and other African peoples.

The Product of Individual Efforts

North America was teaming with the activity of all these groups during the sixteenth, seventeenth, and eighteenth centuries. They interacted in ways that reshaped their societies, and events resulted that led to the birth of the United States. Individuals played important roles in these events, as leaders and as private citizens who represented the conditions and viewpoints of the times. From Pocahontas to John Smith in the early days of colonization and from George Washington to Deborah Sampson in the Revolutionary War, people experienced the times differently. This collection of their experiences provides a mix of perspectives on events that shaped America.

Picture Credits

The photographs and illustrations appearing in *Profiles in American History: Significant Events and the People Who Shaped Them,* Volume 1: *Exploration to Revolution* were received from the following sources:

On the cover: **Courtesy of The Library of Congress:** Christopher Columbus, Pocahontas; **courtesy of The National Portrait Gallery:** Thomas Jefferson.

Courtesy of The Library of Congress: pages 4, 7, 13, 26, 30, 33, 37, 45, 49, 71, 75, 92, 109, 116, 141, 155, 179, 180, 221, 234, 237, 255, 260, 265; **National Maritime Museum, Greenwich, England:** page 53; **The New York Historical Society:** pages 62, 99; **courtesy of The National Portrait Gallery:** pages 65, 183, 193, 203, 210, 218, 225, 243, 251; **courtesy of Virginia State Library:** page 70; **The Bettmann Archive:** page 87; **courtesy of The Smithsonian Institution:** page 90; **Harpers:** page 94; **photograph by Gjon Mili:** page 105; **courtesy of Public Archives of Canada:** page 126; **courtesy of Albert Marrin:** pages 143, 147; **courtesy of The White House Historical Association:** page 162.

Exploration

c. 30,000 B.C.
Asians cross Bering Strait to North America.

c. 12,000- 500 B.C.
Asians spread to South America. Societies form. Mound-builders active in the Mississippi Valley.

c. 1300
Aztec Empire develops in Mexico.

c. 1100
Inca Empire develops in South America.

c. 1000
Leif Eriksson lands in North America.

c. 700 A.D.
Mayan empire peaks in Mexico and Central America.

c. 1400
Pueblo societies irrigate farms in North America.

1492
Christopher Columbus sails to "the Indies" for Spain.

1497
John Cabot claims Nova Scotia and Newfoundland for England.

1521
Hernando de Cortèz destroys Aztec empire.

1585
Walter Raleigh founds Roanoke Colony for England.

1542
Bartolomé de Las Casas protests Spanish treatment of Indians.

1531- 1533
Francisco de Pizarro conquers Incan empire.

1587
Raleigh makes second attempt to settle Virginia.

EXPLORATION

Exploration of the Americas is usually defined as the arrival and examination of the continents by Europeans as if they were the first to discover the area. In fact, this portion of the world had already been occupied for 30,000 years by the peoples now known as Native Americans. Because of this, exploration of the Americas involved far more than an examination of coastlines, mountain ranges, and riverways. It involved contact among the native societies already living in the Americas, the European societies that ventured forth to explore the land, and the African societies brought over to work it. Each of the three groups was a collection of subgroups with separate languages and customs. Native Americans had the Aztec, Pueblo, and Iroquois societies, just as Europeans had the Spanish, French, and English, and as Africans had the Ibo, Ashanti, and Yoruba.

In the 2,000 years before the Europeans arrived, a few native groups shaped their societies into highly developed empires with central cities and written languages. An artful society built great, pyramid-shaped mounds in the Mississippi region of North America over 1,000 years before **Leif Eriksson** became the first European to arrive in North America in 1000 a.d. The Aztec and Incan empires ruled in Central and South America when **Christopher Columbus** landed in the Bahama Islands five centuries later.

Unlike Eriksson's expedition, Columbus's was followed by a

GREENLAND

ICELAND

CANADA

Vikings 1000

Hudson 1610

Cabot 1497

ENGLAND

Gosnold 1602

Gilbert 1595

FRANCE

Cabot 1498

Cartier 1534

SPAIN

CANARY
ISLANDS

AFRICA

Verrazano 1524

De Leon 1513

Columbus 1492-1493

Columbus 1493-1494

Columbus 1502-1504

FLORIDA

CUBA

PUERTO
RICO

HISPANIOLA

Columbus 1498

N
W E
S

▲ **Early European explorations of America**

century-long wave of European explorations. Voyagers from France, Spain, England, Portugal, and Italy began converging on the Americas in the early 1500s. Gold and silver drew them to the Americas at first, their greed quickened by the obvious wealth in the Aztec and Incan empires of Mexico and Peru.

The new societies tried different ways of relating to one another, including trade, conquest, enslavement, religious conversion, and alliance against a common enemy. Choosing conquest, Spain overpowered the native empires of Central and South America in the early 1500s. The Spanish then enslaved many Indians and imported Africans to mine the areas they conquered. The slaves were treated so cruelly that some Native Americans committed suicide to escape bondage. At least one Spaniard, **Bartolomé de Las Casas,** protested the cruel but common practices, writing an account of his people's mistreatment of the Indians.

Expecting to find riches in North America as well, the Europeans were disappointed in their treasure hunt. The Spanish were the first to search in vain. Juan Ponce de León explored in Florida in 1513, and Cabeza de Vaca combed the Texas area in 1534, searching for seven fabled golden cities. The treasure-seekers left empty-handed, and Spanish missionaries became the main European group in these southern areas of North America. Meanwhile, adventurers sponsored by other European countries—mainly France (Giovanni da Verrazano, Jacques Cartier, Samuel de Champlain) and England (John Cabot, Bartholomew Gosnold, Humphrey Gilbert)—explored the east. In the end, the French and English staked their claims on fish- and fur-rich areas of the far Northeast. The English also laid claim to a middle area, Virginia, where they searched for treasure. Unsuccessful in their quest, they finally turned to raising tobacco and other money crops.

It was mainly the English who recognized the value of large-scale settlements. **Walter Raleigh** became the first to found a colony (Roanoke) in Virginia, but had little luck with it. In 1586 Francis Drake stopped at the colony and took most everyone back to England, probably dropping off a few freed black slaves. If so, this was the first contact of three main societies in early North

▲ **Spanish explorers arrive in America**

America—the English, Native Americans, and Africans. (Thirty-three years later Africans were first brought to Jamestown for slave labor.) Native Americans, of course, were in the vast majority then. Altogether about 10 million natives lived in North America north of Mexico—over one-half million near the East Coast—as opposed to only about 100 whites in Raleigh's colony.

North American colonists enslaved Indians in fairly large numbers in the 1600s, a century after the South American colonists began doing so. By that time, however, North America's Indian population was already greatly reduced due to warfare and disease. The greatest Indian killer seems to have been epidemic disease: measles, smallpox, malaria, and the like. Their effects were drastic. From around 1600 to 1700, the native population of 30,000 in Virginia's tidewater region dropped to 1,000. Meanwhile, the white population had swelled to 55,000, and many began importing African slave labor to work the land. It was just the beginning of shifts in the racial balance that would sweep through the country in centuries to come.

Leif Eriksson

c. 960-1025

Personal Background

Leif Eriksson lived sometime between A.D. 960 and 1025. He was born in Iceland to a people who for centuries had been known throughout Europe for their daring, their master shipbuilding and seamanship, and their penchant for exploring other lands. The Vikings, as these people were called, were also famous for their violent raids, their brutal battle tactics, and their lust for silver, gold, and other riches.

Eriksson, who was called Leif the Lucky, seems to have inherited the best of the Viking traits. Bold, confident, and curious about other lands, he was an excellent sailor and a strong and fair leader who commanded respect. Such qualities promised a successful voyage across the icy and rough waters of the North Atlantic to a land previously unknown to Europeans.

The Vikings. For centuries, the bountiful and rugged land of the Vikings, Scandinavia, had provided the people with all their needs. In the fertile soil they grew a large variety of vegetables, fruit, legumes, and grains. They also raised cattle, sheep, pigs, and chickens. In the thick forests they hunted reindeer, beaver, and wolves. From the seas they caught seals, walrus, and whales as well as many kinds of fish. As a result, the Vikings enjoyed a nutritious and varied diet that enabled them to grow large and strong. In fact, they were taller, stronger, and healthier than most other Europeans.

▲ **Leif Eriksson**

Event: Exploration of North America.

Role: Leif Eriksson is believed to have been the first European to journey to North America. He explored the land, named some parts of it, and in one area built a small colony.

▲ **A Viking ship**

The advantages of the land began to turn against them, however, when their numbers swelled to the point where the resources began to run out. Beginning in the eighth century, the Vikings began to venture from their homeland to other European communities. Generations of mastering the arts of sailing and shipbuilding enabled them to safely travel long distances across the seas. Their sturdy and swift crafts, as long as seventy feet, carried heavy cargoes through the rough waters of the northern seas.

At first the Vikings went to the other countries to trade their goods, especially the valuable furs from the animals that roamed their northern forests. But as time passed, they began to invade and plunder far-off lands. Gliding silently in their low boats, they crept onto shore in the dark hours of the morning. Then they raided unsuspecting villages, attacking the people with battle-axes and two-edged swords and stealing all their valuables. Often they sold captured villagers as slaves in other countries.

By the late 800s and early 900s the Vikings sought new lands to settle. Norwegian Vikings began visiting Iceland after it was discovered by Floki Vilgerdsson in the mid-800s. Great numbers of them began to migrate to the large northern island when trouble under the rule of King Harald forced many to flee Norway. On this bleak, cold land of glaciers, volcanoes, sparse forests, and frequent earthquakes, the Viking immigrants set up homesteads, mostly along the coasts. They built low, long houses with stone and sod walls and grass roofs. They grew what food they could on the cold land and also ate birds' eggs, fish, and wild game. By the middle of the 900s, Iceland's population had grown to about 30,000 people.

Erik the Red. Eriksson's father, Erik the Red, arrived in Iceland about 960, when rulers banished him and his own father, Thorvald Osvaldsson, from their native Norway. Fifteen-year-old Erik had been made an outlaw and exiled to Iceland because he and his father had repeatedly feuded with their neighbors and were even involved in some killings.

In his new home, young Erik met his wife, Thjodhild, who came from a leading Icelandic family. The couple set up a homestead on some fertile land given them by Thjodhild's family. Erik worked hard at establishing himself in the community. But even now, the fiery red-haired Viking could not stop fighting with his neighbors. Once again, his feuding led to bloodshed and murder. As a result, by the early 980s Iceland's lawmaking courts, called *Althings,* had deemed Erik an outlaw and banished him for three years from the country.

Now an exile, Erik recalled the story of a distant cousin who some fifty years earlier had been blown off course while sailing west of Iceland and there spotted signs of land. Erik set out on an expedition to find this land, and within a short time he and his crew of about thirty men, probably including young Leif, were sailing around the rocky cliffs of the east coast of the largest island in the world. The expedition sailed southwest and then a short distance north before landing at what is now Julianehaab.

Erik was pleased to find a land that promised good conditions for settlement. The skies abounded with birds and the surrounding seas held plenty of fish. Deep fjords coursed in through the land from the sea. Beside these waterways lay green pastureland that rested below steep mountainsides. The land also had more trees than the barren Iceland.

Still, many glaciers covered the cold land and Erik's choice for a name seemed odd. The *Greenlanders' Saga,* a written account of the country, offers some explanation: "[He] named the country he had discovered Greenland, for he said that people would be more tempted to go there if it had an attractive name" (Humble, p. 13). After spending three years exploring the new land, Erik returned to Iceland eager to convince others to migrate to Greenland. He was anxious to found a new settlement, where he would rule while owning and controlling all the land he wished. With so much space and power, Erik stood a much stronger chance of getting along with his neighbors than he had in the past.

The Viking Sagas

The ability to memorize stories and laws and recite them word for word was highly prized by Vikings. Many nights they gathered around a communal fire to hear a storyteller recount tales of people and events long past. Such storytelling was not only entertaining, it also helped preserve family histories and pass knowledge down through generations. Around 1200, these sagas were finally put into writing. This is how we know about Eriksson's discovery and his family's explorations.

His mission proved successful, for in 986 he set out for the newly discovered land leading twenty-five ships filled with about 750 people. The voyage across was rough and dangerous, and only fourteen ships, holding about 300 to 400 settlers, made it. Some sank while others turned back to Iceland. Traveling with his parents and his two brothers, Eriksson, probably in his teens by now, was among these first settlers of Greenland.

Bjarni Herjolfsson. The new settlers had barely unloaded their ships when reports of sightings of yet other lands to the west of Greenland reached them. Bjarni Herjolfsson, a Norwegian trader and farmer, had traveled to Iceland to spend the winter with this father. There he learned that his father had migrated with Erik and the other settlers to Greenland. After getting a description of Greenland's location and appearance, Bjarni set back out to sea to join his father. However, the voyage was rough and stormy, and, like their countryman years earlier, Bjarni and his crew were blown off course to the shores of another land. The *Greenlanders' Saga* describes their adventure:

> Then the fair wind failed and northerly winds and fog came on, so they had no idea which way they were going. These conditions lasted many days. Eventually they saw the sun again and could determine the quarters of the heavens.
>
> They hoisted sail and sailed all that day before sighting land. (Irwin, p. 11)

The land they sighted was not Greenland, but a more distant land: North America.

From the description he was given, Bjarni knew they had not reached Greenland; he saw no glaciers, only low hills and many trees. Showing little curiosity and a single-minded determination to join his father, Bjarni refused to explore this strange land. He and his men did not even leave their boat, but just kept sailing. Traveling northeast, they again encountered rough weather and again spotted land. Still, Bjarni would not stop. They continued sailing, hoping to reach Greenland before their supplies ran out. The lost crew sighted land yet another time before finally reaching Greenland. Bjarni, who had unknowingly passed up the opportunity to be the first European to discover North America, steered his boat to Greenland's shores. Amazingly, he landed within a short distance of his father's home.

Participation: Exploration of North America

Leif Eriksson—Explorer. Back in Greenland, settlers listened to Bjarni's reports with interest and curiosity about this other land. However, none showed any desire to venture out in search of the place that Bjarni described. The weary settlers had just risked a dangerous voyage across the cold Atlantic and spent many months building homes and setting up farms. All they wanted to do was settle in and establish their new colony.

One young man, however, listened to Bjarni's stories with rapt attention while planning someday to travel to this far-off land. The idea of discovering and exploring new lands excited Eriksson, who was eager to follow in his famous father's footsteps. Also, as the colony grew, the people began to run out of wood. Eriksson knew that if he could find this wooded land that Bjarni described, he would be hailed as a hero for providing his people with this valued and much-needed resource.

Eriksson sought out Bjarni and pressed him for details of the journey he had taken years earlier. He asked Bjarni to tell him as much as he could about the route he had traveled and the land he had sighted. Leif even asked Bjarni to sell him his ship, for the Vikings believed that a ship "remembered" where it had sailed before.

Eriksson wanted his father to lead the expedition. He believed that Erik at the helm would bring good luck on the journey. Grudgingly, Erik agreed. He was by now a fairly old man. Plans changed, however, when a horse threw Erik and the old Viking injured his leg. The superstitious people considered the accident a bad omen and Eriksson decided to lead the expedition himself.

The voyage to the new world. In about 1003, some fifteen years after Bjarni Herjolfsson had sighted land to the southwest of Greenland, Eriksson and his crew of about thirty set out to explore the land. Like other sailors of the time, Leif had no compasses, maps, or charts to guide him on this journey to the unknown. He used the position of the stars and the sun to help determine his direction. He also relied on Bjarni's detailed description of his voyage, noting how many days he sailed, what landmarks he saw, and the varying color and temperature of the water.

Heading northwest, Eriksson and his men sighted land after sailing about 600 miles. The *Greenlanders' Saga* describes the event:

> They found first the land that Bjarni found last. They sailed in close to shore and cast anchor, then put off a boat and went ashore. They could see no grass. Inland lay great glaciers, and from these glaciers to the sea the land was one great slab of rock. This country seemed to them worthless. Leif said, "At least we've done better than Bjarni—we've come ashore. Now I'm going to give this country a name and call it Helluland [meaning Slab-land or Land of Flat Rocks]." (Irwin, p. 37)

▶

Eriksson lands on North America

The explorer traveled on and soon sighted another land, which was flat, wooded, and had long expanses of white-sand beaches. Eriksson named this land Markland, which means Forest-land. After landing here and looking about them, the men continued their voyage and soon sighted an island, on which they made landfall. Here, according to the *Greenlanders' Saga,*

> The weather was fine, and they saw that there was dew on the grass. They happed to touch the dew with their hands, and when they licked their fingers it seemed to them they had never tasted anything so sweet. (Irwin 1980, p. 38)

Where Was Vinland?

For years, historians have argued about Eriksson's route to North America and the lands he found. Some believe that Vinland could have been as far south as Virginia, while others believe it was much farther north, above Labrador in present-day Canada. Eriksson's comment that day and night were of nearly equal length has given experts the most valuable clue to Vinland's location.

Some experts place Eriksson's Vinland in Cape Cod, Massachusetts, along the coast of Maine, and in Newfoundland, Canada. In 1960 Helge Instad, a Norwegian, seemed to have solved the mystery when he found the remains of a Viking settlement in L'Anse aux Meadows, on the northern tip of Newfoundland. However, some are still unconvinced and continue searching for the mysterious Vinland.

Vinland. When Erikkson found a stretch of land with excellent pastures, rivers filled with salmon, and thick forests, the men set out to build a campsite. They chopped wood and built houses and explored the surrounding area. To their delight, they found vineyards of grapes, which they thought would be a valuable cargo to take back to Greenland. The men spent their days chopping wood and gathering grapes and vines and loading the cargo onto their ship. Then they settled into their new home for the winter.

In spring, Eriksson and his men set out on their return voyage to Greenland. Before they left, Eriksson gave the new land a name—Vinland, or Wine-land, after the grapes they had found there.

Back to Greenland. On the trip home Eriksson spotted fifteen shipwrecked Greenlanders stranded on a reef. He rescued the sailors and brought them back to Greenland. This rescue, combined with his successful voyage to unknown lands, earned him the nickname he would carry for the rest of his life: Leif the Lucky.

Soon after Eriksson returned to Greenland, his father died.

Eriksson replaced Erik as the law speaker and leader of the Eastern Settlement. With his new responsibilities, Eriksson left his exploring days behind him. He settled into his life as community leader and would never return to Vinland.

Aftermath

Later explorations. Exploring seems to have been in the blood of the Eriksson clan, for soon after Eriksson returned, his two brothers each set out on their own expeditions. First, Thorvald ventured back to Vinland with a crew of about thirty men. They had little trouble finding Eriksson's camp, where they settled in for the winter. He and his men spent a longer time here than Eriksson and his crew had, and thus had more opportunity to explore the surrounding area. Though they discovered signs of human life—a grain storehouse—they did not encounter the native people.

During the second summer of their exploration, the crew sailed to an area with a deep fjord that Thorvald liked very well. "This is a lovely place," Thorvald said. "I will make my home here someday" (Jensen, p. 36). But soon trouble struck, when he and his men for the first time encountered Native Americans. The Vikings called them "Skraelings," meaning "savages" or "screechers." While exploring the land, Thorvald and his crew came upon about nine Native Americans sleeping on a beach under boats made of skin. For no apparent reason, Thorvald and his men attacked and killed all but one.

The next day Thorvald was killed when boatloads of native people came to avenge the death of their tribesmen. An arrow struck him beneath his shoulder. He died in the land he had come to settle. His men returned to Greenland without his body and told their waiting countrymen the story of their journey.

Back home, the youngest Eriksson brother, Thorstein, heard the story and resolved to return to Vinland to retrieve his brother's corpse. He and his wife, Gudrid, and about twenty-five other adventurers set out for the new land. Their voyage was marked by strife and hardship. A series of storms sent them off course and wandering across the Atlantic for months. In the end, they landed back in Greenland. That winter, Thorstein and many of his crew were stricken by a disease. Thorstein Eriksson died without ever having set foot on Vinland.

Later Gudrid remarried and ventured back to Vinland with her new husband, Thorfinn Thorsdarsson, nicknamed Karlsefni. With an expedition of 160 men and women, they left in the spring of 1011 with the goal of settling Vinland.

Historians are not certain whether the settlers found Eriksson's houses, but they did set up camp and stayed for three years. During this time Gudrid had a son, Snorri, the first white child born in North America. The settlers had much contact with the local people. They traded milk and cheese and red cloth, all strange and exotic to the Native Americans, for valuable furs. Although the Viking settlers at first got along with the native people, conflict arose when one of Karlsefni's men killed a native for trying to steal weapons. After this, relations between the Vikings and the Native Americans were no longer peaceful. Before long, the settlers realized that life in the new land had grown too dangerous and they sailed back to Greenland.

The final expedition. The last recorded voyage to Vinland ended in brutal murder and in infamy for Eriksson and his family. Eriksson's half-sister, Freydis, decided to follow in her brothers' footsteps and lead her own expedition to the new land. Eriksson agreed to let Freydis "borrow" the homes he had built in the new land; even though he had no intention of ever returning, he refused to give them to her permanently. Eager to be on her way as the first women to organize and head an expedition to the new world, Freydis formed a partnership with two brothers from Iceland. In two ships filled with sixty to seventy people, the expedition set off for Vinland.

Apparently, Freydis was as hotheaded as her father, Erik. From the beginning, her group fought and argued with the group led by the two brothers. The feuding groups spent a winter together at Eriksson's campsite barely communicating. One morning it seems that Freydis decided to do something about the situation. She told her husband that the brothers had hit her and roughed her up—a lie. She demanded that her husband take revenge.

In chilling detail, the *Greenlanders' Saga* tells what happened next:

When [Freydis's husband] could bear her taunts no longer, he ordered his men to get up at once and take their weapons. This they did, and went straight to the brothers' house. They entered while the men were asleep, and seized them and tied them up. Each man, when he was bound, was led outside.

As they came out one by one, Freydis ordered each man killed.... Only the women were left, and no one would kill them.

"Hand me an ax!" cried Freydis. Someone did, and she herself killed the five women and left them dead. (Irwin, p. 97)

Freydis threatened her crew with death if anyone told of what happened when they returned to Greenland. However, when they sailed back in the spring, people started talking. When Eriksson soon heard the rumors, he committed the only act of violence that he is known to have committed: he tortured three of the crew members until he was sure they were telling the truth about Freydis. Saddened and horrified, Eriksson did nothing, though it was his responsibility as law speaker to punish criminals. "I do not have the heart to punish my sister as she deserves," he said. "All I can say is that she and her family will never prosper" (Jensen, p. 41). Indeed, Eriksson's prophecy seems to have come true, for this tragic and brutal account is the last mention of Leif Eriksson or his family and descendants in the Viking sagas.

When Did the Viking Explorations End?

Although the Viking sagas make no more mention of other explorations or settlements in North America after the early 1000s, some believe that Vikings were traveling and settling in the new land through the 1300s. There is quite a lot of evidence to support this view. In 1898, for example, a farmer in Minnesota found a stone inscribed with the runic alphabet (Viking writing). Dated 1362, the Kensington Stone, as it is called, describes an expedition of about thirty Vikings traveling from Vinland. Other Viking artifacts have been found beside waterways north of the Kensington Stone.

For More Information

Humble, Richard. *Exploration Through the Ages: The Age of Leif Eriksson.* New York: Franklin Watts, 1989.

Irwin, Constance. *Strange Footprints on the Land: Vikings in America.* New York: Harper & Row, 1980.

Jensen, Malcolm C. *Leif Erikson the Lucky.* New York: Franklin Watts, 1979.

Christopher Columbus

1451-1506

Personal Background

Christopher Columbus's time and place of birth could hardly have been more ideal for shaping his destiny. Two years after his birth, Muslim Turks conquered the Christian city of Constantinople, or present-day Istanbul, Turkey, cutting off a large part of the trade between Europe and Asia. Constantinople had been the meeting point for the trade routes between the two continents, sitting as it did on the Mediterranean and Black seas. To reach Asia, European merchants would sail across either of the seas and then travel overland on a long and difficult journey. With these paths now closed, it became increasingly important to find a direct route to Asia by sea.

As a boy, Columbus may or may not have been aware of this search for a new sea route to Asia. Growing up in Genoa, Italy, though, he could not have helped but develop a strong sense of the sea and knowledge of the art of sailing. Genoa's location on the Ligurian Sea, which leads out to the Mediterranean, made it a powerful and thriving trading port, especially during the Middle Ages. By the time Columbus was born, Genoese fleets had achieved world-renown for their sailing expertise.

Family, marriage, and children. Although they lived in a city where seafaring was the major industry, Columbus's family did not make their living off the sea. His parents, Domenico Colombo

▲ **Christopher Columbus**

Event: Exploration of the Western Hemisphere; European discovery of Latin America.

Role: Christopher Columbus was the first European to journey across the Atlantic Ocean to the Western Hemisphere and claim some of the land for a European sovereign. Although earlier explorers, such as the Viking Leif Eriksson, had landed on the North Atlantic coast, Columbus's "discovery" led to migration and colonization, increased trade, and the interaction of peoples that earlier had been unknown to one another.

and Susanna Fontanarossa, worked as weavers, following a family tradition on the Colombo side of at least three generations. Domenico also earned some of his living selling cheese and wine. As a member of his local guild, he probably held a position of some standing in his lower-middle-class community.

Columbus and his three brothers and one sister may have received some schooling through their father's guild. For the most part, however, Columbus attained only a basic education in the rudiments of reading, writing, and arithmetic.

He may have been ashamed of his humble origins, for he spoke little of his childhood in his later years. His craving for social standing may have been partly realized in 1479 when he married Felipa Perestrello e Moniz, a Portuguese woman of noble blood but little money. Within a year the young couple had a son, Diego, and not long after, Felipa died. Years later, Columbus developed a relationship with a much younger woman, Beatriz Enríquez de Harana. Though they never married, she also bore him a son, Ferdinand, who was to become Columbus's biographer.

Columbus's Appearance

Surprisingly, there are no trustworthy likenesses of the famous explorer. No artist painted Columbus during his lifetime. By most accounts, including his son Ferdinand's, Columbus was a tall, well-built man. He had blue or gray eyes, a curved nose, a ruddy but light complexion, freckles, and reddish or blond hair that turned white in his thirties. He seems also to have had a strong and striking presence, with a sober expression and a grave but pleasant manner.

Training and education. According to his own accounts, Columbus became a sailor at "a very tender age," probably in his early teens. Very likely, he ventured out to sea to travel to nearby coastal communities buying wool and other goods for his father and selling the finished cloth. By his early twenties, Columbus had become an accomplished mariner. While sailing on numerous business expeditions and on whaling ships, he strengthened and sharpened his keen, almost instinctive understanding of the stars, the ocean currents, and the wind.

In 1476 misfortune changed the course of the young mariner's life, directing him toward his destiny as an explorer. While traveling on a fleet of ships carrying valuable cargo, Columbus and his shipmates were attacked by French pirates off the coast of Portugal.

Luckier than most of his mates—many were killed—Columbus jumped his sinking ship and, wounded and exhausted, swam the six miles to shore.

He spent some time in Lagos, Portugal, recovering from his wounds and then traveled on to Lisbon, where his brother Bartolomeo owned a bookstore and mapmaking business. In Lisbon—the heart of the navigational world and probably the most lively and forward-moving city of the day—Columbus learned the art of cartography, or mapmaking, while making full use of his brother's book collection. Columbus poured over books on topics ranging from philosophy to geography to astronomy to cosmography, or the study of the structure and physical features of the world.

Religion. Columbus must also have read a great deal on the subject of religion for, like many of the people of his time, he was a devout Catholic. According to his contemporaries, he lived a life more strictly religious than most. He fasted regularly, avoided foul language, and practiced his religion with sober and fervent devotion. He saw God's hand in all his endeavors, especially in his dangerous and daring crossing of the Atlantic. Columbus believed his life's mission was to spread the Christian faith to other lands and saw himself as a divine messenger guided by God. So strong was his belief that he signed his name *Xpo FERENS,* or "Christ-bearer."

> **The Many Names of Columbus**
>
> Columbus has come to be known and was known in his own lifetime by many names. His English name is a variation of his Italian birthname, Cristoforo Colombo. In Spain, he is called Cristóbal Colón. His son Ferdinand called him Colonus.

Participation: "Discovery" of the Americas

Current thought and culture. It is a myth that during Columbus's time most people thought the earth was flat. In fact, educated people accepted that the earth was a sphere—every European university taught this geographical concept. However, what the experts of the day could not agree on was the earth's size. Most estimates placed it at about two-thirds its actual size.

While learned men argued about the earth's dimensions, noblemen, merchants, and seamen clung to the hope of finding a direct sea route to the Indies. Fired by descriptions from the travels of thirteenth-century Venetian explorer Marco Polo, European traders looked greedily to Asia, calculating the wealth they could make. Marco Polo had written of a land abundant with gold, pearls, rubies, and other precious metals and stones. He also described delectable spices and the animals of the continent, such as monkeys and elephants, which were unknown and entirely exotic to Europeans. Eager to use Asia's bountiful resources, Europeans sought new ways to reach the enormous, far-off land.

Thus the idea of traveling west across the Atlantic to the eastern shores of Asia was not entirely new by the time Columbus developed his plan. But in the late fifteenth century the thought of sailing across the "green sea of gloom," as the vast ocean was called, was as grandiose and frightening as the thought of flying to the moon became to people living before the 1950s. The person who could overcome the physical, mental, and emotional barriers of braving the gloomy sea and, in the process, discover a direct route to Asia's riches, would be assured instant fame and glory.

The Enterprise of the Indies. The fifteenth century was a time of great discovery. Explorers were finding new lands faster than mapmakers could chart them. Prince Henry of Portugal, a leader in this quest for exploration, earned the nickname Henry the Navigator by encouraging cosmographers, mapmakers, and mariners from all over the world to come to his kingdom to develop and execute plans for exploration. Thus, Lisbon became the center for world navigation and discovery. Under Henry's patronage, explorers had landed on the Madeira, Azores, and Cape Verde islands and claimed these lands for Portugal.

Although Henry died some twenty years before Columbus arrived in Lisbon, the city was still a thriving navigational and intellectual center. Studying the most current maps of the earth as well as books that laid out theories about its size and structure, Columbus became convinced that he could sail west across the Atlantic to the eastern coast of Asia, or "The Indies." Like others, he believed that the earth consisted of one huge landmass made up of Europe, Asia, and Africa that was flanked on both sides by ocean. Columbus's grand plan and extraordinary venture came about as a result of two enormous miscalculations in geography: he thought the earth was much smaller than it really is, and he imagined Asia to be a great deal wider.

Columbus called his plan "The Enterprise of the Indies." By the mid-1480s he was ready to make what he now saw as his life's destiny a reality. But first he needed financial backing and support. King João II of Portugal listened with interest to Columbus's plan but refused to back him. Deflated but refusing to abandon the expedition, Columbus left Lisbon with his young son, Diego, and headed for Spain.

Ferdinand and Isabella. During this time, Spain was undergoing many changes as it moved toward becoming a major European power. The marriage of Ferdinand and Isabella, the "Catholic Sovereigns," increased the size of the country by bringing together its two great regions. Isabella ruled over the larger Castile region, while Ferdinand held court over the smaller region of Aragon. During their forty-year reign, Ferdinand and Isabella worked to unify Spain into one Catholic nation. To this end, they fought and finally conquered the Moors in Granada in 1492. That same year, they issued a royal decree expelling from the country all Jews who refused to convert to Catholicism. Under their rule, thousands of Jews and other "non-believers" were tortured and brutally killed in the Spanish Inquisition.

As they struggled to achieve Catholic unity, Ferdinand and Isabella also worked to create a new and powerful Spain. Their efforts included conquering other lands, exploring and claiming new territories, and building the country's wealth. So, when Columbus approached them with his bold plan, they listened with open minds and encouraging attitudes. Columbus especially found an ally in Isabella, who had an adventurous spirit and shared the explorer's enthusiasm for spreading Christianity.

That Columbus managed to gain an audience with this powerful royal couple was no small feat. It demonstrates the ambition, drive, and forcefulness of his character. It also proves his patience and persistence. It had taken six long years for Ferdinand and Isabella to finally agree to finance his daring venture.

The voyage. On August 3, 1492, Columbus set sail, leaving port with a crew of about ninety men on three ships known as the *Niña, Pinta,* and *Santa Maria.* At less than 100-feet long, the *Santa*

▲ A sixteenth-century engraving of Columbus's small fleet

Maria was the largest of three. The *Niña* and *Pinta,* called caravels, measured about seventy-feet long. Cargo on the three vessels included water, wine, sea biscuits, olive oil, salt meat, sardines, anchovies, cheese, beans, rice, garlic, honey, almonds, and raisins. Most of the men who had signed on for this voyage were Spaniards.

Life on any ship at the time was difficult and mostly unpleasant. Crew members slept anywhere on board they could find a dry spot. Few were lucky enough to have even a change of clothes. Crowded together in tight spaces, the hard-working men could look forward to only one hot meal a day. During long voyages, the food spoiled and became contaminated with pests. The ships were filthy and unsanitary, often infested with mice, rats, worms, and cockroaches.

On this first voyage, Columbus was keenly aware of the great risk his men had undertaken by coming aboard. He did everything he could to quiet their fears, including keeping two logs, a true one and one that showed a reduced estimation of the distance traveled. Fortunately, luck was with him throughout the long journey. Fair weather and clear skies along with a steady wind at their backs guided the ships safely across the uncharted ocean. After a brief stop in the Canary Islands, off the northwest coast of Africa, the small fleet of ships traveled due west across the Atlantic, eventually landing on islands off North America.

Columbus had few tools at his disposal for accurately gauging the journey. He relied on his mariners' compass and his mastery of a technique called dead reckoning, which involves plotting a course and figuring position using estimates of speed, distance traveled, and direction and strength of the wind. Columbus's skill as a mariner is undisputed: that he made it across this enormous expanse with so little to guide him was a huge accomplishment. In fact, on his first time out he found the best possible route of travel across the Atlantic. It is no wonder that his shipmates held his seafaring skills in high esteem. Michele de Cuneo, who accompanied him on a later voyage, wrote:

> Ever since Genoa was Genoa, there has been no such great-hearted man or keen navigator as the Admiral. He could tell from a cloud or a single star what direction to follow. (Giardini, p. 37)

▲ **Columbus's crew sights land**

Landfall. After more than two months at sea, Columbus and his crew finally spotted land in the middle of the night on October 12, 1492. The next day they anchored their ships and set foot on the land that Columbus would name San Salvador (its native name was Guanahaní), one of the Bahama Islands. Grateful to be finally safe after their long voyage, Columbus and his men explored the "new" land, which Columbus believed to be the Indies. In his journal he described a large and very flat island "with green trees and plenty of water; there is a large lake in the middle, no mountains, and everything is green and a delight to the eye" (Cummins, p. 96).

The native people. Columbus also encountered the native people, whom he dubbed Indians, thinking he had reached the Indies. In fact, the people called themselves Arawak. They lived in thatched huts and farmed the land, growing such foods as maize, yams, and cassava. Tall with brown skin and straight black hair, the Arawak were a trusting, generous, and friendly people. They imagined their strange-looking visitors to have arrived from the heavens.

As Columbus explored the surrounding islands, he also met other native tribes, including the more primitive Lucayas and the richer and more advanced Tainos. Most of the native peoples were peaceful and greeted Columbus and his crew with hospitality, sharing their food and goods.

Columbus viewed the natives as individuals who would readily accept Christianity and be easily subdued. He wrote to the king and queen of the potential for using the Indians as slaves either in Europe or on their own land. Considering this hidden attitude, Columbus was fairly respectful toward the native peoples in the beginning and treated them with consideration. However, it was not long before conflicts arose. Sailors treated the natives harshly and they in turn rebelled.

Quest for gold. During the next three months, Columbus and his men explored the surrounding islands, including Hispaniola (Haiti and the Dominican Republic) and Cuba. As Columbus claimed the land for Spain and named the islands, he and his men searched for the gold they had come to seek. Still believing that they had landed on the shores of the exotic Orient, they set about looking for streets of gold and the glittering palaces of the prince, the Grand Khan. The gold rings that some of the natives wore only strengthened their certainty of having landed at their destination. Communicating with the people through gestures, they asked to be led to the gold sites. However, most of their efforts were fruitless. The islands in fact held little gold.

The return voyage. The adventurers returned to Spain with one less ship and fewer crew members. On Christmas Eve in 1492, the *Santa Maria* ran aground off the shores of Haiti. There, in a quickly built fort he called La Navidad, Columbus left thirty-nine of his men, who agreed to stay on the island and continue the search for gold. (When Columbus returned a year later, he found an empty fort. The greedy and lustful first colonists had quarreled among themselves and abused the kindness of the native peoples, demanding gold and raping the women. Stirred to anger and seeking revenge, the natives had attacked and killed all the Spanish sailors.)

In the middle of January, after setting up the fort, Columbus and the remainder of his crew set sail for the long journey home. The trip eastward across the Atlantic began smoothly, but soon Columbus and his men ran into trouble. Strong currents carried them north into increasingly colder weather. A winter storm, marked by lightening and an angry sea, thrashed the *Niña* and the *Pinta* as the crew struggled to save their ships. The fierce storm raged until all the tired men could do was pray. Columbus feared that he would never see land again and that no one would ever hear of his amazing discovery. In desperation, he recorded his triumph, sealed it in a bottle, and tossed it into the sea, hoping that someone someday would find it if he did not survive the storm.

Reception in Spain. Columbus and his men did survive, landing first in Portugal in mid-February and from there making their way to Spain. With some of his crew, six native Americans whom he had brought back with him, some caged parrots, and a sample of gold, Columbus journeyed through the Spanish country on his way to the royal palace. Along the way villagers cheered and looked with curiosity at the exotic people from the other land. When the procession arrived at the Spanish court in April 1493, a festive reception greeted them. The king and queen bestowed on him his new title: "Admiral of the Ocean Sea, Viceroy and Governor of the Islands" that he had discovered. Columbus basked in the glory and relished his long-awaited rewards.

Aftermath

Additional voyages. A little over a year after his first voyage, in September 1493, Columbus set sail for a return trip to the land he had claimed for Spain. This time he set out with a fleet of seventeen ships filled with about 1,300 adventurous men. The ships' cargo included horses, cattle, and large supplies of grain and seeds. The goals of this expedition were to spread Christianity among the native peoples, to continue the search for gold, and to establish some Spanish colonies.

This second expedition was marked by trouble, hardship, and

conflict. Unused to the wet and warm climate, many of the men fell ill. Food rotted in the heat and swarms of mosquitoes plagued the weary travelers. Meanwhile, the native peoples looked with alarm and fear at the large number of visitors, who treated the land as though it belonged to them and who had little regard for their hosts. The greedy and often ruthless visitors instituted slavery, making the Indians toil in the barren mines for gold. Brutal conflicts ensued, leading to bloodshed and murder. Soon, disorder spread through the new colonies, and Columbus struggled for control. He failed, however, and after three years he returned to Spain with little fanfare and no glory. The experience left him so shamed that, in penance, he dressed in a monk's robe, which he wore until his death some ten years later.

Columbus was to take two more voyages, each more troubled than the one before. During his third voyage, to South America, rumors of poor leadership and rebellion had made their way back to Ferdinand and Isabella, and the royal couple sent an officer to investigate the charges. On his arrival, the officer found rotting corpses hanging from the gallows and more prisoners waiting to be executed. Horrified, he concluded that Columbus had indeed mismanaged the colony, and he returned the stunned explorer to Spain in chains.

Back in Spain, still wearing the chains like a martyr, Columbus appealed to Ferdinand and Isabella. The couple, sympathetic to the explorer's pleas, returned to him his papers and belongings, but would not give him back his titles. Surprisingly, they granted the determined explorer one last voyage.

On this final voyage, Columbus set out with only four ships, two of which had to be abandoned because of their poor condition. The writings of his son Ferdinand offer a vivid description of the wretched conditions of this last expedition: "Our ship biscuit had become so wormy that, God help me, I saw many who waited for darkness to eat the porridge made of it, that they might not see the maggots" (Deák, p. 53).

Columbus's death. Columbus returned to Spain after this final voyage, ailing from arthritis and gout and nearly blind. Queen Isabella lay on her deathbed, and the saddened court had no time and little desire to welcome the one-time hero. Indeed, during the last few years of his life the world paid little tribute to Columbus. In 1506 he

▲ **Columbus in chains**

died a bitter and broken man, asking to be buried with the chains that had held him prisoner years earlier. Few attended his funeral. It would take some time for the world at large to acknowledge, understand, and take advantage of Columbus's discovery of a "new" world.

Destruction of the native populations. Colonization on the new land carried with it drastic, lasting effects. Soon after Columbus's discovery, entire native cultures began to disappear at a rapid pace. Probably half of Hispaniola's native population—as many as half a million people—died or were killed during the three years following the second voyage.

Suddenly, after thousands of years on American lands, the native peoples found themselves at the mercy of frequently cruel and greedy strangers. Indians were taken prisoner, made into slaves, tortured, and executed. Some Spaniards raped the native women. Slaves in the gold mines were given three months to collect a certain amount of the precious metal—nearly impossible to find due to the lack of gold on the islands. Yet Indians who could not meet the gold quota were killed or had their hands cut off. Some of them fled into the mountains. Others chose to take their own lives rather than submit to the slavery and cruelty.

At the time, Europeans viewed such treatment of "uncivilized" people as acceptable and justified. One man, however, looked upon the slavery and killing with horror and devoted his life to speaking out against the plight of the Indians. Bartolomé de las Casas, a Spanish bishop who spent forty years in the new colonies, saw the Indians as human beings, equal to whites (see **Bartolomé de Las Casas**). He called them "our brothers, redeemed by Christ's most precious blood, no less than the wisest and most learned men in the whole world" (Déak, p. 51). Presenting his plea in writings, sermons, and direct appeals to the Spanish court, Las Casas fought unsuccessfully to pass laws to protect the native people.

Columbus today. Columbus's fame and reputation have gone through many swings since the discovery. For generations, schoolbooks have celebrated Columbus, presenting him as a hero whose discovery of a new land brought sweeping and beneficial changes to the entire world. Today, however, just past the five-hundredth anniversary of the "discovery," Columbus is viewed with much controversy. Native Americans refuse to celebrate the explorer, seeing him more as an anti-hero who brought cruelty and destruction to their ancestors. Others see him as a daring explorer who paved the way for colonization and change both positive and negative, but who cannot be held solely responsible for the devastation of the native populations.

For More Information

Cummins, John. *The Voyage of Christopher Columbus: Columbus' Own Journal of Discovery.* New York: St. Martin's Press, 1992.

Deák, Gloria. "Everything You Need to Know About Columbus," *American Heritage,* October 1991, pp. 41-54.

Giardini, Cesare. *The Life and Times of Columbus.* New York: Curtis Books, 1967.

Levison, Nancy Smiler. *Christopher Columbus: Voyager to the Unknown.* New York: Lodestar Books, 1990.

Bartolomé de Las Casas

1474-1566

Personal Background

When he was still a teenager, Bartolomé de Las Casas stood on the streets of Seville with the crowds of people welcoming Christopher Columbus back to Spain. The young Las Casas watched as the explorer paraded in front of the throngs of people with his shipmates, six Native Americans, and several caged, brightly colored parrots. There were amazing trophies too: native masks and ornaments, gold and other precious metals. Las Casas stared with awed delight at a large ball that one of the Indians carried. This ball, made from the juice of a tree that grew in the new world ("new" to the Europeans, that is), bounced twice as high as any ball made in Spain. The exotic spectacle and the glimpse of a world that a year before had been completely unknown to Europe captured the young man's adventuring spirit. In a few years, he himself would set off across the ocean to that land so far away.

Early years. Very little is known about Las Casas's family and early years. He was born in 1474 in Seville, a city in southern Spain. His father, Pedro, was a simple merchant and his mother, who was probably Isabel de Sosa, owned a bakery.

Interestingly, it is known that Las Casas's father and three uncles, Francisco, Diego, and Gabriel de Peñalosa, sailed on Columbus's second expedition. In fact, Pedro may even have been on the

▲ **Bartolomé de Las Casas**

Event: Struggle for the rights of Native Americans.

Role: A priest, and later bishop, who was an early colonist of the newly "discovered" Americas, Bartolomé de Las Casas witnessed the abuses inflicted on the Native Americans by the Spanish settlers. He spent his life fighting to defend the rights of the Indians. His writings later had some influence on attitudes toward Indians as well as African slaves in the English colonies.

first voyage in 1492, for his name is listed on the register of the *Santa Maria.* In the new world, Pedro acquired some property in Hispaniola and eventually made his home there. Returning to Spain in 1498 on a ship filled with Native American slaves, he presented his son with a young Indian boy to use as a slave. At the time, Las Casas was studying theology and law at the University at Salamanca, northwest of Madrid. Apparently, he developed a friendly relationship with the boy, who later returned to his native land a free man. Soon afterward, Las Casas journeyed with his father to the new world.

The new world. By 1502 records show that Las Casas was living in Hispaniola. He seemed to have taken an immediate interest in the native peoples, for he studied their culture and learned their languages. A gifted interpreter, the Spaniard learned as many as twelve Native American dialects.

Although Las Casas may have been more interested in the native peoples, his attitudes and life-style varied little from those of his fellow Spanish colonists. He joined his countrymen, including conquistadors Hernán Cortés and Diego Velázquez, in using the Indians for selfish purposes and seizing their land. Las Casas served as a soldier in a struggle in eastern Hispaniola against Indians. Later, he lived as a planter on the land his father had given him, using Indians as slaves to cultivate and farm the acreage. During this time, he did not question his own actions or beliefs or those of his countrymen.

In 1512, after being ordained a priest, Las Casas accompanied Velázquez on his invasion of Cuba. As Velázquez and his men pushed across the island to subdue the natives, they used tactics typical of these early settlers, marching into a village, capturing the chief, and then sometimes burning him at the stake. Velázquez and his soldiers met with little resistance, however, because the Native Americans did not have the weaponry or the manpower to fight them. In one of the villages, though, brutal Spaniards massacred hundreds of Indians. As the Spanish conquered the island, they divided the Indians among themselves and made them slaves.

Las Casas, numb to the injustice of these practices, took the slaves he had acquired to the land that was now his and had them work it for profit and gold. Although he said he treated and fed them well, Las Casas admitted that at the time he was more interested in the gold they might find than in converting them to the Christian faith. In his own words, he cared "more about his possessions and his mines than about the Christian teachings; for he was just as blind as the secular [non-religious] settlers" (Las Casas, p. 20).

Spanish attitudes toward Indians. Las Casas treated the Indians no worse than most of his countrymen. Along with other explorers, he was simply following royal decree that dictated how the Native Americans should be approached and handled.

Queen Isabella, who had sponsored Columbus's voyages, had given specific instructions to early explorers. Foremost, they were to convert the native peoples to the Catholic faith. She insisted that the natives be made to work—to cure them of their "excessive liberty" and idleness—but also that they not be taken as slaves. (Isabella believed that forcing the Indians to work would help them develop Christian virtues, while also bringing a profit to the gold-hungry Spanish kingdom.) Ignorant of the richness and depth of their culture, Isabella wanted to transform the Indians into the image of Europeans. She advocated that they wear clothes, receive instruction in religion, reading, and writing, and let go of such "bad habits" as frequent bathing, which the Queen believed "does them much harm" (Wright, p. 210). (The next century would find English colonists ready to transform the natives of North America in much the same manner.)

When Isabella died in 1504, Ferdinand ruled alone. He cared little about converting the Indians to Christianity but a great deal about the gold that could be mined from their lands. Under Ferdinand's rule, the Spaniards took greater liberties in forcing the native peoples to work for them. They had the Indians toil at growing food, mining gold, and diving for pearls while paying them no wages and feeding them barely enough to survive. These early settlers had no intention of dirtying their own hands by laboring in the land they had come to conquer. So stubborn were they not to work that during a time when Indian labor was in short supply in Hispaniola, Spaniards chose to die of starvation rather than labor on the farms.

The primary motive for the explorers and for the Spanish in

conquering the new land was greed. They wanted the profits that came from the gold, pearls, and other treasures that the land offered. The only way for them to get their hands on this booty was to use the Indians. At the same time, however, the growth of Protestantism in Europe was threatening the strength of the Catholic Church, which was losing its numbers to the new religious sect. The Church saw the millions of Indians in the Americas as a perfect source of new members. Against these two powerful forces, money and religion, the rights of Native Americans stood little chance of being respected by the invading Spaniards.

Participation: Contact with Native Americans

The Native Americans. When Columbus's three ships first reached the shores of the new world, the native peoples looked on the explorer and his crew with awe and welcome. The men in the strange wooden boats seemed to come down from the heavens. For thousands of years, the native groups had lived on the rich and peaceful land, hunting in the forests, fishing in the seas, and growing food. They were skilled artists, crafting jewelry and ornaments from gold, silver, and other materials found nearby. The various peoples had their own customs regarding marriage, religion, diet, and war. Some groups had more elaborate customs than others.

> ### Different Types of Missionaries
>
> Catholic priests from Spain and France had to learn about the life-styles of the Native American peoples before converting them to the Catholic Church. In contrast, Protestant ministers in the English colonies generally stayed close to their colonial settlements, venturing out only when the natives were called together to listen to a sermon. As a result, most Protestant ministers learned little about the native life-styles (Jennings, p. 56).

After Columbus and his crew landed in what they perceived as the new world, the lives of the Native Americans would change forever. Even under the best of circumstances, without brutality or forced slavery, strangers from such a different civilization would have disrupted their lives. The disturbance to the native peoples' hunting and food-gathering practices brought famine. Europeans carried over sicknesses unknown to the Native Americans, which their bodies could not fight. Thousands died of diseases such as smallpox, measles, and influenza.

▲ Queen Isabella I of Spain

On top of these "natural" disruptions, the Indians faced violence and conquest from a better-armed people. Their bows and arrows and their darts and stones could not fight off the fast horses and sharp swords of the Spaniards. Because of this, within a few short decades after Columbus's discovery the Indians found themselves enslaved and living in misery. Each year, their numbers decreased by hundreds of thousands or, by some estimates, even millions.

Antonio de Montesinos. Although most Spaniards believed that their actions and attitudes toward the Indians were morally correct, it was not long before some colonists began to rise up in defense of the native peoples. Before Las Casas, another voice spoke out fiercely against the Spanish treatment of the Native Americans. One Sunday in 1511 at a church in Hispaniola, Antonio de Montesinos, a Dominican friar, gave a seething sermon protesting the abuses toward the Indians.

> Tell me, by what right or justice do you keep these Indians in such a cruel and horrible servitude? On what authority have you waged a detestable war against these people, who dwelt quietly and peacefully on their own land? . . . Why do you keep them so oppressed and weary, not giving them enough to eat nor taking care of them in their illness? For with the excessive work you demand of them, they fall ill and die, or rather you kill them with your desire to extract and acquire gold every day. . . . Are these not men? Have they not rational souls? Are you not bound to love them as you love yourselves? (Hanke, p. 17)

The Spanish colonists listened in stunned silence as the friar thundered these radical views at them. No one had ever questioned what they were doing. As they saw it, Columbus had claimed this land for Spain, making the Indians Spanish subjects, and they had come over from Spain to become wealthy off the gold of the land. It was their right as Spaniards to impose their will on the native peoples. They were only following the wishes of their king. Furthermore, they were forcing the Indians to convert to Christianity, so they were doing God's work as well. Shocked and offended, the colonists hurried to the house of the governor of Hispaniola, Columbus's son Diego, and demanded that he do something about this outrage.

Conversion to the cause of the Indians. Las Casas may or may not have been in the church to hear Montesinos's fiery sermon. In any event, he certainly would have heard about it. Nevertheless, he was unmoved by the friar's message. He took no steps to change his treatment of or attitude toward the Indian peoples, and he continued using the same practices he had for the decade he had lived in the new world.

Then one day in 1514, while preparing a sermon, Las Casas had an experience that would completely and forever change his life. Reading his Bible, the forty-year-old priest came upon a verse that struck him:

> I came upon a place in the book of Sirach, chapter 34, where it says: "The poor man has nothing but a little bread; whoever deprives him of it is a murderer. Whoever does not give the worker his wages is a bloodhound . . . " I thought about the misery and slavery in which the native people are living here. . . . And the more I thought about it the more convinced I was that everything we had done to the Indians so far was nothing but tyranny and barbarism. (Las Casas, p. 23)

From that moment on, Las Casas devoted his life to fighting for "the justice of those Indian peoples, and to condemn the robbery, evil, and injustice committed against them" (Boorstin, p. 631). He immediately gave up his property and freed his Indian slaves. He delivered sermons similar to the one Montesinos had given two years before, again to angry and shocked congregations. He journeyed back and forth across the Atlantic reporting to King Ferdinand, and later Charles V, on the miserable conditions of the Indians.

For years Las Casas worked tirelessly to bring about change. Though he did receive a somewhat sympathetic audience in the throne and some laws were instituted, in practice, little changed in the American colonies.

Las Casas considered it a great victory, then, when in 1520 King Charles granted him some land so that he, now a bishop, could put into effect a scheme that he had devised for dealing with Indians. Las Casas planned to set up peaceful, free villages in which Indian peoples would live and labor among peasant families brought over from Spain. The families would teach the Indians how to work as well as instruct them in the Catholic religion. But this utopian plan was doomed from the start. Indian peoples were revolting in the area that Las Casas wanted to settle while Spanish peasants whom he had assembled deserted him to join raiding parties in the colonies. The failure crushed him. His hopes dashed, Las Casas retreated to a monastery and lived in isolation for nearly a decade.

Description of the mistreatment. While in the monastery, Las Casas began working on a book that would help further the cause of the Indians. Published in 1542, *The Devastation of the Indies: A Brief Account* outlines in ugly detail the cruelties and horrors that the Spanish conquistadors had inflicted on the Indians since arriving in the new world a half-century earlier. Las Casas's descriptions of these brutalities shocked officials back in Spain and, later, people around the world.

In his book, Las Casas describes the Spanish methods for conquering the native peoples. Through unjust wars, they overtook villages and communities, slaying the rulers and young men and then enslaving the survivors. In some places, they raped the women in front of their mates and threw infants against cliffs or into rivers to their deaths. Sometimes they strung up their victims just above the ground and lit fires beneath them, burning them slowly to their deaths.

Las Casas also describes the vicious practice of throwing captives and slaves to the dogs. There were Spaniards who punished rebels by cutting off their hands and hanging them around their neck. Hopeless against such cruelty, Indians killed themselves in large numbers. When a village or community was emptied of its men, the remaining women and children usually starved to death.

The horrific accounts of enslavement, torture, and murder continue through Las Casas's book, which goes on for about 100 pages. Incredibly, he claimed:

> No matter how extensively I wrote, I haven't related more than one ten-thousandth of all destruction wrought in that country, of all murders and violence and horrors and meanness, as it continues until today. (Las Casas, p. 144)

Nonetheless, Las Casas painted a vivid enough picture for the Spanish Crown to finally act to protect the Indian peoples.

The New Laws. In 1542, after fighting for the rights of the Indian population for nearly forty years, Las Casas achieved a measurable victory. Charles V, disturbed and horrified by Las Casas's accounts of the cruelties toward Indians, signed into law ordinances that would protect the Indian peoples. These New Laws, as they were called, established procedures "for the government of the Indies and good treatment and preservation of the Indians" (Hanke, p. 91).

The New Laws covered governmental and administrative matters in the territories and also detailed specific guidelines for the treatment of Indians. First, the laws decreed Indian peoples could no longer be enslaved. Spaniards who owned slaves without the proper papers would lose them; owners who had an unreasonable number of slaves would have some taken away; and those who had been found to mistreat their slaves would be forced to give them up. The laws also prohibited the deadly practice of pearl fishing, in which Indians were forced to dive about thirty feet into the cold sea and remain underwater for several minutes. Furthermore, in Hispaniola, Puerto Rico, and Cuba, where the Indian population had been severely reduced due to conquest, disease, and starvation, Indians would not be required to work at all so that they could recover and begin to repopulate. Finally, the laws gave details for the appropriate treatment of Indians; if a landowner did not follow them, he would lose his property to the Crown.

Not surprisingly, the laws outraged the Spanish settlers. They resented this threat to their landholdings and future income by their Spanish countrymen who lived safely and comfortably across the sea. They felt that they had been working loyally and with commitment to furthering Spain's wealth and glory and were greatly displeased at this "reward" for such service. So they spoke out viciously against the New Laws, and as a result, many of the ordinances did not come to pass. In Peru, for example, the viceroy commissioned to oversee them was beheaded immediately upon his arrival. In Mexico, the commissioner, at the urging of the colonists, agreed to suspend some aspects of the law. Still, many colonists returned to Spain with their families, claiming they could no longer take the risk of living in the new world. Throughout the colonies, officials sided with the colonists over the Spanish government, realizing they could do little to enact the laws in face of such strong opposition. Sadly, in 1545, Charles V withdrew the New Laws.

Aftermath

Final efforts. Las Casas continued fighting against slavery and for laws protecting the Indian peoples until the end of his life. In 1550 he became embroiled in a dispute with the prominent theologian and historian Juan Ginés de Sepúlveda about the morality of the treatment of Indians. Although Sepúlveda lost the famous debate, Las Casas's victory did nothing to improve the condition of the Indians. However, he continued speaking out against the Spanish cruelties in the hope that one day people would realize that forcing Indian peoples into slavery and killing and torturing them was not a good way to go about converting them to Christianity. In *The Devastation of the Indies,* he recounts the story of a chief about to be hanged who was told he would not go to heaven if he did not convert to Christianity before he died. The chief asked if the Spanish Christians went to heaven and, receiving a positive response, told his executioners that in that case he would much prefer hell after his death. In the end, Las Casas spent more than fifty years of his life fighting for the Indians. He died in 1566 at the age of ninety-two.

Reactions to Las Casas' work. Although the printing press was still fairly new, *The Devastation of the Indies* was translated into several different languages, including English, French, Dutch, German, and Italian, and published throughout Europe. The book had a powerful effect on European attitudes toward Spain, toward converting the native peoples in the new world to Christianity, and, later, toward slavery.

For centuries, other European powers and individuals presented Las Casas's book as proof of Spanish cruelty and inhumanity and used it for political purposes. For example, in the late 1500s Walter Raleigh thought to distribute the text to Peruvian Indians so they would side with the English against their Spanish enemies. In the 1600s, when the first Pilgrims set off for the new world, their destination was in part determined by Las Casas's account, for they chose to avoid colonizing near the Spanish. They wanted be far out of "reach of so cruel and murderous fanatics" (Hanke, p. 55). As late as the nine-teenth century, Spanish revolutionaries in South America used Las Casas's work to support their struggle for independence from Spain.

The book also had some effect on the way the English treated the Native Americans when they began colonizing in North America. They chose not to attempt to convert the native people using the "barbarous and cruel" methods of the Spanish, which gave them "a Disgust against the Christian Religion" (Hanke, p. 57).

Slavery. Interestingly, when *The Devastation of the Indies* first came out and for centuries after, there was little discourse about Las Casas's condemnation of slavery. Rather, people focused on the cruelties of the Spanish as justification for prejudice against them. Over the next three centuries the world would slowly come to agree with Las Casas's conclusion that slavery was inhumane and un-Christian.

Some, however, have accused Las Casas of being responsible for the use of Africans as slaves. In his early writings he stated that African peoples should be substituted as slaves because they were stronger and had better constitutions than Indian peoples. He continued to view African slavery as acceptable until the late 1540s, when he wrote that "Negro slavery was as unjust as Indian slavery and for the same reasons" (Hanke, p. 63). After this change of heart, Las Casas deeply regretted his earlier stance.

Unfortunately, some would later use his words to support using Africans as slaves. In the United States, southerners in favor of slavery defended their views by using Las Casas as an example. Either they did not know of his reversal of position or they chose to ignore it. Thus, Las Casas remained a controversial and influential figure in the centuries following his death.

For More Information

Hanke, Lewis. *Bartolomé de Las Casas: Bookman, Scholar, and Propagandist.* Philadelphia: University of Pennsylvania Press, 1952.

Jennings, Francis. *The Invasion of America.* Chapel Hill: University of North Carolina Press, 1975.

Las Casas, Bartolomé de. *The Devastation of the Indies: A Brief Account.* Translated by Hans Magnus Enzenberger. New York: The Seabury Press, 1974.

Wright, Louis B. *Gold, Glory and the Gospel: The Adventurous Lives and Times of the Renaissance Explorers.* New York: Atheneum, 1970.

Walter Raleigh

c. 1552-1618

Personal Background

Little is known of Walter Raleigh's early years. He was born around 1552, the son of Walter Raleigh, a member of the English gentry, or the upper-middle class. Raleigh's father owned several ships, which he used for lawful trade and for privateering, or attacking Spanish treasure ships. At the time, Spain and Portugal were the two world powers, exploring, discovering, conquering, and bringing home riches. England had as yet hardly entered the race. She and Spain were bitter enemies, though, because of their different religions: most of the Spanish population was Catholic while most of the English population was Protestant.

Family life. Raleigh's father married three times. His third wife, Katherine Gilbert, was a widow with three sons, John, Humphrey, and Adrian. Humphrey, in particular, would greatly affect his stepbrother Walter's life. Katherine had three more children in this new marriage: Carew, Walter, and Margaret. Walter, then, was the fifth son of a third marriage. He had little chance of inheriting the family fortune. Rather this ambitious youth, the future Sir Walter Raleigh, would have to make his own fortune.

Soldiering in France and Ireland. Raleigh became a soldier, following in the footsteps of his father, who was also a naval officer. While a teenager, Raleigh volunteered to fight in a bloody civil war in France. Returning home, he attended Oxford University.

▲ **Walter Raleigh with his son Wat**

Event: Exploration of the Eastern Seaboard of the United States; founding of Roanoke Colony.

Role: Claiming the Eastern Seaboard for England, Walter Raleigh was the first Englishman to found colonies in America. He established, through representatives, two very different settlements at Roanoke. Though both met dismal ends, the second colony served as a model and showed what was necessary for North American colonies to succeed.

In 1580 Raleigh volunteered for service in Ireland. The English had begun to build their empire by planting colonies here. Some of the Irish had rebelled against the English, who then seized the rebels' lands for themselves. In Munster, Raleigh's stepbrother Humphrey Gilbert, an officer, lined the path to his tent with the heads of dead men to instill fear in the Irish. On one occasion, Raleigh himself carried out orders to brutally slaughter a group of Irish families after they had already surrendered. Raleigh spent eighteen months in Ireland and captained 100 soldiers.

Young Raleigh, who was an independent thinker, began acting on his thoughts. Not yet thirty, he became a commissioner of Munster and, during his term, concluded that he should become familiar with the problems of the Irish. He traveled widely to learn of their lives and concerns, gaining the people's respect. Returning to the English court, Raleigh, tall, attractive, and self-assured, stated his views of Irish problems so well that Queen Elizabeth I took special note of him. Their relationship blossomed, and he became the queen's favorite.

Raleigh and the queen. Raleigh was soon a constant presence at the queen's court, delighting her with his wit, wisdom, and the poetry he composed for her. Recognizing the intelligence of Raleigh's advice, she called him her "Oracle." His appearance appealed to her, too. He fell into a role occupied through the years by several dashing young men who surrounded the "Virgin Queen." Each of these favorites, as one nineteenth-century author described it, had "in his air and manner all the ardor and devotion of a lover" (Tarbox, 1884). The thirty-year-old Raleigh stepped into this position for the nearly fifty-year-old queen.

The queen showered gifts on her "Oracle." In 1583 Raleigh received the right to collect money each year from every winemaker in the country. In 1584 he was granted control of the export of England's popular woolen cloth. In 1585, the right to govern tin-miners. In 1586, vast estates in Ireland (40,000 acres). And in 1587, the job of captain of the queen's guard. This last prize kept him always near the queen.

During these years Raleigh became perhaps the most hated man in England. He offended commoners by flaunting his good fortune. He had no patience for those less quick-witted than he. Six-feet tall and thirty-five years old, he wore a pointed beard, jeweled shoes, a pearl earring, and silks. England's poor blamed him for their poverty: "No man is more hated than him, none more cursed daily of the poor, of whom in truth numbers are brought to extreme poverty through the gift of the cloths to him" (Williamson, p. 29).

Meanwhile, Raleigh carried on, driven as much by visions of an English empire as by his own fortune. He was in fact quite willing to pour his own wealth back into the country for patriotic as well as personal gain. Some of his plans proved successful; others would, in the end, destroy him.

Participation: Exploration of North America

First efforts at exploration. In 1578 Raleigh's stepbrother Humphrey Gilbert had won permission from the throne to explore and claim any lands in the Americas not yet occupied by a Christian king. That same decade Raleigh sailed for the West Indies, his first trial at exploration. Badly beaten in a battle against Spanish ships along the way, Raleigh returned to England with new knowledge of how fierce an enemy the Spanish were and of how seasick ocean travel would always make him.

In 1583 Gilbert planned a colony in America, offering land to would-be settlers and sketching out a government, churches, and other institutions. His enthusiastic stepbrother Raleigh, by then the queen's favorite, invested in the venture, building the *Bark Raleigh,* a ship he planned to command himself during the voyage. The queen would hear nothing of it, however; Raleigh was not to leave her side. So without him but with five vessels, including the *Bark Raleigh,* Gilbert reached Newfoundland and claimed it for England. Disaster struck on the return voyage: eighty sailors on one ship drowned and Gilbert's vessel was lost in a violent storm. Several months later, in 1584, Raleigh himself won a patent to plant a colony in North America. He would plan and finance it but never voyage to the continent himself.

Durham House. Among the queen's gifts to Raleigh was Durham House in London, which became a center of activity. Here,

Raleigh enlisted experts in all fields to explore the Eastern Seaboard for a site on which to found a colony. Richard Hakluyt, an instructor at Oxford, wrote on the benefits of expanding Elizabeth's empire. Thomas Harriot and Lawrence Keymis, two Oxford students, collected newly created maps of the continent's coastline and information on ship design. Harriot taught navigation to the pilots whom Raleigh planned to use, and the artist John White joined the team to help record findings.

Purposes for Founding a Colony in North America

- Set up a base for English shipping and privateering
- Provide more jobs for the English
- Spread the Protestant religion
- Acquire wealth for individuals and for England
- Prevent the Spanish from expanding their empire
- Increase the power of England in the world
- Find new natural resources for England

Raleigh would become involved in three major voyages to North America. The first voyage was launched in April 1584. Upon crossing the Atlantic, the expedition searched for a site that would support a colony. Within six months the explorers returned with some of the native people, descriptions of the rich countryside, and samples of skins and pearls. The queen, as a reward, bestowed knighthood on the project's leader, thereafter known as Sir Walter Raleigh. The Virgin Queen also allowed the area to be called *Virginia* in her honor. In the name of England, Elizabeth then appointed Raleigh lord and governor of this large stretch of eastern North America. The land was his to dispose of as he pleased, except he was to pay the queen one-fifth of any precious metals found there.

Roanoke. In 1585 Raleigh launched a second expedition with high hopes. It carried the first English colonists to North America, more than 100 military men. Altogether, ten vessels sailed under Raleigh's cousin, Richard Grenville. Their mission was to seize a deep-water harbor and make it a base for English shipping. Here, privateers who raided Spanish ships on the high seas would have a safe harbor. For protection from Indians and Spaniards, the harbor (and colony) would be occupied by soldiers, who would be rotated home after a period of service.

► Early Roanoke and surrounding area

Je Port oder Meerhafen der Landschafft Virginia ist voll Inseln / die da verursachen / daß man gar beschwerlichen in dieselben kommen kan. Dann wiewol sie an vielen orten weit von einander gescheiden sind / vnd sich ansehen lässet / als solte man dadurch leichtlich können hinein kommen / so haben wir dannoch mit vnserm grossen schaden erfahren / daß dieselben offne Plätz voll Sandes sind. Deßwegen haben wir niemals können hinein kommen / biß so lang wir an vielen vnnd mancherley örtern mit einem kleinen Schiff die sach versucht haben. Zuletzt haben wir einen Paß gefunden / auff einem sonderlichen ort / der vnsern Engelländern wol bekannt ist. Als wir nun hinein kommen / vnd eine zeitlang darinn on vnterlaß geschifft hatten / sind wir eines grossen fliessenden Wassers gewar worden / dessen außgang gegen der Inseln / von welcher wir gesagt haben / sich erstrecket. Dieweil aber der Inngang zu demselbigē Wasser deß Sandes halben zu klein war / haben wir denselben verlassen / vñ seyn weiter fort geschifft / biß daß wir an eine grosse Inseln kommen sind / deren Einwohner / nach dem sie vnser gewar worden / haben alsbald mit lauter vnd schrecklicher stimm zu ruffen angefangen / dieweil sie zuvor keine Menschen / die vns gleich weren / beschawet hatten. Deßwegen sie sich auch auff die Flucht begeben haben / vnnd nicht anders dann als Wölffe vnd vnsinnige Leut / alles mit ihrem heulen erfüllt. Da wir ihnen aber freundtlich nachgeruffen / vnd sie widerumb zu vns gelocket / auch ihnen vnsere Wahr / als da sind Spiegel / Messer / Puppen / vnd ander geringe Krämerey (an welchen wir vermeyneten sie einen lust haben solten) fürgestellt hatten / sind sie stehen bliebē. Vnd nach dem sie vnsern guten willen vnd freundtschafft gespürt / haben sie vns gute Wort geben / vnnd zu vnser ankunfft glück gewündschet. Darnach haben sie vns in ihre Statt / Roanoae genannt / ja daß noch mehr ist / zu ihrem Weroans oder Oberherrn geführet / der vns freundtlich empfangen hat / wiewol er erstlich sich ab vns entsetzte. Also ist es vns ergangē in vnser ersten ankunfft der newen Welt / so wir Virginiam nennen. Was nun für Leiber / Kleydung / art zu leben / Feste vnd Gastereyen die Einwohner daselbst haben / das wil ich stück für stück nach einander einem jeden vor die Augen stellen / wie nachfolget.

Thomas Harriot and John White became members of this first settlement. White's job was to draw maps of the land and to sketch the native people; Harriot's, to describe in writing their customs and the type of wealth the land might provide. Their leader, Grenville, dropped them off at the chosen site, an island called Roanoke, in present-day North Carolina. He then sailed back to England to pick up supplies and more colonists.

Meanwhile, the colony at Roanoke foundered. Short of food and supplies, the men found the site a poor one for their purposes. They quarreled—among themselves and with the Algonquian Indians living nearby. In the spring of 1586, the explorer Francis Drake, who was on one of his voyages, stopped at Roanoke to drop off supplies and men, including, it is thought, some freed African slaves. If so, there followed the first contact among what was to become the three main societies in colonial America: Native American, English, and African. The Roanoke colonists, to Drake's surprise, begged him to carry them back to England in his ships. They had come expecting quick riches and an easy life in a land full of gold and pearls. Instead, they had found a country that demanded slow pioneer farming on soil that would, only in time, yield the resources needed for survival.

Missing Drake by a short while, Grenville arrived at Roanoke with some more colonists. Surprised that the first colonists had abandoned the settlement, he dropped off a small holding party of fifteen men, then returned to England.

The artist John White and the writer Thomas Harriot, who had gone back to England with Drake, created *A Brief and True Report of the New Found Land of Virginia* (1588). Their book portrayed the first images of life in America ever seen by Europeans, with drawings of its people and wildlife as well as maps of Raleigh's Virginia (present-day North Carolina and Virginia). Among the crops mentioned in the report was tobacco. Raleigh soon became convinced that tobacco had medicinal benefits. He was seen everywhere smoking a long silver pipe and carrying a gold tobacco case.

The Lost Colony. In 1587 Raleigh sent out a third major expedition to North America. Many lessons had been learned from the earlier attempt at colonization. Recognizing that Roanoke was a poor site (the harbor was small and nearby Indians were unfriendly), Chesapeake Bay was chosen for the new colony. It was decided that leadership would be civil, not military, and the artist White was named governor. Along with him would voyage families who intended to stay, rather than military men who planned to return home. Fourteen families participated, making a total of 114 colonists in all. Seventeen were women, including White's pregnant daughter Eleanore Dare (her child Virginia became the first English person born on the continent), and nine were boys. The remaining eighty-eight colonists were men born in England and other European countries. Their goal was to build an English-American settlement, the City of Raleigh.

> ### Voyages Sponsored by Raleigh to the New World
>
> **1584** Expedition finds site for colony in North America
>
> **1585** First colony lands at site, called Roanoke
>
> **1586** Supply ships return to find colony deserted
>
> **1587** Second colony lands at Roanoke
>
> **1590** John White returns to the deserted colony
>
> **1595** Raleigh makes first voyage to Guiana, South America
>
> **1599** Raleigh begins sending search parties to Roanoke
>
> **1618** Raleigh makes final voyage to Guiana

The party set out for Chesapeake Bay. Piloting the expedition was Simon Fernandes in ships supplied by Raleigh. As agreed, Fernandes stopped at Roanoke to pick up the fifteen men left there by Grenville the year before. They had disappeared. It was learned they escaped from an Indian attack. After hearing this news, the new colonists intended to continue on to Chesapeake Bay. But Fernandes refused to ferry them any farther. It was late in the season for privateering, he insisted, and he must set sail immediately. Fernandes left the colonists at Roanoke, taking White, who had to return to England for supplies, with him.

White visited Raleigh as soon as he arrived, and both men threw themselves into preparations for White's return to America. Raleigh tried to send out a small supply ship right away, but it never sailed and White's trip was also delayed. The queen forbade ships to leave due to a crisis at home: Spain was sending its fleet, or armada, to crush the English navy. Raleigh was needed to defend his country in this conflict.

Meanwhile, White kept searching for investors with money to support the Roanoke colonists he had left behind. In 1589 Raleigh struck a deal with some merchants who would send money, supplies, and ships to Roanoke. In 1590 Raleigh arranged for White to sail back to his family at Roanoke. Finally, after three years, he returned, only to find an empty colony.

The search for these lost colonists began. The only clues left were a post with the word "Croatoan," the name of a nearby island, carved into it, and a trench with buried chests, which the Indians had already dug up and rifled through. Poor weather forced a puzzled White to leave for England without searching any further. For close to ten years little was done to solve the mystery.

Meanwhile, in 1595, Raleigh sailed to South America. He was searching for El Dorado, the Incan city of gold, to lay its treasures at the queen's feet. Raleigh planned to find the mythical city and establish new colonies of natives in this area for Elizabeth. But his plan failed. Raleigh, now in his forties, returned home empty-handed. Although Elizabeth was disappointed, she had another project for him.

In 1596, under Elizabeth's orders, Raleigh assembled men and supplies to capture treasure ships at Cadiz, the main port of Spain. The attack was a huge success, and Raleigh fought splendidly. During the battle, however, a cannonball struck his ship, sending splinters into his leg. Raleigh would limp because of this injury for the rest of his life.

Back in England his skill in battle had begun to reverse his poor standing with the public. "I never knew the gentleman until this time," one citizen remarked, "and I am sorry for it, for there are in him excellent things beside his valour" (Williamson, pp. 102-103).

Still, there was no news of the lost colonists in Virginia. Around 1599 Raleigh began sending parties to search for them. Two vessels that he sent to Chesapeake Bay in 1603 failed to locate

The Colonists vs. the Indians

The 1587 Roanoke colonists attacked Indians gathered around a fire as revenge for their massacre of fifteen white men left by Richard Grenville in 1586. But the colonists attacked the wrong Indians. Slowly, John White began to realize the enormous mistake. "The people sitting around the fire had included women and children as well as men. White tried to explain, saying that Indian men and women dressed so much alike that it was impossible to distinguish them, particularly in the still-dark morning.... It was a sad day for the colony. Not only had they again offended their only friends, but they had failed to teach their enemies [a lesson]" (Kupperman, p. 117).

▲ The English fleet battling the Spanish Armada

even the Bay, and one man was killed by a party of Indians. Raleigh, by then, had lost his rights to America, which depended on whether his colony still existed. Unfortunately, it did not.

Aftermath

From Roanoke to Jamestown. Though clues have surfaced over the years, the fate of the lost colony is still unknown. From 1607 onward the settlers at a new colony at Jamestown were instructed to search out the lost colonists. The Indian chief Powhatan, who ruled much of the region at the time, claimed the colonists had been massacred a short time before the English arrived to settle Jamestown. Most of the colonists had, it seems, trudged from Roanoke to Chesapeake Bay, where they lived in peace among the Chesapeake Indians for twenty years. Then Powhatan, listening to the advice of his priests, decided to wipe out the Chesapeakes so they would not destroy him.

In search of English survivors, Captain John Smith, leader of the Jamestown colony, sent some scouts southward over the uninviting marshlands between Jamestown and Roanoke. Rumor had it that seven of the colonists (four men, two boys, and one girl) had escaped and lived among the Chowan Indians of North Carolina, but they were never seen. A last search for the colonists occurred in 1622. Since then more clues, such as writings the colonists may have carved into stones and tree trunks, have surfaced.

Raleigh and Indians. Raleigh's own attitude toward and relations with Native Americans seems to have changed over the years. When he first applied for a patent to colonize North America, he regarded them as savages who would welcome a kind English ruler. A Native American named Manteo returned with the first expeditions from Roanoke. Raleigh befriended Manteo and had him crowned Lord of Roanoke, wanting him to serve as a sort of feudal lord over the other natives. Later, Raleigh met other Native Americans and voiced his admiration for their courage and thoughtfulness. This contrasted sharply with the first impression the English made on the Indians in North America: "The Indians … were not at all convinced of the superiority of European culture. As they looked at the relative helplessness of the English in Roanoke, they judged otherwise" (Kupperman, p. 116).

During his later expeditions to South America, Raleigh befriended many tribal leaders, especially in Guiana. For the last thirty years of his life, he dreamed of the English replacing the Spanish as the major European power in South America. With this in mind, he encouraged these chiefs to side with the English against the Spanish.

Prison Life. In 1592 Raleigh had secretly married Elizabeth Throckmorton, a lady-in-waiting to Queen Elizabeth. They were able to keep the marriage hidden until Bess, as she was called, became pregnant and began to show. The queen, angry and jealous at the prospect of sharing the affections of her "suitor," imprisoned the couple in the Tower of London. After a few months, when news reached England that one of Raleigh's vessels had captured a treasure ship, he regained the queen's favor and was released.

Soon, however, Elizabeth died, and Raleigh again found himself imprisoned in the Tower. James I, the king who had succeeded Elizabeth, felt threatened by the popular and powerful Raleigh. The king drummed up false charges against Raleigh, accusing him of plotting against the throne. James stripped Raleigh of all the honors Elizabeth had bestowed on him and sentenced him to be hanged, drawn, and quartered. The public, outraged at this unfair treatment, plainly favored Raleigh. One countryman commented: "Whereas when I saw Sir Walter Raleigh first, I would have gone a hundred miles to see him hanged, I would, ere we parted, have gone a thousand to save his life" (Williamson, p. 142).

At the last minute, in 1603, Raleigh's death sentence was changed to life in prison in the Tower of London. He was allowed visitors, and his family lived there with him for a while. Raleigh's first son died. His second son, Wat, a saucy youth, was deeply loved by Raleigh. Raleigh also cared greatly for the king's son, Henry, for whom he wrote the *History of the World*. Based on the belief that God controls history, the work was written to guide the prince into becoming the finest king possible. Raleigh never finished the work, stopping when Prince Henry died at age eighteen. Nevertheless, the *History of the World* was printed and widely read by rulers in the seventeenth century.

Besides writing in prison, Raleigh began inventing medicines. His medicines helped revive the prince for a short while when he was on his deathbed. But they failed to rescue Raleigh from the stale prison air; he suffered two strokes while in the Tower. Yet his dreams of discovery remained alive. Raleigh pleaded to return to Guiana to search for the gold he was sure was there. The king finally agreed to let Raleigh go, promising to pardon him if he returned with gold.

Disaster. Raleigh had heard of Jamestown colony while in prison and ached to stop there on the way to Guiana. He did not, however, because 100 of his crew threatened to stay there and not go on to South America.

Raleigh's voyage of 1618 was difficult from the start. The sixty-two-year-old Raleigh grew ill with fever. His son, Wat, who had come along, journeyed onward with Raleigh's friend Lawrence Keymis to find a gold mine while the sickly Raleigh stayed behind to guard the path of retreat. On the way Wat was killed in a fight with Spanish soldiers, and Keymis failed to find the mine. Raleigh, hearing the bad news, lost his temper and blamed Keymis, who then killed himself with a knife. Only years later would modern equipment uncover the gold that, as Raleigh firmly suspected, lay buried in Guiana.

Raleigh returned to England without any gold for the king. Moreover, his promise not to fight the Spanish had been broken in the conflict that claimed his son's life. The king ordered the explorer's death. The night before he was executed, Raleigh added two lines to an old poem he wrote:

> Even such is Time, which takes in trust
> Our youth, our joys, and all we have,
> And pays us but with age and dust:
> Who in the dark and silent grave,
> When we have wandered all our ways,
> Shuts up the story of our days.
> But from that earth, that grave, that dust,
> The Lord shall raise me up I trust. (Ross, p. 207)

The next morning Raleigh was beheaded in one of the most famous death scenes in history. Untidy but cheerful (this was a worthy way to die, he felt), he directed his own execution.

Raleigh handled the ax that was to behead him: "Sharp medicine," he joked, but "a sure cure for all diseases" (Kupperman, p. 157). When he stretched out his arms, he instructed the executioner, it was time to let the ax fall. But when Raleigh threw out his arms, the executioner hesitated. So Raleigh shouted, "Strike!"

After his death Raleigh became a hero in England and in America. The English saw him as the first leader to carry the Protestant religion and English culture to the rest of the world. The

Americans recognized him as responsible for the arrival of the first English settlers in North America. It happened at Roanoke—twenty-three years before the English planted their colony at Jamestown. Later, the Americans would use ships named after Raleigh in their Revolution, their Civil War, the Spanish-American War, and World War II.

In the end, Raleigh's 1587 plan was the model for every successful colony that followed. It called for a corporation of merchants to support a colony, for families to settle the colony together, and for gifts of land to attract colonists. Raleigh had operated on two separate beliefs: first, that the discovery of gold would bring England and himself fortune and fame, and second, that fame and fortune rested on the discovery and production of everyday goods, like wood or cloth. In his lifetime he searched for gold. So did the first Roanoke colonists and the first Jamestown settlers. Only after a decade of failure did the leaders of Jamestown seek families as settlers and offer them land to attract them. One of the Jamestown colonists, John Smith, fought for his vision of a great English empire just as Raleigh had. In fact, he has been thought of as the Raleigh of the 1700s. But Smith, unlike Raleigh, operated on the belief that the production of everyday goods promised more success than the discovery of gold. "Let not the meanness of the word *fish* distaste you," Smith argued, "for it will afford as good gold as the mines of Guiana … with less hazard … and more certainty" (Jones, p. 135).

> ### Ships Sailing to Roanoke
> Most ships used on the Roanoke voyages were small and privately owned. One of the vessels, the *Moonlight,* could hold only eight tons. It carried forty voyagers and seven cannons.

For More Information

Jones, H. G., ed. *Raleigh and Quinn: The Explorer and His Boswell.* Chapel Hill: North Carolina Society, 1987.

Kupperman, Karen Ordahl. *Roanoke: The Abandoned Colony.* Totwa, New Jersey: Rowman & Allanheld, 1984.

Williamson, Hugh Ross. *Sir Walter Raleigh.* Westport, Connecticut: Greenwood Press, 1978.

Tarbox, Increase N., ed. *Sir Walter Raleigh and His Colony in America.* Boston: Prince Society, 1884.

Colonization

1565
▼
Pedro Menéndez Avilés Marquez founds St. Augustine, Florida, for Spanish.

1585
▼
Walter Raleigh founds Roanoke Colony for English.

1587
▼
Raleigh makes second attempt to settle Virginia.

1620
▼
Plymouth Colony founded.

1608
▼
Samuel de Champlain founds Quebec Colony for French.

1607
▼
Jamestown founded; **John Smith** meets **Pocahontas.**

1604–1640
▼
English people establish colonies in the Caribbean. They import African slaves.

1622 ▶ Chief Powhatan fights war to oust Jamestown colonists.

1623–1625
▼
New Netherlands founded, renamed New Amsterdam.

1629
▼
John Winthrop founds Massachusetts Bay Colony.

1637
▼
Massachusetts banishes **Anne Hutchinson.** New England colonies war against Pequot tribe.

1664
▼
English people capture New Amsterdam and rename it New York.

1731–1732
▼
James Oglethorpe helps found Georgia Colony.

1712
▼
Slave rebellion in New York.

1692–1695
▼
Salem Witch Trials judges sentence **Bridget Bishop.**

1681
▼
William Penn founds Pennsylvania; he recognizes rights of local tribes to land.

1739 ▶ Stono Rebellion in South Carolina.

COLONIZATION

Colonization, or the growth of European settlements in America, occurred during the first 200 years of United States history. First came the Spanish, then the English, French, and Dutch, with the English becoming the most powerful of the immigrant populations.

In some cases a company paid out money for the colony. Other colonies were financed by single owners, or sole proprietors. But whether they owned the colony or not, certain individuals figured greatly in the development of settlements from Massachusetts in the north to Virginia and Georgia in the south.

Begun for various reasons, the colonies owed their growth to the Native American, European, and African populations on the continent. The contact among societies, which had started in the days of exploration, continued in the colonial period. Tribes of Indians traded corn to famished colonists and taught them to fish in American waters. Whites, Indians, and blacks produced foods and marketable crops for the colonies, working as servants or slaves.

In the early 1600s conditions in Europe were making it difficult for many to survive and prosper. Religious groups were persecuted in various areas and there was a shortage of land, especially in England. Landless nobles saw an opportunity to acquire vast estates in America. The chance to own land attracted common folk,

▲ Ten European settlements established in America before 1700

too. Across the social classes, Europeans began looking to the Americas as a haven from the "Old World."

English investors poured their money into Jamestown, Virginia, founding a military colony intent on discovering gold. Barely surviving with the help of **John Smith** and others, the colony changed direction. Its promoters finally focused on slow growth by working "free" land instead of quick riches through the discovery of gold. The land, however, was not free, but belonged to Indian tribes, a fact recognized at the time by William Penn of

Pennsylvania and few others. He pledged to pay the Indians for every acre before selling it to settlers. Elsewhere a tug-of-war for land developed, in which there were peaceful dealings and conflicts between Indians and whites. **Pocahontas** and her father, Chief Powhatan, dealt peacefully with the newcomers until the chief, growing wise to the European thirst for Indian land, lost patience and fought. Afterward, the English convinced themselves they were entitled to native lands. In their eyes, Indians became obstacles to remove.

While colonists in Virginia came mostly for profit, those in New England came for religious freedom as well as profit. The *Mayflower* and its load of Pilgrims landed on Cape Cod, Massachusetts, in 1620, beginning a steady migration from Europe. Nine years later a settlement of Puritans, the Massachusetts Bay Colony, was founded at present-day Salem. Another settlement of Puritans was later founded at Boston.

The Puritans experimented in their new home. Actually, the whole continent became a type of social laboratory for leaders with different visions. The Puritan vision was that of a society living in strict harmony with the Protestant religion as practiced by the colony's leaders. Such a rigid viewpoint resulted in the birth of other settlements, such as Rhode Island, whose founder, Roger Williams, felt the Bay Colony was too strict. It was Williams who first introduced the idea of separation between church and state to the colonies. The strict Puritan outlook also led to punishment for disobedient colonists such as **Anne Hutchinson,** and to the Salem Witch Trials. **Bridget Bishop** was one of the first to be persecuted in these trials held by Puritans, who themselves had suffered persecution in England. And to fulfill yet another vision, Georgia began as a refuge for prisoners. **James Oglethorpe** saw the southern colony as a haven for "criminals" locked up in crowded English jails for owing money that they had no likely way of ever repaying.

Tensions marred relations among the different groups from the start. Almost every colony experienced such difficulties that its ownership eventually shifted to the king, making it a royal colony. Still, far from home, the settlers exercised some self-government through their colonial assemblies. Only in Pennsylvania was this assembly

The figure of the Indians fort or Palizado in

NEW ENGLAND

And the maner of the deſtroying

It by Captayne Vnderhill

And Captayne Maſon.

Hear enttra Captayne Vnderhill

The Indians howſe

Their Streets

Hear Enttra Captayne Maſon

▲ Attack on the Pequot fort at Mystic, Connecticut

chosen by all the colony's free males. Other areas required their voters to meet several qualifications: be male, belong to a church, and have enough property.

Even in Pennsylvania, women were denied the vote, though at least the colony allowed them to become ministers. In contrast, Massachusetts Bay Colony condemned Ann Hutchinson for daring to preach, or in its view, daring to act as a "man" rather than a "woman." Colony leaders would later execute one of Hutchinson's followers, Mary Dyer, for acting too independently.

In New England, as in Virginia, trouble also erupted between the colonists and Indians. The Pequot War, occurring fifteen years after Powhatan's rebellion in Virginia, began at Mystic River, Connecticut, in 1637. Fighting a confederacy of tribes led by the Pequot Indians, colonists here torched an Indian village and killed men, women, and children. Warriors who fell captive to the colonists in later fighting were shipped to the Caribbean Islands as slaves.

Trouble between African slaves and colonists would erupt a century later, in the 1700s, after a rise in the slave trade. It was a triangular trade, from a port in North America to West Africa to the Caribbean Islands and then back to a North American port. Most of the slaves were dropped off in the Caribbean at first, but as time passed an increasing number of them were shuttled to North America. Desperate for a work force to raise tobacco in the area around Chesapeake, Virginia, merchants turned first to indentured servants—poor Englishmen who were promised free land after seven years labor. The service was brutal; its volunteers suffered malaria and cruel work regimes. Only about one in twenty survived the full term. Yet for several generations Virginia had many more white servants than black slaves. Then the cost of slaves from Africa dropped, and so did the supply of white servants. The result, by the early 1700s, was a shift from mostly white to mostly black laborers in the fields. With it came a change in the balance of free and slave populations, followed by revolts such as the Stono Rebellion in South Carolina, where blacks came to outnumber whites by two to one.

John Smith

1579-1631

Personal Background

Privateer. Born in Willoughby, Lincolnshire, England, in 1579, John Smith seems always to have been destined for the military. By the age of sixteen he had left home and traveled to France, where he became a private in the French Army. At that time France was at war with Spain over control of the Netherlands, and Private Smith fought in Flanders until 1600, when he left for Italy. On the ship near Italy he was discovered to be a Protestant and thrown overboard, only to be rescued by pirates. He remained a soldier of fortune. His career took him to Transylvania, where Duke Sigmund Bathor was fending off Turkish invaders. Much in his early escapades, told by Smith himself, might have been exaggerated. In 1604 he supposedly killed three Turks in man-to-man combat, for which he was knighted by the duke. Later that year Smith was captured by the Turks and sold into slavery to the Tartars of Eastern Europe and Asia. He killed his owner and escaped to Morocco.

Virginia Company. Returning to England, the soldier of fortune caught the attention of King James I. When a group was organized to establish a colony in Virginia, Smith was persuaded to join as one of its leaders.

THE PORTRAICTUER OF CAPTAYNE IOHN SMITH ADMIRALL OF NEW ENGLAND

These are the Lines that shew thy
That shew thy Grace and Glory,
Thy Faire-Discoueries and Fowle-
Of Salvages, much Cwilliz'd by
Best shew thy Spirit and to it G
So, thou art Brasse without—but G

▲ John Smith

Event: Founding of Virginia Colony at Jamestown.

Role: Although not the elected head of Jamestown, John Smith, by virtue of his military experience and his personality, soon became leader. The colony, set in a malarial swamp and surrounded by Indians whose attitude to the whites was unknown, faced starvation. Smith is credited with saving its settlers in the cruel winters of 1609-10 and 1610-11, when their population had dwindled from over one hundred settlers to sixty.

Participation: The Virginia Colony

Raleigh and Gilbert. Earlier some of the coastline of Virginia had been explored by Walter Raleigh and his stepbrother Humphrey Gilbert, who had financed a settlement on an island south of Chesapeake Bay, Roanoke. Although this colony was unsuccessful and the settlers disappeared, the venture provided useful information to the king. He later granted investors of the Virginia Company of London a patent to settle another colony, allowing expansion 200 miles north and south of the James River, stretching from sea to sea. (One of their assignments was to search for Raleigh's missing colonists.) On December 19, 1606, the 104 colonists (men and boys) set sail in three ships under the direction of Christopher Newport. This was not the group of Protestant farmers and cattle raisers that would later colonize Plymouth, Massachusetts. Rather, the members of the Virginia party were nearly without farming experience. They were carpenters, laborers, jewelers, perfumers, and gold refiners sent to establish a colony for profit. In fact, there were more "gentlemen" officers—men with little work experience—than non-officers, and this was to take a toll on the Jamestown Colony.

Leaders of the colonists. On board the ships, Smith, Bartholomew Gosnold, and George Percy established themselves as leaders among the passengers. However, Smith was accused at sea of inciting a mutiny with the suggested intent of murdering his superior, Captain Newport, and making himself king of Virginia. The accusation was serious; a gallows was prepared for Smith's execution. It is perhaps an indication of his own strength and personality that "Capt. Smith, for whom they [the gallows] were intended, could not be persuaded to use them" (Horne, p. 167).

Protector of the colony. Nevertheless, Smith was still under arrest when the company anchored in Chesapeake Bay near the Powhatan River (renamed the James River in the king's honor) on May 13, 1607. Immediately the settlers were attacked by hostile Indians and two were wounded. The colonists then opened the sealed box in which their instructions from the king had been kept secret. Smith was named the second of seven councillors chosen to guide the colony. Although Smith was among the seven, he was not allowed to participate at first. The council elected Edward Maria

Wingfield president of the council and governor of the colony for the year 1607. Largely under Smith's direction, the colonists constructed a central building, then strengthened their settlement. Smith next volunteered to search the surrounding territory for food. That first summer was a terrible one. Unable or unwilling to plant sufficient crops, the settlers found it necessary to live almost entirely on fish and crabs. Fifty of the party died.

Wingfield proved an unworthy leader—not strong enough to deal with the Indians even though several nearby chiefs expressed their willingness to live in peace. Somewhat reluctantly, a few of the Indians had even traded with Smith for food.

Disagreement. In September 1607, several councillors, including Smith, petitioned for Wingfield's removal from office. He was replaced by John Ratcliffe, who guided the colony until September 8, 1608. Yet more and more obviously Smith was becoming leader of the colony. According to his own statement, his goals were "erecting towns, peopling countries, informing the ignorant, reforming things unjust … and gain to our native Mother Country" (Horne, p. 167). Smith was an able organizer, though harsh in his dealings at times with his own countrymen as well as the Indians.

Surveying Chesapeake Bay. Late in 1607, Smith volunteered to lead a party to explore the area around Chesapeake Bay. The party, including Smith, two white men named Robinson and Emry, and two Indians, traveled up the James River, where they encountered some hostile Indians and were forced to land in a bog:

The savages … followed him with 300 bowmen led by the king Pamunkee, who, searching the turnings of the river, found Robinson and Emry by the fireside. These they shot full of arrows and slew. (Horne, p. 168)

Pocahontas. Smith was captured by an Indian named Opechancanough. Turned over to the priests, they judged the Englishman harmless. Afterward he was taken around the Indian territory and at one point invited to shoot his pistol at a target. Smith knew he couldn't hit a target so far away, but he also knew he had to leave the impression of being powerful. So he secretly damaged his pistol, then made excuses that it was broken so he could not shoot it.

Later, Smith was taken to Chief Powhatan. It was during this period, Smith claimed, that he was rescued from death by the chief's daughter, Pocahontas. Some historians accept Smith's tale, while others dismiss it as much exaggerated. Nonetheless, Smith related that he was captured and bound to a tree and held captive for a month before killing two of the Indians. Recaptured, he was condemned to death by Powhatan until the chief's twelve-year-old daughter, Pocahontas, interfered on his behalf. Apparently, the young girl persuaded the chief to change the death sentence to a type of slavery, having Smith make hatchets and bells for the Indian warriors. Smith had imagined other treatment: "So fat they fed Mee, that I much doubted [feared] they intended to have sacrificed mee to the Quioughquosiche, which is a superior power they worship" (Horne, p. 169). As the story goes, Smith finally convinced the chief to free him in exchange for two cannons and a grindstone.

John Smith's Description of Powhatan

"There came skipping in a great grim fellow, all painted over with coale mingled with oyle; and many Snakes and Weasel's skins stuffed with moss, and all their tayles tied together, so as they met on the crown of his head in a tassel; and round about the tassel was a coronet of feathers." (Smith, p. 48)

Smith returned to find the people of Jamestown near starvation and John Ratcliffe, the colony's leader, preparing to sail for England in the colony's only remaining ship. Smith immediately recruited other colonists to help stop Ratcliffe, whereupon Ratcliffe attempted to have Smith executed for the deaths of Robinson and Emry, Smith's murdered companions. Fortunately, Smith was cleared of all charges, and the atmosphere grew less strained when Pocahontas appeared. She came leading a train of Indians bearing food. By Smith's account, during his years in the colony this would occur repeatedly.

Smith fulfilled his commitment to Powhatan by offering his representative two large cannons and a millstone. The two cannons weighed 3,000 and 4,500 pounds, a weight the Indians were not able to move, so the offer was declined.

Governor Smith. Smith became governor of the Virginia Colony to serve for one year beginning in September 1608. Seeing that some colonists were reluctant to labor and that their religion was being abandoned, he directed the building of a church and forced the "gentlemen" of the party to work. His directives of early 1609 forcefully stated his position:

Countrymen! You see now that power seateth wholly in myself. You must obey this now for a law—he that will not work shall not eat. I protest by that God that made men, since necessity hath no power to force you to gather for yourselves, you shall not only gather for yourselves, but for those that are sick. They shall not starve. (Horne, p. 171)

As governor he continued to chart the region. In 1608 and 1609 Smith led two parties that mapped out the coastline of Chesapeake Bay, traveling, by his own estimate, 3,000 miles.

Early in 1609, according to Smith, he had another narrow escape from the hands of Powhatan. With the people of the colony hungry, the captain led a party to Werowocomoco, Powhatan's home base, to secure food. Powhatan was by this time familiar with the power of English weapons and demanded payment in swords and guns. Smith refused, and the two argued until Powhatan grew weary and turned to other plans. He would give the Englishmen the needed corn, but delay its delivery to allow time to kill them all. The plan was to supply a meal to the English during the delay, then attack them when they laid their weapons aside to eat. Once more, according to this account, Pocahontas came to the rescue, warning the English. Smith sent a message to Powhatan that convinced him the plan would fail, and it did.

The English party then traveled to the village of Opechancanough to secure food. As the story is told, they arrived to find that this chief's armed warriors vastly outnumbered them. Smith crashed into Opechancanough's tent, grabbed the larger Indian by his hair, and threatened to kill him unless his demands were met. The party thus secured the needed food for the colony, but the incident added to Opechancanough's hatred for the colonists, which grew into a commitment to eliminate European settlements in America. Later, when he replaced Powhatan as the supreme chief, Opechancanough tried to accomplish this goal. In 1622 and again in 1640, his warriors attacked Jamestown and its surroundings, massacring hundreds of colonists. These attacks would, in turn, leave the colonists with the long-lasting belief that they were entitled to destroy Indian villages.

Smith did return to Jamestown with his cargo of food but his remaining time in the colony was to be brief. A second party of

King Powhatan comands CiSmith to be flayne, his daughter Pokahontas beggs his life his thankfullnes and how he fubiected 39 of their kings. reade history.

▲ Powhatan commands Smith to be executed

colonists arrived in August 1609 with a new charter won by Smith's old foe, Christopher Newport. Smith refused to give up his rule to the new leaders, but when his one-year term expired, he gave the task of governing the colony to George Percy without waiting for the next appointed governor to arrive.

Smith then went outside the village of Jamestown to build his own home. He wanted, it seems, to establish English settlements outside Jamestown. In the process, he accidentally exploded a bag

▲ **Native Americans massacre early settlers**

of gunpowder he was carrying and tore a large wound in his hip. His clothing caught fire. To extinguish it, he jumped into the river and almost drowned. The experience left him too weak to continue his struggles for the welfare of Jamestown. Some accounts maintain simply that his enemies forced him out of his leadership position in the colony. In either case, at the end of September 1609 Smith set sail for England, never to return to Jamestown. Certainly some of the settlers would miss him. His departure and the feelings of these colonists were reported by Richard Potts and William Phettiplace, two of the sixty survivors of the winter of 1609-10:

What shall I say? but thus we lost him that in all his proceedings made justice his first guide and experience his second; ever hating baseness, sloth, pride and indignity more than any dangers; that never allowed more for himself than his soldiers with him; that upon no danger would send them where he would not lead them himself; that would never see us want what he either had, or could by any means get us; that loved actions more than words, and hated falsehood and covetousness worse than death; whose adventures were our lives, and whose loss our deaths. (Horne 1894, p. 172)

Aftermath

The year 1609 found barely 100 survivors remaining in Jamestown. Late in that year these residents were joined by 400 English newcomers who had set sail in nine ships in June. The old residents of Jamestown were too weak to help these newcomers, who themselves were weak from the trip. According to Smith, just before he left the colony:

Though there be fish in the sea, fowls in the air, and beasts in the woods, their bounds are so large, they so wild, and we so weak and ignorant, we cannot much trouble them. (Hawke, p. 95)

Smith had, through force and persuasion, established friendly relations with the Indians, particularly with Powhatan, but the new colonists in their weakened state robbed, stole from, and otherwise mistreated the Indians. The Indians in turn took advantage of the weak colonists and held them within the fortifications of Jamestown and destroyed their livestock. That winter the people of Jamestown were reduced to eating dogs, cats, rats, snakes, toadstools, horse-hides—nearly anything available. When other ships arrived in May 1610 with 175 new colonists, they found only 60 of the 500 inhabitants of Jamestown alive. Prepared to abandon the settlement, the inhabitants had already boarded ship and set sail down the bay when Lord De La Warr's fleet of relief ships arrived, bringing great quantities of supplies and 300 more settlers.

De La Warr turned the colony into a military beachhead and established martial law to save the settlement. Jamestown became the capital of Virginia and a farming community. It flourished until it was partly destroyed in a rebellion in 1676. Then Williamsburg became the territorial capital. By 1722 Jamestown became nothing but a heap of rubble with only three or four liveable, inhabited houses.

Meanwhile, Smith had already embarked on a new phase of his career. In 1608 he had written *A True Relation of Virginia,* and now he returned to writing and mapmaking to promote the growth of America to the English. In 1612 he published the results of his explorations of Chesapeake Bay in *Maps of Virginia.* Two years later he returned to America to chart the coastline of New England (his name for the region). Some credit him with naming Boston, Massacusetts at this time.

Smith remained a soldier and in 1615 entered a battle between the English and the French. Captured by the French, he was imprisoned at Rochelle, where he found time to write the results of his New England survey in *Description of New England* (1616). His work as a soldier and mapmaker won the respect of King James I, who named him Admiral of New England.

> ## The Writings of John Smith
>
> *A True Relation of Virginia,* 1608
> *Maps of Virginia,* 1612
> *Description of New England,* 1616
> *New England Trials,* 1620
> *General Historie of Virginia, New England, and the Summer Islands,* 1624

In his fight to establish a British empire in America, Smith combined writing and action. He created a powerful case in England for such an empire and demonstrated a degree of leadership in America that few could match. Smith lived in Virginia but grew strongly attached to New England too. In fact, he spoke of Virginia and New England as his children, "for they have bin my wife, my hawks, my hounds, my cards, my dice, and in totall my best content" (Jones, p. 129). Smith died in London, England, on June 21, 1631.

For More Information

Hawke, David. *The Colonial Experience.* Indianapolis: The Bobbs-Merrill Company, 1966.

Horne, John. *Great Men and Famous Women.* Vol. 5. New York: Selmar Hess, 1894.

Jones, H. G., ed. *Raleigh and Quinn: The Explorer and His Boswell.* Chapel Hill: North Carolina Society, 1987.

Pocahontas

c. 1595-1617

Personal Background

The Powhatans. Around Chesapeake Bay and inland, across one-fifth of present-day Virginia, lived a number of Native American groups ruled by several chiefs. During the early 1600s their population ranged from 8,000 to 9,000, and they paid allegiance to an overall chief, Powhatan. Though spread throughout the large area, their center of government, the royal village, was located on a river just twelve miles from Jamestown. The Indians had seen white men earlier—English, French, and Spanish ships had explored the bay off and on for nearly 100 years before the founding of the Virginia Colony. No one, however, had threatened their claim to the countryside.

Indian life. The Powhatan Indians lived in long houses, built by bending saplings and binding them together, then covering the sides with woven mats or bark and the roof with thatch. Men roamed the village clad in knee-length shifts of rabbit skin. They painted designs of black, red, and white on their bodies and ornamented themselves with copper jewelry, pearls, and occasionally garter snakes around their necks. Women dressed in short, animal-skin aprons and bone necklaces enhanced with feathers and beads. In the warm seasons children seldom wore any clothing. The Indians provided for themselves by hunting, fishing, and farm-

Ætatis suæ 21 Aº. 1616.

Matoaks als Rebecka daughter to the mighty Prince
Powhatan Emperour of Attanovghkomouck als virginia
converted and baptized in the Christian faith, and
Wife to the Worll Mr Tho: Rolff

▲ **Pocahontas**

Event: Settlement of Virginia Colony (Jamestown).

Role: Pocahontas was a daughter of the Indian chief who controlled the area around Chesapeake Bay. She befriended the Jamestown settlers. Regarding her as an exception in a group of otherwise savage Indians, the English considered her a heroine. She, in their view, rescued the colonists from starvation and was responsible for any friendship they received from the Indians.

ing, raising mostly corn. Despite using swords and axes made only of wood, stone, or bone, Powhatan's followers were a fearsome group given to such practices as the ritual torture of captives.

Pocahontas. Powhatan had several wives, some of whom bore him single children, then seemed to disappear from the history of the village. About 1595 one of these wives gave birth to a daughter who became the chief's favorite. Bright, independent, and mischievous, she was named Mataoka, but she became known as Pocahontas, "the playful one."

By the time the Virginia Colony settlers had arrived, Pocahontas was nearly eleven years old. Her first trip to Jamestown occurred, it seems, when she was twelve. Like most Indian children of her day, she wore no clothes and her hair was cropped close to her head, except for a long, braided lock at the back. Her mission on that first visit was to get the colonists to release some Indian prisoners. Afterward, she made social visits to the town. From the beginning she seems to have felt comfortable with the villagers even though their ways were strange to her. Earliest recollections of the settlers reveal Pocahontas as a sometimes playmate of the several boys of Jamestown who were nearly her age. Certainly she was a spirited child. She would "gett the boyes forth with her into the markett place and make them wheele, falling on their handes turning their heeles vpwardes, whome she would follow . . . all the Fort over" (Rountree, p. 44).

Participation: Virginia Colony

Pocahontas and John Smith. Apparently, Jamestown leader John Smith treated the young girl with kindness and friendship. She probably admired him, knowing her father's regard for Smith, and he probably thought of her as no more than a child. Still, he learned some Indian words from her and taught her some English. This early association would serve them both well in the future.

Smith claimed that Pocahontas saved his life. Linking her closely to the Jamestown community, the incident was told in Smith's early writings and in greater detail in an account written twenty years later. Its truth has since been called into question, along with other details that have been corrected over the years. Smith, for example, wrote that Pocahontas sent food to save Jamestown from starvation. Historians now know that it was her father, Powhatan, who sent the desperately needed food.

Pocahontas's rescue took place in the dead of winter. On December 10, 1607, Smith led a party traveling by boat to trade for corn with the Chickahominy, a group loyal to Powhatan. When the river up which they traveled became narrower, Smith left the boat and continued by canoe with two white traders and two Indian guides. Farther on, the party decided to make camp. The two traders, Robinson and Emry, began to set up camp while Smith explored the land ahead. He soon found himself surrounded by Indians armed with bows and arrows. Although he tried to escape, Smith was captured and taken to Opechancanough, uncle of Pocahontas and a chief under Powhatan. Smith, certain that the Indians intended to kill him, presented his ivory compass to the Indians, making them believe that he possessed magic.

The prisoner was then taken to Werowocomoco to stand trial before the great Chief Powhatan. Here he dined in a manner befitting someone who was about to be ritually killed. (Elsewhere the Powhatan Indians had already killed another of the Smith party, dismembering him and burning the body parts.) After dinner Smith was given water in which to wash and feathers with which to dry himself. Then two great stones were rolled into place: Powhatan intended to have him killed by crushing his head against the stones. Pocahontas stepped forward and pleaded for Smith's life. As a favorite daughter, the twelve-year-old was in a privileged position. Powhatan listened to her pleas and decided to lighten the punishment. Instead of killing Smith, he held him as a prisoner. (The story detailed twenty years later described how Pocahontas lay down beside Smith, whose head was being held against the stones, and placed her own head over his as if to shield him from the blows of the executioners.)

His life spared, Smith helped his cause with more "magic," sending a piece of paper to Jamestown that would "speak" to the settlers, who then responded as the note had requested. Finally, he was sent back to Jamestown, commanded by Powhatan to send the Indians two cannons and a grindstone. (Smith kept his promise, offering the Indians who led him home two cannons, each weighing

▲ Arms and armor typical of the early Massachusetts settlers

close to 4,000 pounds, and a heavy millstone. As Smith had hoped, the Indians refused to cart off the heavy offerings.)

Jamestown. The same day that Smith returned to Jamestown, January 2, Pocahontas came to the village with a group of Indians to bring provisions. According to Smith's later records, the Indian princess repeated her supply mission every four or five days until her father forbade her to visit Jamestown. By late 1608 Powhatan had changed his attitude toward Jamestown. When the colonists had first arrived, Smith had told the chief that the English had landed only to repair some damaged ships and escape bad weather. Now, nearly two years later, Powhatan realized that these visitors were staying. The chief lost patience and began making war on the colonists. Though they still sometimes traded food with the colonists in hopes of winning European weapons, Powhatan's people harassed the colonists at every opportunity.

A second rescue. Nevertheless, in the desperation that came with a difficult winter, Smith led still another party to Werowocomoco to obtain food in January 1609. The account of this incident suggests that Pocahontas played a large role in it, too. She was present at the meeting, during which Smith asked for food and Powhatan demanded payment in swords and muskets. The two bargained for hours until Powhatan apparently decided that the bartering was futile and left the meeting.

Later, the chief sent a gift of a pearl necklace to Smith, who, with his men, had returned to his own camp discouraged. Then one of the chief's warriors came to report that Powhatan had changed his mind, that the colonists would be given the food they wanted. When it arrived, the Indians refused to load the food onto Smith's ships. Powhatan's plan was to keep the settlers in their camp until they grew hungry. Then, when they laid down their weapons to eat, his men would descend on them and destroy the party. In the night, the story continues, Pocahontas sneaked into the camp and warned the colonists of the plan. Food arrived shortly thereafter and with it more demands from Powhatan. Smith's response convinced the chief that the colonists were prepared for battle and Powhatan withdrew. Once more Pocahontas, according to the story, had rescued a group of colonists.

Powhatan's massacre. Powhatan, however, was not prepared to abandon his plans to eliminate the threat of colonization. Smith had returned to Jamestown to find that a new ship had brought a new charter and a call for a new governor. While awaiting the new governor, Smith turned over his command to George Percy and withdrew from Jamestown, preparing to build himself a home on a nearby island. The troubles of the colony were now in the hands of Percy.

In the fall of 1609 Powhatan sent a young white boy, Thomas Savage (who had earlier been left with him as a hostage), to the colony with supplies. Unsuspecting, Percy sent Savage and another young man of the colony, Henry Spelman, back with a gift for Powhatan. The chief promptly used Spelman as a tool to carry out his plan. He sent a message back to the colony, asking for the colonists to sail a shipload of copper pots to his village; in return he would fill the ship with corn. Again Spelman acted as messenger; the ship would be sent.

Sixty-two colonists manned two ships carrying the copper. When the ships arrived at Powhatan's base, the Indians were armed and ready for battle. They overwhelmed the colonists and killed all but one young boy, Samuel, who was taken prisoner, and one other colonist, Jeffry Shortridge. This treachery contributed greatly to the horrors suffered during the dismal winter of 1609-10, from which only 60 of over 450 colonists survived.

Pocahontas, it is claimed, had not agreed with her father as he planned for war or for the massacre of the ships' crews. Although she could not violate Powhatan's order not to visit Jamestown, she did spend more and more time away from his new capital, Rasawrack. Soon after the massacre she moved to live with the more peaceful followers of Powhatan, the Potomacs. Now she plotted to help the hostage boys escape. She and the chief of the Potomacs visited Rasawrack and befriended Samuel, Henry Spelman, and Thomas Savage. When they prepared to return home, the three young men stole away with the two Indians, conducted safely by some of Powhatan's men. Savage betrayed them, though. He had been treated like a son by Powhatan and now was loyal to him. He returned to warn Powhatan of the escape. Powhatan sent messengers to order Pocahontas and Chief Pasptanze to return. In the struggle Samuel was killed with an axe wielded by one of Powhatan's men, but Spelman escaped. He later received aid from Pocahontas and eventually returned to Jamestown.

Henry Spelman. Pocahontas's aiding Spelman had an effect on the colony. Word was sent to England that there was some hope of making peace with the Indians and her kindness to Spelman was given as proof. Lord De La Warr, the new governor, wrote glowingly of the friendly Potomacs and downplayed the war with Powhatan. More settlers were encouraged to come to the colony and it began to expand beyond Jamestown. The new charter allowed expansion 200 miles north and south of Old Point Comfort, including much of today's Virginia, Maryland, Delaware, and North Carolina.

Pocahontas's kidnapping. With her father's order to avoid Jamestown and with Smith now returned to England, Pocahontas had few dealings with the settlers for the next several years. Smith had left without saying goodbye, and the colonists informed her he was dead. Seven years later she discovered that he was still alive. The lie made her furious.

During this period the colony grew, though war with Powhatan and his followers continued. Then in 1612 Pocahontas again became the center of attention in Jamestown. Captain Samuel Argall, a ship-master of earlier immigrations, returned to Jamestown and immediately reestablished his good relations with the Potomacs. In December 1612 Argall secured about 1,100 bushels of corn from these Indians. In April 1613 the captain again returned to the Potomacs.

This time Argall resolved to kidnap Pocahontas as a means of forcing Powhatan into a lasting peace. He bribed two Indian friends with a copper kettle and they lured Pocahontas aboard his ship. She was not allowed to leave. For her freedom, Powhatan agreed to pay in corn but refused to give up some missing guns Argall wanted. Raids between the groups continued and for almost a year Pocahontas remained at Jamestown. Remembering her past assistance, the older colonists treated her like a princess. Powhatan sent a message that he wished Argall to treat his daughter well, and then he ignored her plight.

Pocahontas's stay in Jamestown was a learning experience. Several of the men gave her lessons in English manners and religion. Then the leaders decided to make her a showpiece to advertise the Virginia Colony: a model Indian princess. She was given into the care of the reverend Alexander Whittaker, whose family taught her

▲ **The first Europeans learned much from the Native Americans, including methods for grinding corn**

to dress like an English lady and to pray to the Christian God. She began to attend Christian services and to study the catechism. Although she was unable to read English, Pocahontas proved to be a fine student. Soon she could recite such Christian doctrines as the Apostle's Creed, the Lord's Prayer, and the Ten Commandments. In the spring of 1614 Pocahontas took the vows of Christianity, was baptized, and received the Christian name Rebecca.

Rebecca. Among the young men who instructed Pocahontas in English ways was twenty-eight-year-old John Rolfe. Rolfe, who had lost his wife on the journey to the colony, had become a leader in the colony. Even before Pocahontas became the Christian Rebecca, Rolfe had thought about taking her as his wife. On April 5, 1614, after winning approval from Powhatan and from the heads of the colony, Rolfe and Rebecca were married in Jamestown. Pocahontas's two brothers and her uncle Opechancanough witnessed the marriage. Pocahontas had become a symbol of Indian-colonist unity—"another knot to bind the peace." When Powhatan was satisfied that the marriage was a happy one for his daughter, he sent a message of peace to Jamestown that spoke of the then-governor Thomas Dale:

> There have been too many of his men and mine slaine, and by my occasion there shall never be more … for I am now olde and would gladly end my daies in peace: if you offer me injurie, my countrie is large enough to goe from you. This much I hope will satisfie my brother. (Woodward, p. 166)

Powhatan was growing old and had long been losing his power. Other chiefs would take over and war against colonists would continue. However, for a short time peace came to Jamestown. Pocahontas lived as the wife of a planter and in 1615 gave birth to a son, Thomas. The few years that followed became the golden age of relations between the Powhatan Indians and the English. The colonists hired the Indians to hunt for them and trained them to use guns. It was during this time that Rolfe learned about tobacco, introduced it as a moneymaking crop to Jamestown, and himself became a successful grower. But the tobacco farms that followed would ruin any hopes of peace between the Indians and the settlers of Virginia in the future.

Virginia Families Descended from Pocahontas

- Blair
- Bolling
- Lewis
- Randolph (John Randolph was a U.S. senator from Virginia)

Pocahontas in England. The next year Pocahontas began her final act of support for the colony. Always in need of money, the Virginia colonists had petitioned King James for help but found him indifferent to their needs. Therefore, the colonists proposed to raise the needed cash through a lottery held in the yard of St. Paul's Cathedral in London. The lottery was so successful that the organizers proposed another plan to raise money to establish a religious school in

Virginia. To attract contributions, the colonists would send to England a real Indian princess, Pocahontas. On June 12, 1616, Rolfe, Pocahontas, and several Indians (carefully chosen by the governor of Virginia Colony) arrived at Plymouth, England, aboard the *Treasurer.*

Aftermath

Pocahontas. For a year Pocahontas served as Lady Rebecca in public relations for the Virginia Colony. The officials of the Virginia Company of London had planned that she be treated as royalty, and she was recognized as a princess there. Met at the dock by a vice-admiral of the British navy, she was escorted to London, where wealthy merchants and officials welcomed her. The Indian princess appeared in the royal court in a red-and-gold English dress, which increased the royal air of her bearing.

Pocahontas was a slight woman, and the grueling tour of banquets and calls upon the social elite of London began to wear on her. Soon illness would keep her away from the social whirl. All in all, the visit to England was a success for the Virginia Company and Pocahontas, though her own health suffered.

Pocahontas, who contracted a lung disease, escaped the foul air of London in the English countryside. There she was visited by John Smith, whom she thought was dead. Startled, and furious, it was a few hours before she could bring herself to speak with him.

The last days in England were spent introducing Pocahontas to the Rolfe family at their estate at Heacham. In March 1617 Rebecca, Rolfe, and their son, Thomas, were scheduled to set sail for Virginia from Gravesend, a port at the mouth of the Thames River. However, while waiting for the ship Pocahontas again fell ill. She died of a respiratory infection (perhaps pneumonia or tuberculosis) and was buried at St. George's Parish Church in Gravesend. She was twenty-one or twenty-two years old when she died.

John Rolfe and Jamestown. Pocahontas's husband left his son in the care of his family in England and returned to Virginia. There he devoted his time and efforts to developing the tobacco industry and to improving the economy of the colony. He became a member of the first representative legislature in America. His work and that of others gave Virginia Colony an orderly government and made the colony productive.

But when Rolfe first returned he found the colony inhabited by about fifty soldiers living in decaying houses and with poor storage areas and churches. Desperate to make money, the colonists had planted tobacco even on the streets of the colony. The new governor, Samuel Argall, set out to repopulate Jamestown and make it productive. Powhatan held to his declaration of peace but continued to lose power among the Powhatan Indians. And shortly after Rolfe's return, the great chief was replaced by Opechancanough. He had once lived in Spain and served the Spanish in Mexico under the name Luis de Velasco. In his new home he had been adopted as a brother by Powhatan. A militant leader, Opechancanough had plans to rid the country of the colonists. In 1622 he organized a blow to the colonists. Only the people living directly in Jamestown were forewarned. The massacre resulted in the deaths of 347 settlers, including Rolfe, and again put the Virginia Colony on uneasy footing. The massacre also left the survivors feeling entitled to lay ruin to Indian villages. Opechancanough again fought the colonists in 1640 and killed many of them. Nevertheless, the colony grew and prospered, expanding beyond Jamestown until by the 1690s the town was nearly abandoned.

Thomas Rolfe. In 1635 the twenty-year-old son of Pocahontas returned to Virginia and the home in which he had been born. He found that in his absence his grandfather Powhatan had willed him 1,200 acres stretching along the James River. Thomas secured permission of the Virginia General Assembly to visit his Indian relatives, after which he returned to the colony and became a successful tobacco planter. He married an English woman and their children and grandchildren started families whose descendants are still wealthy and prosperous Virginians. Among them, through seven generations, are educators, statesmen, lawyers, judges, and ministers as well as successful planters and businesspeople.

For More Information

Bridenbaugh, Carl. *Jamestown, 1544-1699.* New York: Oxford University Press, 1980.

Rountree, Helen C. *Pocahontas's People.* Norman: University of Oklahoma Press, 1990.

Woodward, Grace Steele. *Pocahontas.* Norman: University of Oklahoma Press, 1969.

Anne Hutchinson

1591-1643

Personal Background

Anne Hutchinson came to be known as a religious trouble-maker and, indeed, that was her heritage. Her father, Francis Marbury, lived in the small town of Alford in Lincolnshire, England, about 20 miles north of Boston, England, and 125 miles from London. There he earned a reputation as a religious rebel.

Anglican Church. In the early 1500s, King Henry VIII broke away from the Catholic Church in order to divorce his wife Catherine and established the Anglican Church in England. By 1556, when Hutchinson's father was born, Queen Elizabeth I had come to the throne, positioned herself as the head of the Church of England, and defeated the Spanish Catholics. England became a country of great religious activity, with Anglican bishops and ministers taking dominant positions in the government and courts. People loyal to the queen were pressing for church rites, teachings, and rituals that would clearly separate their new church from Catholicism. In this atmosphere, some small groups wanted to change the church even more, to rid it of any formal ritual that would suggest a relationship with the Catholics. These people were called Puritans.

Francis Marbury. Bridget Dryden, who would marry Francis Marbury, was the daughter of a large estate owner in central England. Many in her family were Puritans, and at least one relative

▲ Anne Hutchinson

Event: Religious conflict in Massachusetts Bay Colony.

Role: At the time that Anne Hutchinson lived in Massachusetts Bay Colony, its citizens were governed by ministers and laymen of a church growing increasingly rigid in its rituals. Hutchinson was one of the leaders advocating greater freedom of worship. Although banished from the colony for her actions, she joined others, such as Roger Williams, whose actions increased religious freedom in the American colonies.

had been imprisoned in the Tower of London for suggesting religious reforms. About 1571, a young Anglican minister, Francis Marbury, began to teach and preach at the church in Northampton near the Dryden estate. Although Marbury had been educated at Cambridge University, he soon found that many of the Anglican ministers were not well educated but appointed to their positions by the ruling bishops for political reasons. The young minister so openly opposed this lack of an educated clergy that in 1578 he was arrested and sent to jail. After he was released, Marbury, now a widower, chose to move from Northampton. He married Bridget Dryden and settled in Alford. There Marbury supported his growing family by preaching and teaching at St. Wilfred's Church.

Early life. Anne Hutchinson was born in July 1591. At the time, her father was again in trouble over his quarrels with the Anglican leaders. They accused him of being a Puritan and, even though he won his trial, he was forbidden to preach again for several years. This was a benefit for Anne, for now her father could spend his time tending the fields near their home and teaching his young daughter. Anne learned to read through the Bible and an account of her father's first trial, which he had published.

The Marbury home was a busy one. Bridget Marbury gave birth over the years to twelve more children and Anne was expected to help her mother care for them. In addition to managing her household, Anne's mother spent much of her time helping others. She was a skilled midwife, and assisted the women of the community whenever they were giving birth. As she grew older, Anne accompanied her mother on these goodwill visits, and in time she herself became a midwife.

British royalty and the church. Meanwhile, James I had become king of England and proved to be a religious fanatic himself. He asked Parliament to enact a law against witches (many of those who wanted reforms in the Anglican Church were thought to be witches, or messengers of the devil). The law called for witches—most of whom were women—to be hanged.

Anne Marbury and William Hutchinson. Finally, the need to earn a living convinced Marbury to give up trying to reform the church. He applied for a position at a church in London and the

Marbury family moved to this city of 325,000 people. There, after several successful appointments in the church, Marbury died in 1611, leaving 200 British pounds to each of his twelve living children and stating that the girls must stay with their mother until they married. Twenty-one was a late age for a woman of that time to still be single, but on August 9, 1612, Anne did marry. William Hutchinson was a textile merchant whom she had known since her days in Alford. Establishing their home once more in Alford, the Hutchinsons lived there for twenty-two years and had thirteen children who lived to adulthood.

Religion in England. Alford was far enough removed from London for religious differences to develop. Several women in the communities around Alford became preachers even though women preachers were not recognized by the Anglican Church. In Boston, only twenty-four miles away, a young and powerful minister, John Cotton, preached more and more often on Puritan themes. Anne Hutchinson had plenty of opportunity to hear about Cotton since Alford was a market town. Every Tuesday, people would come from far and near to shop at the market and to gossip. Cotton had read about John Calvin, a religious leader of Geneva, Switzerland, and had adopted his beliefs.

One of these beliefs greatly influenced Hutchinson. Anglican bishops of the day were setting rules of conduct for people and judging them for their actions if they broke the rules. This was known as salvation through good deeds, or the Covenant of Works. Cotton, on the other hand, taught that people were sinners and they could only be saved by complete faith in God; their *faith* was more important than their *actions*. This belief became known as the Covenant of Grace. Depending on people to judge themselves, the Covenant of Grace placed responsibility for a person's actions directly on the person himself or herself, rather than tying the person's actions to the demands of the church. The Hutchinsons began to visit Boston to hear Cotton preach.

Massachusetts Bay Colony. A new king of England, Charles I, brought heavy taxes and a poor economy to the land. Meanwhile, freedom to worship continued to be an issue for many. In 1622 Cotton was arrested for preaching ideas not approved by the Anglican Church. He was able to avoid punishment but, as conditions grew

▲ John Cotton

more desperate, he began thinking of leaving England. Meanwhile, another preacher, John Wheelwright, who thought much like Cotton, married William Hutchinson's sister. Before long, he, too, was in trouble with the leaders of the Anglican Church. In 1633 Cotton sailed for New England aboard the *Griffin*. One year later, the Hutchinson family followed on the same ship. Their two older children had gone to the Massachusetts Bay Colony earlier. A couple years later, Wheelwright and his wife, Mary, joined the group in Boston.

Participation: Massachusetts Bay Colony

Beliefs. Before the *Griffin* even landed, Hutchinson was already in trouble for her beliefs. On board the ship bringing them to the new country was a preacher, Zechariah Symmes. Arrogant and given to five-hour sermons, Symmes sometimes preached doctrine with which Hutchinson disagreed. Hutchinson was outspoken about her disagreements and vowed to prove him wrong when they landed. However, Symmes was able to strike the first blow.

Shortly after arriving in Boston, the Hutchinsons applied for membership in the First Church of Boston. (In those days, people were strongly examined about their beliefs before being allowed church membership.) Any member of the church could object to the application and require an investigation. William Hutchinson was immediately accepted into membership, but Symmes objected to Anne Hutchinson's application. She was forced to wait a week and then endure a hearing held by Governor Thomas Dudley, Cotton, and Symmes. It was to be only the first of several times Hutchinson would find it necessary to defend herself from her foes.

Soon, as she had done back in England, Hutchinson began to hold weekly meetings to discuss the Sunday sermons of the ministers. At first these were intended for women, and only a handful of women attended. However, Hutchinson's gentle, helping nature (she continued to call on those in need and act as a midwife), and ability as a speaker soon attracted greater crowds. Once she had heard a preacher tell about his revelation that England was about to be destroyed. She was excited that others received revelations, for Hutchinson maintained that whenever she had done anything of

▲ **Hutchinson preaching**

worth, an inner spirit had revealed it to her beforehand. After a time men joined the women to hear Hutchinson speak; she addressed them from a large chair overlooking her audience. By 1637 Hutchinson would be holding two meetings each week in her home, "wherto sixty or eighty persons did usually resort" (Winthrop, p. 284).

Massachusetts Bay Colony was established in an atmosphere of religious freedom, but it had changed to a rigid Puritan way. The ministers and high lay officials of the churches were becoming the law of the colony—both setting rules and trying those accused of breaking them. Hutchinson thought that they were preaching the Covenant of Works and disagreed with them. Her weekly meetings grew increasingly outspoken in favor of changing the government so that people—and not their ruling ministers—would be responsible for their own actions and that they would be admitted to heaven through belief in God (the Covenant of Grace).

The years 1635 and 1636 were important years for Hutchinson. In 1635 the ship *Defence* arrived in Boston with 200 new settlers. Among them was a young man of wealth and possibly influence at the British court, Henry Vane, and a new minister for the First Church of Boston, John Wilson. Vane was soon attending Hutchinson's meetings and agreeing with her ideas. Reverend Wilson, on the other hand, was a strong opponent. In 1635 he, John Winthrop, a fanatical Puritan and one of the founders of the Massachusetts Bay Colony, and other leaders succeeded in expelling another free thinker from the colony, Roger Williams. Given six weeks to leave the colony, Williams went into the wilderness and established the community of Providence in present-day Rhode Island.

Hutchinson had been telling her listeners that only two ministers, Wheelright and Cotton, besides her were teaching the right doctrine, a doctrine that meant that people could have freedom of religious belief. In 1636 her message grew stronger. She began to compare John Cotton and Wilson in a way that was unfavorable to Wilson. Her future grew brighter for a moment in the summer of 1636 when Vane was elected governor. But the colony had begun to take sides for and against Hutchinson. On her side were Vane, Cotton, and Wheelwright, as well as most of the people of Boston, who would have defended her right to speak.

John Winthrop, the governor of the colony, had organized its founding in 1630. As he did so, he aimed to fulfill his dream of creat-

▲ **People whose religious views differed from those of the authorities were whipped**

ing a "city on a hill," or a city in which people of one belief lived without religious prejudice. Differences of opinion among the people of the city disturbed him. One disturbance was removed when Roger Williams was banished. Now Winthrop turned his attention to Hutchinson. Joining him in opposition to her was Wilson and many of the ministers of churches outside Boston.

During the winter of 1636 letters began to be sent among the leaders of both sides. At one time, Wilson and Winthrop persuaded Cotton to eavesdrop on Hutchinson's meetings to see if there were any unacceptable messages. Cotton reported none. Still, the letters were written and pressure grew to rid the colony of Hutchinson and her, according to Winthrop, "dangerous errors." The arguments grew more heated and focused on more and more trivial issues. The bickering grew too much for the twenty-four-year-old governor,

Vane, who threatened to return to England but was persuaded to finish his year as governor. However, Vane was criticized by a second minister, Hugh Peter, who joined Wilson in his attacks. Wilson was forced to explain these accusations against the governor and was unable to do so, which made him more bitter toward Hutchinson.

Still, the parties to the controversy gathered at Cotton's home and invited Hutchinson to join them. Hutchinson responded to their questions so satisfactorily that the meeting eventually broke up with everyone seemingly satisfied. Meanwhile, a foreshadowing of coming events occurred in March 1637. Hutchinson's brother-in-law, Wheelwright, was called to court to defend one of his earlier sermons. Led by Winthrop, the court found him guilty of sedition (or rebellion and contempt for disobeying the government). Most people of Boston, however, disagreed with this verdict, so the members of the court delayed sentencing until after the 1637 summer election of a new governor.

The atmosphere in Boston was so heated that Winthrop successfully led an action moving the government across the Charles River to Cambridge. In the May elections, Hutchinson and her followers supported Vane, but their support meant little, for women were not allowed to vote. Winthrop was elected governor. Shortly thereafter Vane left for England and Wheelwright was banished from the colony. Finally, in November 1637, Hutchinson was brought to trial before a court headed by Winthrop. Winthrop had made himself the attorney general, foreman of the jury, and chief justice in this trial. His opening statement set the stage for the trial:

> If you be in an erroneous way we may reduce you so that you may become a profitable member here among us, otherwise if you be obstinate … then the court may take such course that you may trouble us no further. (Adams, p. 236)

Although she had traveled five miles through the snow to reach the trial and was pregnant with her fifteenth child, Hutchin-

Hutchinson's Family in Prison

According to John Winthrop, Anne Hutchinson "infected" other members of her family with her beliefs. Called before the governor in Boston, her son-in-law, a Mr. Collins, was charged with a letter he had written accusing the colony's churches and ministers of being anti-Christian. Collins and Hutchinson's son Francis were both thrown into prison.

son ably responded to the challenge. "I am called here to answer before you, but I hear no things laid to my charge" (Adams, p. 236).

As the trial progressed through the testimony of five ministers and her witnesses—including Thomas Leverett and Cotton—Hutchinson appeared to have won the day. But in the end she delivered a tirade against those who accused her. It turned the tide of opinion and Hutchinson was banished from the colony. Due to her pregnancy she was allowed to remain under house arrest until the spring.

Held in the home of the reverend Thomas Welde, Hutchinson awaited another hearing. This time a church council heard about twenty-nine gross errors she was accused of making. At this hearing she was harshly scolded for nearly nine hours, defended only by her son Edward and a friend, Edward Savage. Even her long- time friend Cotton turned on her, accusing her supporters of encouraging Hutchinson in her evil ways and telling the women present that Hutchinson had led them astray. The real reason for her trial may have come from the reverend Peter, when he accused Hutchinson of being a husband rather than a wife, a preacher rather than a hearer, and a magistrate rather than a subject. He was accusing Hutchinson of behaving more like a man rather than a woman of his day.

At the end of the questioning, Cotton was requested to expel Hutchinson from the church. Cotton, however, persuaded Wilson to do so. It was a task that Wilson undertook with pleasure:

> The Church consenting to it we will proceed to excommunicate.... Forasmuch as you, Mrs. Hutchinson, have highly transgressed and offended ... and troubled the Church with your Errors ... I do cast you out ... and deliver you up to Satan.... I command you in the name of Christ Jesus and of this Church as a Leper to withdraw yourselfe out of the Congregation. (Ilgenfritz, p. 100)

Hutchinson's actions had led to a movement for religious freedom that would continue in the coming years. In hindsight, she also served as an early champion of the rights of women.

Aftermath

Exile and final years. Seventy-five men of Boston had protested the final verdict. Immediately after his victory, Winthrop ordered these men to surrender their weapons or to acknowledge that they had sinned in their protest. All surrendered their weapons, but only thirty-five acknowledged that they had erred in supporting Hutchinson.

Hutchinson's husband had traveled to what was to become Rhode Island in search of a new home. With the help of Roger Williams, he received permission from the Narragansett Indians to build a home on an island called Aquidneck. In the spring of 1638 Hutchinson gathered the children still living with her and moved to Aquidneck. There she continued to teach and preach, and the Hutchinson family flourished. In 1642 William Hutchinson died. By this time Massachusetts Bay Colony had grown so large that it threatened to take in other colonies as far distant as New York. New York, however, was in Dutch hands. Fearing that Aquidneck Island would soon fall to Massachusetts, Hutchinson gathered her young children and moved to Long Island, New York. There she established a home near present-day New Rochelle, New York, which was claimed by the Dutch.

Hutchinson Daughter Survives

One of Hutchinson's daughters was carried away by the Indian people who killed her mother and others in her family. The child was about eight years old when taken and remained with the tribe for four years. By then she had forgotten her own language and all her friends. Much to her dismay, she was returned to the Dutch when the parties finally made peace.

The director-general of the Dutch colony at that time was William Kieft. He had taken charge of a poor but spreading colony in 1637 and had shown very little ability to deal on friendly terms with the nearby Indians. Kieft demanded tribute of the Indians and made war on them at the slightest cause. His poor dealings resulted in a large Indian uprising in 1643 against the Dutch living on the outskirts of the colony. Anne Hutchinson and five of her children were killed in these Indian raids.

For More Information

Ilgenfritz, Elizabeth. *Anne Hutchinson*. New York: Chelsea House, 1991.

Williams, Selma R. *Divine Rebel: The Life of Anne Marbury Hutchinson*. New York: Holt, Rinehart, and Winston, 1981.

Winthrop, John. *Winthrop's Journal, History of New England: 1630-1649*. Edited by James Kendall Hosmer. New York: Barnes and Noble, 1959.

Bridget Bishop

16??-1692

Personal Background

Witchcraft in the colonial world. The seventeenth century was a time of great religious excitement both in Europe and America. The turmoil over religious beliefs may have led to the search for witches, which reached a high point in the colony of Salem, in present-day Massachusetts, in the late seventeenth century. It had been widely believed even before the Puritans left England that witchcraft was a well-practiced profession in Europe. (A witch, it was thought, made a pact with the devil in exchange for supernatural powers.) In the fifteenth and sixteenth centuries, thousands of people, mostly women and children, were tried and sentenced to death for this crime in Germany.

Witchcraft had been a crime long before the trials in Massachusetts Bay Colony. The ancient Hebrews and Romans were convinced that some people had the power to enchant others or take the shapes of animals, and they believed that these people obtained their powers by making an agreement with the devil. In Europe during the sixteenth century, especially during the period of intense religious upheaval known as the Reformation, there was a renewed interest in witches. Tests for witchery, including a test to "swim" the suspected witches, or to dunk them in water until they were ready to confess their evil ways, became popular.

▲ **A woman condemned as a witch is led to execution**

Event: The Salem Witch Trials.

Role: The first of twenty colonists accused of practicing witchcraft in Salem, Bridget Bishop was convicted and put to death during the panic of 1692. In that year hundreds were accused and more than fifty tried and convicted of being practicing witches. Some "repented" their imagined sins. Others, like Bishop, maintained their innocence until their deaths.

In England, King James II was an ardent believer in the evil of witchery. He had written a description of the antics of witches, which he spread throughout England, and offered a reward for exposing one of those who followed the devil. In the colonies, the brilliant preacher Cotton Mather had been caught up in the study of witches and had written about them in *Memorable Providences Relating to Witchcraft and Possessions.* Suspected witches were being brought to trial as early as the 1630s, and over the years many had been banished or put to death. Each colony came to hold witchery as a crime punishable by death.

Bridget Bishop. By the 1690s, it seemed no one was safe from the devil. Even upstanding citizens in Salem and the surrounding communities were being accused of witchery. So who better to suspect of being a witch than Bridget Bishop?

Little is known of Bishop's early life, though she was noted for her unusual ways. She dressed gaudily for her day, outfitting herself in red bodices for daily wear and in laces, often brightly dyed, for evening. (Samuel Shattuck, who dyed many of Bishop's laces, would later testify against her at her trial.) She made quite a picture, dressed in her famous black cap, black hat, and red bodice looped with laces of different colors.

Bishop owned two taverns, one in Salem Village and one in Salem Town. She got along well with the men—especially the young ones—who patronized these taverns. Much to the dismay of her neighbors, she allowed them to play "shovel board" (shuffle board) at all hours. One neighbor had even found it necessary to storm the tavern late one night and throw the playing pieces in the fire to quiet the merriment. Later, the incident was used against Bishop when her accusers remembered that the very next day that neighbor had become "distracted," or suffered a breakdown.

Bishop's temper alone was enough to make her suspect. All the community knew that often when her second husband bounced his wagon across the stream to their house, a loud and bitter argument followed. Before that, she had become the Widow Wasselbe when her first husband died under mysterious circumstances. Some, even then, had suspected her of causing Wasselbe's death. Later she married Thomas Oliver, but that marriage had not lasted.

She finally married a successful lawyer, Edward Bishop, but sometimes she still called herself Bridget Oliver.

In 1679 Bishop had been accused of practicing witchcraft, but was rescued by the testimony of her minister, John Hale. Later, in 1687, she was again accused, and again acquitted. These charges stemmed from several claims against Bishop. She had been accused at least once of contributing to the death of a neighbor, and more than once of causing someone she had argued with to become ill. She had also been charged with taking part in the devil's sacraments on the Witches' Sabbath. On this day, it was believed, those faithful to the devil gathered together in the woods to worship him. The devil, in turn, would leave his mark on the body of each witch, a sign that he and the witch had made an agreement.

Witch trials. Throughout the colonies the signs of a witch were well known: administering sacraments in the devil's name on the Witches' Sabbath, and dancing wildly and nude at the celebration in the forest; body blemishes where the devil had left his mark; being able to transform oneself into cats, dogs, or other animals; casting spells; practicing magic; and even nursing snakes. As in Europe, different colonies resorted to torture to extract the truth from suspected witches. Even before the Salem Witch Trials of 1692 to 1695, there had been more than 100 accusations of witchery in the colonies.

Bridget Bishop's History with the Law	
1670	Accused of fighting with husband
	Fined or subjected to ten lashes
1678	Accused of swearing at her husband
	Sentenced to stand in public square for one hour
1679	Claimed husband's property at his death
	Awarded property on condition of settlement of debts
1687	Accused of witchery
	Acquitted
1687	Arrested for theft of brass fitting
	Committed to Salem jail pending judgment
1692	Accused of witchery
	Sentenced to death by hanging

Participation: The Salem Witch Trials

Origin. In 1692 a group of young Salem girls, for no apparent reason, began falling into wild fits and imagining that people's spirits—preparing to do evil—were separating from their bodies. Often they saw these people carrying the devil's book (in order to enlist others in their evil causes) and, just as often, they saw these people in the company of a dark man (presumably the devil in human form). These girls kept company with a female slave from the West Indies named Tituba, who was reported to have practiced some forms of magic. Spurred on by an overzealous witch-hunter, the minister Samuel Parris, the girls made accusation after accusation against Bishop and other suspected witches.

Examination. On April 19, 1692, Bishop was summoned to be examined by a preliminary court headed by John Hathorne (ancestor of the writer Nathaniel Hawthorne). Also summoned that day were Giles Corey, the elderly husband of Martha Corey who once seemed ready to name his wife a witch but now stubbornly defended her; Abigail Hobbes, accused of falsely baptizing her own mother in the name of Satan; and Mary Warren, a servant girl whose imprisonment while waiting for this examination drove her insane.

The first part of the examination had the accusers confront the accused. The young girls had been instructed, perhaps by Parris, in what to do. When Bishop raised her arm, they did too. When she was asked whether she was a witch and she answered "I do not know what a witch is" and rolled her eyes, the girls rolled their eyes too. They acted as though Bishop controlled them. Although the girls' actions did not seem to trouble Bishop, it influenced the opinions of the authorities. Bishop was sent to Salem Prison to await trial.

Trial. The Court of Oyer and Terminer met at Salem in June 1692. Acting as chief magistrate, or judge, was Deputy Governor Stoughton. Bartholomew Gidney, Samuel Sewell, John Richards, William Sergeant, Wait Winthrop, and Nathaniel Saltonstall served as additional judges.

Since much of the testimony against her had been brought out in the examination, Bishop was already convicted in the minds of many in the town. There was little real evidence against Bishop, but the colonists believed their certainty alone could determine her guilt. Cotton Mather, the most powerful minister in the area, described the trial and the colonists' attitudes: "There was little occasion to prove the witchcraft, this being evident and notorious to all beholders" (Starkey, p. 153).

Nevertheless, the judges listened to the parade of accusers. Bishop's earlier history was repeated: the noisy shovel board games late at night at her tavern, her bad temper, her first husband's mysterious death. Also, witnesses reported that as she was led to court, Bishop's sideward glance at the church had caused a board to detach from a wall and fly across the room.

Some women of the community searched Bishop's body for the always-evident sign that she had made a commitment to the devil. After sticking pins in her, they found an unusual spot, which they testified about in court.

Samuel Shattuck testified that Bishop was a flamboyant dresser who often came to him to have various pieces of lace dyed. Some of these pieces seemed too small for a woman to wear, he noted. (It was well known that witches often used dolls to represent their victims when casting spells; Shattuck implied that this was how Bishop used the lace pieces.)

William Stacy recalled that at age twenty-two he had been stricken with smallpox and that it was Bishop who nursed him back to health. (Bishop was said to have had power over men, which grew as she became older.) Later, however, Stacy had begun to doubt Bishop, and had talked with others about her. For this, he said, Bishop had plagued him. Once, he testified, the wheel of his wagon had stuck in a hole in the road. When he stepped out to look at it, however, the hole had disappeared. Now, although he was a decent father and husband, Stacy said, the shade of Bishop plagued him in his sleep.

Samuel Gray, Richard Corman, and Jack Louder were also pestered by the image of Bishop as they slept. Sometimes her image turned into a black pig, a monkey, the feet of a cock, or the face of a man. Gray suspected that because the men had declined her friendship she had punished their families. Bishop, Gray testified, had been the cause of the deaths of his and Shattuck's sons (she had first driven Shattuck's son insane) and of the daughter of another.

The most damaging testimony was given by John Bly. Bishop had employed him to tear down a cellar wall in her former house.

Inside the wall, he claimed, he had found dolls ("poppets") made of rags and hogs' bristles with pins stuck through them.

Bishop's own testimony worked against her too. She was found guilty of telling lies, since some of the details she gave conflicted with what others said. Also, according to the court, early questioning had supposedly showed knowledge of witchcraft, yet Bishop claimed to have no knowledge of it.

Any evidence in Bishop's favor was not allowed. While they were in jail, Bishop had asked Mary Warren, one of the other accused witches, about the claims made against Bishop. Warren told Bishop that the girls had manufactured the evidence against her. Bishop attempted to use Warren's statements in court, but the authorities would not permit the remarks of a person they considered insane to go on the record.

Bishop's son would have testified on her behalf, too, but he had been arrested after beating the truth about the false accusations out of an Indian servant and then accusing the girls who were the prime witnesses in all the trials of game-playing. He had even suggested that beatings might return the girls to their senses, too.

In the end, there were no witnesses to defend Bishop. Even John Hale, the minister who had defended her in 1687, was now convinced of her guilt. Meanwhile, the young girls continued to be bothered by the evil cast upon them, they were convinced, by Bishop.

Sentencing. Bishop was found guilty of witchery and sentenced to be hanged, but hanging was forbidden by an old Massachusetts law. Conveniently, an old colonial law that made witchcraft a life-or-death offense was "discovered" and, on June 8, 1692, again passed into law. On June 10, High Sheriff George Cowan reported that he had hanged Bridget Bishop on Gallow Hill from the branch of a large oak tree.

Aftermath

More arrests. The young girls who accused Bishop were taken into the care of the minister Samuel Parris and, under his urg-

▲ Even upstanding citizens were accused of being witches

ing, named their tormentors one after another, even people from other towns with whom they had little acquaintance. The slave, Tituba, was arrested for witchery, mostly for her suspected influence on the girls. Seeing the benefits of cooperation, Tituba confessed and became a prime witness against others accused. (She was not the only confessor-turned-accuser. When a man, known in the records as G. B., was brought to trial, he found himself accused by a half-dozen people who claimed to have been bewitched and by eight more who had previously been accused and who had confessed.) A rash of charges arose so that it was dangerous to testify in favor of an accused witch; it seemed no one was safe from the charge of witchery. By the time the frenzy in Salem subsided, some 200 people had been accused, 55 had been tortured, and 20 put to death.

Bishop was not the first to be accused by the young women who pretended to be enchanted. However, few of the victims had histories as suggestive of witchery as Bishop. Among those executed was Rebecca Nurse, seventy-one years old in 1692 and nearly deaf. Nurse had nearly won the hearts of those in court but made the "mistake" of not being able to hear one of the last questioners. Her failure to answer the question she could not hear resulted in her death.

Martha Corey had been brought to trial with the expectation that her aging husband, Giles, would testify against her. When he refused and even defended her, she was condemned without his testimony. Then, accused of lying, Giles was subjected to torture to determine the truth. He was forced to lie down while stones were stacked on him to force him to talk. In the end, he was crushed to death while remaining silent.

Sarah Good, also found guilty, was executed, and along with her, her young daughter—perhaps the youngest of the condemned witches. When Sarah Cloyse, Rebecca Nurse's sister, stormed out of the court that had accused her sister, she herself was accused and condemned. The testimony of her own eight-year-old daughter helped to convict Martha Carrier. The records indicated: "This rampant hag, Martha Carrier, was the person, of whom the confessions of witches, and of her own children among the rest, agreed that the devil had promised her, she should be queen of hell" (Hall, p. 515). George Burroughs was a Harvard graduate who left his post as minister of the Salem Village church in 1685 over a salary dispute. He had not had any of his children baptized, and this was enough to see him convicted of witchery.

After Salem. Just as witchery had been a crime before the Salem affairs, it continued to be long afterward. In Europe the witch hunts continued, particularly in Germany, until 1782. From 1484, when witch hunting increased after a papal order was issued, until 1782, an estimated 300,000 women were executed for witchery. Witch torture was popular in England until the last recorded witch trial of a women and her nine-year-old daughter, in 1716. Finally, in 1736, King George II abolished prosecution for witchcraft in England and Scotland.

Reaction against the witch trials of Salem began while the trials were still being held and finally resulted in a slowing of the frenzy by 1695. Then the citizens of Salem and the Massachusetts Bay Colony began to rethink their actions. In 1697 John Hale wrote *A Modest Inquiry into the Nature of Witchcraft,* in which he admitted, "We walked in clouds and could not see our way. And we have most cause to be humbled for the error" (Starkey, p. 263).

By 1709 the tides had turned. Twenty-one of those accused for witchery demanded and were finally paid for the financial losses they had incurred as a result of their imprisonment. The next year the Massachusetts Bay General Court agreed to absolve any of those who had been suspected of witchery if that person or a relative requested it. Even the church withdrew from its position. Rebecca Nurse was one of those exonerated and reinstated in the church long after she had been put to death. No one came forward to clear the name of Bridget Bishop.

The last-known court case involving witchery in the United States occurred in 1915.

For More Information

Boyer, Paul, and Stephen Nissenbaum, eds. *Salem Village Witchcraft.* Belmont: Wadsworth Publishing Company, 1972.

Hall, David D. *Witch-hunting in Seventeenth-Century New England.* Boston: Northeastern University Press, 1991.

Starkey, Marion L. *The Devil in Massachusetts.* Garden City, New York: Doubleday, 1969.

James Edward Oglethorpe

1696-1785

Personal Background

Family life. Full of energy, independently wealthy, and a bachelor, James Edward Oglethorpe was thirty-five years old when he dedicated himself to the founding of Georgia Colony. He had been raised for such a role. His parents had given their son and daughters a strong religious and moral upbringing. Thus Oglethorpe grew up with ambition, a sense of duty, and a healthy dose of self-confidence. And seeing his mother involve herself in political causes gave him an example he would follow.

Training. Oglethorpe, the son of Eleanor and Theophilus Oglethorpe, was born in London, England, on December 21, 1696. As befitting the son of a well-to-do family, he attended Eton College and then Oxford University. The army commissioned him as an officer at an early age. Thereafter history would give him two faces: on one hand, Oglethorpe would be known as a skillful fighter (he was trained in the harsh atmosphere of ground combat and rose to general in the British Army); and, on the other hand, he would involve himself in causes on behalf of those less fortunate than he.

At age seventeen Oglethorpe enlisted in the Austrian army and became aide-de-camp to its commander, Prince Eugené. He proved to be an able officer and soldier, helping the prince lay siege to and retake the city of Belgrade. Returning to London at twenty-six,

▲ **James Edward Oglethorpe**

Event: The settlement of the Georgia Colony.

Role: James Edward Oglethorpe planned to resettle the unemployed of England in the southernmost reaches of English North America. Backed by a company of trustees, he intended to give people who were out of work the chance to start anew as independent farmers in a colony named after King George. Oglethorpe directed the development of Georgia in its early years. In laboring for its survival, he interacted with surrounding Creek and Cherokee Indians as well as the Spanish and French. In striving to achieve his goals for the colony, Oglethorpe established several unusual policies regarding slavery, liquor, and the Indian trade in Georgia.

Oglethorpe was elected to the British Parliament. He was to serve in Parliament from 1722 to 1754, although his occupations would take him far from London much of the time.

Social causes. Oglethorpe, like other English colonists (see **John Smith**), knew the value of writing in support of the causes he championed. In 1728 he authored a pamphlet called *The Sailors' Advocate* on behalf of the rights of sailors. A few years later (1730-32) he authored *Some Account of the Design of the Trustees for Establishing Colonys in America.* In *Some Account* he disclosed a plan to resettle the unfortunate of England in America. The work showed him to be well read in the experiences of those colonists who went before him. His writing recalled the argument put forth by Walter Raleigh (whose colony predated Oglethorpe's by 150 years) on how both England and her out-of-work citizens would benefit from such a colony. Specifically, his first aim was to resettle prisoners thrown into jail because they could not pay their debts.

Oglethorpe in Parliament

- Supported the education of homeless children.
- Defended seamen against impressment.
- Aided Moravians in need.
- Attempted to reduce taxes on the poor.

In the early 1700s English people were sent to debtors' prison for failure to repay even the smallest debt. Of course, while in prison the debtors had no way to earn the money to repay the amounts they owed. So their debts grew as they remained in poorly kept jails, waiting for friends or relatives to come to their aid. The hopelessness of the debtors' situation became the subject of frequent speeches by Oglethorpe in Parliament. Apparently, one of his friends had been sent to debtors' prison, and his death while there prompted Oglethorpe to act. He headed a special committee of Parliament assigned to investigate the plight of the debtors. Oglethorpe's work as chairman of this committee would result in the freeing of debt-ridden but otherwise law-abiding citizens in numbers that reached from 10,000 to 100,000.

Georgia Plan. Considered criminals, these debtors could not be set free in English society. Oglethorpe's solution was to arrange for some of them to be released from jail to settle in America. His timing for this request to King George II was excellent. Of the English colonies in America, the Carolinas occupied the southernmost position. Plantation owners there were prospering and sending money and crops to England, though they lived in fear of nearby Spaniards and Indians. South of the Carolinas lay a great expanse of land that had been claimed by Spain as early as 1660; the British had claimed it by 1665. Spaniards were living in Florida at the time and there were French living along the coast at present-day Biloxi, Mississippi, and Mobile, Alabama. Some of this land, in British eyes, was theirs, even though earlier British attempts to settle it had failed. A portion of what is now Georgia had remained in King George's hands, though. Now the wealthy colonists of South Carolina urged the king to occupy it with a string of forts to their south for protection, in particular from the Spanish in Florida.

Oglethorpe and about twenty others petitioned the king for a charter to settle the same area. Oglethorpe wrote to the king about the benefits of granting the charter:

> When hereafter it shall be well-peopled and rightly cultivated, England may be supplied from thence with raw Silk, Wine, Oil, Dyes, Drugs, and many other materials for manufactures, which she is obliged to purchase from Southern colonies. (Keller, p. 88)

The Georgia Plan called for a colony vastly different from South Carolina. In the older colony, rice plantations along the tidewater had already given rise to a very wealthy class of planters, many of whom seemed to spend their time in idle chatter and gambling while African American and Native American slaves did much of the hard labor. In fact, South Carolina impressed Oglethorpe as a model *not* to follow for a colony of freed prisoners who aimed to live a new, morally uplifting lifestyle. Indeed, South Carolina had placed its slave population on the worst legal footing of all the colonies. By a 1691 act, for example, the punishment for any slave who committed violence against a white person was to have his nose slit and face burned. A half-century later South Carolina's slaves would rebel against such policies, seizing guns to fight whites in the Stono Rebellion. Similarly, poor relations with Native Americans in the colony brought violence. War broke out in 1715, with the Yamasee Indians killing over 400 white settlers. Looking to South Carolina to learn what policies to avoid, Oglethorpe set out to create his model society in Georgia.

Articles of charter. In 1732 Oglethorpe and nineteen other trustees obtained a charter from the British Parliament to establish a new colony on land between the Altamaha and Savannah rivers. It was an unusually long document defining how the new colony of Georgia should be directed. All religions were to be tolerated except for the Catholic faith. Trustees were not to own land (so Oglethorpe owned acreage in South Carolina though he lived in Georgia), and women could not inherit it. The entire colony would be given back to the king after twenty-one years. Under these terms, Oglethorpe led a party of 114 settlers to America aboard the *Anne,* arriving there early in 1733.

The land that had been chartered lay fifty or sixty miles south of the colony at Charleston in what is now South Carolina. Anxious for friendly relations with his native neighbors, Oglethorpe had written to the governor of Charleston asking that he alert the neighboring Indians of the new colony's arrival. He wanted them to know that he would purchase land from them fairly and that he desired to live in peace. Oglethorpe would inspire the Indians to trust him to a much greater degree than other leaders. They sensed his genuine concern and respect for them. At the moment, though, Oglethorpe was busy with the trustees in England selecting the candidates most likely to work hard and keep the peace. The trustees advertised for people:

> Of reputable families, and of liberal or, at least, easy education; some undone by guardians, some by lawsuits, some by accidents of commerce.... These are the people that may relieve themselves and strengthen Georgia by resorting thither, and Great Britain by their departure. (Barck, p. 275)

In the end the 114 candidates selected to settle Georgia did not include many poor people of London. The colony in its early years would see the arrival of some persecuted groups, including Moravians and Jews. Apparently, Oglethorpe, like many of his contemporaries, held anti-Semitic, or anti-Jewish views. He did, however, accept the Jews as colonists and valued the few doctors among them, who later would prove useful to the community. His ideal colonist would change over the years to meet demands of colony life. Later, when defense became his primary concern, he preferred Germans, Highland Scots, and married soldiers as settlers.

Atlantic crossing. Aboard ship, Oglethorpe took firm control. He followed procedures he had suggested in *Some Account,* launching the passengers into a new morally uplifting lifestyle right away. He saw to it that their sleeping quarters were cleaned with vinegar during the voyage and that their bedding was aired. He practiced strict discipline and encouraged them to pray. Intending that men have the upper hand in the colony, he punished a wife, Anne Cole, for beating her husband, by using a folk custom called skimmington, a sort of parade conducted by her peers to ridicule her. A boy, Samuel Clark, died and was buried at sea. Afterward another passenger threatened to stir up trouble, so Oglethorpe "came behind him & gave him a good kick on ye arse" (Spalding, p. 9). The voyage taught the colonists to regard Oglethorpe as their strict leader. In truth, though, he never was given official authority to govern them.

Settlement. Oglethorpe left the colonists in Charleston, setting out for Georgia. Sizing up the terrain, he chose Yamacraw Bluff as the site for the first township, Savannah. It overlooked the fresh-water Savannah River, could be easily approached by ocean-going ships, and lay close to Carolina. On one side, the town would be protected by the bluff; on the other, by marshes. Hurrying back, Oglethorpe fetched the colonists, who made the two-night voyage to Savannah. The next day each family received "an iron pott, frying pan, and three wooden bowls, a Bible, Common Prayer Book," and split boards to make "clapp board houses"; two days later everyone got "a musket and bayonett, cartrige box and belt" for self-defense (Spalding, p. 12). The trustees had agreed to provide for the colonists for a year, after which they were to be on their own. In *Some Account,* Oglethorpe outlined his plan:

Trustees shall

1. Accustom colonists to salt provisions before departing.

2. Equip colonists with clothing from head to foot after boarding ship.

3. Provide bedding.

4. Furnish kitchen utensils, working tools, and seed.

5. Supply colonists with provisions for one year.

In exchange the colonists are obligated to

1. Obey the directors of the colony.

2. Assist each other and fortify the town as commander sees fit.

3. Build houses for selves and sow lands for next year's provisions.

4. Divide land and houses among selves; in payment, labor one day a week for public (to provide supply of products for times of war or sickness).

5. Not leave colony for two years without a license, to be issued if the person repays sum spent on that person.

6. Male settlers aged 17-45 practice with and use weapons to defend colony. (Based on Oglethorpe, pp. 27-29)

Savannah. Oglethorpe directed the construction of Savannah. Built to protect English America from the Spanish and other southern enemies, the entire colony was to consist of townships. Savannah was the first. Laid out in four sections, it surrounded a large central square, the gathering place in case of trouble. Each section centered around another square and was subdivided into house lots for the colonists, with gardens and farms to the rear.

The early settlers came well prepared. Oglethorpe had succeeded in persuading the king to accompany the grant with a gift of 10,000 pounds and the trustees and their friends had added money. Some of the money was spent on tools for building and planting and tents in which to live while the wooden homes were being constructed. In the next few years, King George II would invest over 100,000 English pounds to support the Georgia Colony.

The first colonists were industrious workmen—carpenters, weavers, bootmakers, farmers, merchants, clerks—who quickly set to building the town and even planning for other nearby settlements. Much like the Puritans of Massachusetts Bay Colony, the Georgia colonists intended to set an example for the rest of the world. The plan was for its settlers to grow neither too rich nor too poor so they could not own more than 500 or less than 50 acres of land. Meanwhile, they would construct forts and protect the rest of the colonies from England's enemies in America. Each farm in the colony was required to raise fifty mulberry trees on which silkworms would spin cocoons. The idea was for Georgia to supply Britain with silk; however, once Oglethorpe learned more about Georgia's climate and soil (which were not well suited to raising mulberry trees), he did not press the colonists to meet this requirement.

Oglethorpe himself showed little interest in accumulating wealth or living in luxury. In England he had always lived in plain country houses. Now he stayed in a tent on the edge of the bluff even after the others moved into their newly built homes. Sometimes he even slept outdoors in his cloak.

Native Americans. Oglethorpe appreciated the Indian approach to material wealth. He regarded the Native Americans as a shrewd lot who set an example for others to follow:

> The Indian dwellings are in their corn fields and have dirt floors. In these Mansions, they live much more contented than our great men in palaces ... They think the English very unwise who Waste Life in Care and Anxiety merely to heap up Wealth. (Spalding, p. 84)

Oglethorpe followed up his early message of friendship to the Indians by holding a meeting in May 1733 of eight tribes (100 warriors) from the Creek nation. Promising to compensate the Indians if traders in any way harmed their property, the trustees aimed to eliminate the stealing and cheating that troubled South Carolina. Oglethorpe presented each chief with a hat, shirt, and lace-trimmed coat, and he gave every warrior a gun. In particular, Oglethorpe became fast friends with Chief Tomochichi and the half-Indian Mary Musgrove, whose husband was a trader.

Trip to England. In 1734 Oglethorpe was recalled to England, partly because of money. The trustees were upset at how easily he spent their funds on silk production, prizes to boost the spirits of the colonists, and so forth. A poor record keeper, Oglethorpe failed to furnish receipts as proof of the purchases he claimed to have made. So he returned to explain himself in person.

While in London, Oglethorpe skillfully promoted the colony and managed to achieve the passage of three acts on slavery, liquor,

▲ Oglethorpe meets with Indian chiefs

and the Indian trade. He brought along the aging Chief Tomochichi, his wife, Senauki, his son, Toonahowi, and five warriors. They spent eighteen months in England, with the Chief receiving royal treatment. King George sent his own horse and coaches to carry Tomochichi to the palace. Oglethorpe kept busy playing host to the Indians, hoping to impress them with English society.

Meanwhile, back in Georgia, war threatened. Oglethorpe feared an attack by the Spanish and wanted to enlist the Indians' support. An Indian Trade Act was passed to insure fair exchanges with Native Americans, who would come to the support of the English in the event of war. Anyone trading with Georgia Indians had to get a license and put down money as a guarantee that he would observe the colony's rules. Parliament passed a second act to forbid liquor in Georgia, and a third to forbid blacks. The banning of Africans was introduced to eliminate the possibility of slavery in the colony. Oglethorpe blamed slavery for ills in white society. He believed that slavery deprived white colonists of the benefits of hard work; slave owners became preoccupied with luxury and material gain. By his own admission, Oglethorpe was also concerned for the welfare of blacks. He did not want to "occasion the misery of thousands in Africa . . . and bring into perpetual Slavery the poor people who now live free there" (Oglethorpe, p. 76). But he limited his argument to the effect slavery was sure to have on Georgia. He never tried to bring reform to the other colonies and, in fact, it was promised that any escaped slaves found in Georgia would be duly returned.

Return to Georgia. Over the next few years, adventurers from Scotland, Germany, Switzerland, and Austria volunteered to join the original colony. Oglethorpe himself helped a party of Germans reach Georgia and build the settlement called Ebenezer, and saw that each family got a pig, a cow, chickens, ducks, and geese. These later settlers were joined by others from England, but the trustees grew more and more lax in their selection. Eventually, the newly arrived were being referred to as "the scourings of London's streets" (Keller, p. 89). At the same time there was a flow of migrants moving from South Carolina into Georgia.

Oglethorpe left England with a new set of colonists. On board he warned them that Georgia's land was uncleared, the climate hot, and flies abounded. He parceled out garden seeds, turnips, cabbages, and beans and instructed this new group on the fine points of house building. This was a more realistic Oglethorpe, hardened to the rugged demands of southern frontier life. In some ways, though, he remained the same. He still kept matters in his own hands, tending to make all the important decisions himself.

Oglethorpe returned to find the colony in disarray. The colonists feared an invasion from Spain, and their relations with the Indians had soured. The leader picked up where he left off, continuing to preoccupy himself with major and minor concerns. His military experience stood him in good stead now, as defense began to consume most of his time. With the threat of the Spanish invasion looming large, Oglethorpe became absorbed with the task of building forts on the mainland and on nearby islands. He sketched out the fortified town of Frederica down to the details of how the walls should be sloped. Meanwhile, newcomers grumbled about the restrictions on liquor and slaves. Their protests reached the trustees, who grew uncomfortable with their investment. Oglethorpe visited England again to assure them that the colony was still a worthwhile venture. He returned to Savannah in 1738 with a regiment of British soldiers. This third stay in Georgia would be his last.

Military command. Changing from colony builder to military leader, Oglethorpe prepared his regiment for battle. Two other concerns besides the Spanish troubled Oglethorpe: colonists in Carolina objected to policies in Georgia, and troublemakers had managed to enter the colony. Though he had little time to deal with these concerns, he was reluctant to let others decide any aspects of daily life in the colony. Though the threat of war continued to escalate, he still preoccupied himself with nonmilitary concerns. For example, he became involved in an investigation of two murders. He even joined an expedition to pull weeds in central Savannah.

Almost daily there were alarms that the Spanish would invade. To calm the situation, Oglethorpe set off to visit not only the Creek but also the Cherokee Indians. They promised their support. The Cherokees would supply 600 warriors, and he in return would send them 1,500 bushels of corn. By then Chief Tomochichi had died, and Oglethorpe was relying on Mary Musgrove for advice.

War of Jenkins' Ear. Meanwhile, Spanish soldiers from St. Augustine, Florida, and elsewhere pushed northward and encouraged the Indians to join them in driving out the English. Oglethorpe had left the Spanish with almost no Indian allies, but they still threatened war. An accident involving Captain Robert Jenkins, commander of the ship *Rebecca,* added to the need for protection from the Spanish. In 1738 Jenkins, a trader for the English South Seas Company, reported that he had been stopped by Spanish ships, accused of smuggling, and then had his ear cut off in punishment. This was not an isolated event: Spanish seamen had been seizing British ships at will for some time. Now, however, hearing Jenkins' story, the English declared war on Spain.

The War of Jenkins' Ear began October 23, 1739; Oglethorpe was ordered to lead his army in an attack on the Spanish town of St. Augustine. He laid siege there for a month in 1740, then retreated

▲ Oglethorpe fought the Spanish at Bloody Marsh and Amelio Island

without success. Weakened by fever, the general suffered a physical and mental collapse. He recovered to hold off the Spanish in a counterattack on Georgia two years later.

Battle of Bloody Marsh. War raged at sea up and down the coasts of North and South America. In 1742 Oglethorpe's men repelled the Spanish attack at Frederica. However, by this time the Spanish had raised a large force at their base in Havana, Cuba. Oglethorpe met this force of between 7,000 and 8,000 men in the Battle of Bloody Marsh. The Spanish were so thoroughly defeated in this battle that Oglethorpe declared a day of general thanksgiving on July 24, 1742. He was not hailed as the saving hero of the colony, though, but became a target of criticism. The Trustees had placed in Savannah a secretary, William Stephens, whom Oglethorpe did not keep informed during the battle. The settlers panicked during

119

the invasion; besides their fear of the Spanish, the people and their cattle had been struck by fever. And they had no word from Oglethorpe. Oglethorpe also spent much of his own money on supplies for the troops under his command and was again accused of mismanagement.

Oglethorpe again returned to England to defend his record and recoup his fortune. He was cleared of all accusations, but his ties to the Georgia colony weakened after 1743, when he remained in Europe. Historians recognize Oglethorpe as the driving force in Georgia's early days and credit him with the colony's survival. Yet they also fault him for not sharing leadership and attempting to handle all concerns himself.

Early Leaders of Georgia Colony

James Edward Oglethorpe, 1732-1743

William Stephens, 1743-1751

Henry Parker. 1751-1754

Aftermath

New success. Back in England Oglethorpe found himself embroiled in an uprising against King George. His military prowess still celebrated, Oglethorpe was appointed major general and placed in charge of troops guarding the king. Oglethorpe defeated the intruders and pursued them toward France and Scotland. Once again, however, he was rewarded with criticism. Powerful people in England accused him of failing to do his duty and allowing some enemies to escape. He was court-martialed but soon cleared of all charges against him.

In 1744 Oglethorpe married at the age of forty-eight, after which he visited the Georgia office in England less and less often. Instead he pursued his military career, fighting under a false name in Europe in the 1750s. The British army promoted him to full general in 1765 and placed him in command of all the king's forces. A decade later Oglethorpe was offered command of the British army during the American Revolution. He refused. In fact, he tried to effect a compromise to keep the colonies in the British Empire.

Changes in Georgia. Back in Georgia, citizens of the 1740s and beyond began to undo some of Oglethorpe's work. They smuggled in rum and petitioned to import slaves. Without slaves, they argued, Georgia could not compete with the other colonies or bring riches to the trustees. Relations with Georgia's Indians broke down as well. In 1742 the limit on the amount of property a person could own soared from 500 acres to 2000 acres. That same year the ban against liquor was removed. In 1750 slavery became legal, and in 1752 the trustees turned over the colony to the king. Within two years it would be ruled like other British colonies, by a colonial assembly and a royal governor.

The colony's territory was extended to the St. Mary's River in the south and to the Mississippi River in the west. In 1775 Georgia rebels expressed their support for other colonial rebels by seizing a powder magazine in Savannah from which they were able to send 13,000 pounds of gunpowder to the Continental Army. In April 1776 Georgia, youngest of the thirteen colonies, voted to join the others in pursuit of independence. By then Georgia had imitated South Carolina. Far from the colony of modest farmers that Oglethorpe originally envisioned, it had become home to a class of wealthy landowners. They kept rice plantations in the tidewater region and African American slaves to work them. Elsewhere in Georgia, small struggling farms were the rule.

For More Information

Barck, Oscar Theodore, Jr., and Hugh Talmage Lefler. *Colonial America.* New York: Macmillan, 1958.

Keller, Allan. *Colonial America: A Compact History.* New York: Hawthorne Books, Inc., 1971.

Oglethorpe, James Edward. *Some Account of the Design of the Trustees for Establishing Colonys in America.* Athens: University of Georgia Press, 1990.

Spalding, Phinizy. *Oglethorpe in America.* Chicago: University of Chicago Press, 1977.

French and Indian War

1622-1675
Indians try to dislodge colonists in Powhatan's War, the Pequot War, and King Philip's War.

1689-1744
French and English wars—King William's War, Queen Ann's War, King George's War—spread to America.

1755
French and Indian War declared. General James Braddock loses to the French and Indians in Ohio Valley.

1754
George Washington sent to drive French from Ohio River Valley.

1752
French build chain of forts from Lake Erie south to Ohio River.

1756
England declares war against France in Europe on May 18, beginning the Seven Years' War.

1758
Robert Rogers leads Rangers on victory march through Great Lakes area. Iroquois side with English.

1759
British defeat French at Quebec.

1763
Britain and France agree to peace in Treaty of Paris.

1761
British navy captures Martinique, Grenada, and Havana, Cuba.

1760
Montreal falls to the British.

1764
Pontiac fights Pontiac's War in Ohio Valley.

FRENCH AND INDIAN WAR

Fought from 1754 to 1763, the French and Indian War was the final conflict between France and England for control of North America. It became part of a broader fight that erupted on the battlefields of Europe in 1756 as the Seven Years' War. For more than a century the Old-World powers had engaged in a series of wars that finally culminated in this bloody conflict.

French and British soldiers, some colonists, and many Indians participated in the fighting in North America. Most of the Indian tribes sided with the French, who were, in their view, the lesser threat to their lands. While colonists joined in the fighting, Britain and France sent over the bulk of their forces from Europe.

For much of the 1700s, nations struggled for power in the world at large. France, Britain, Holland, Italy, and Spain were contending for empires, and their disputes involved nearly all the countries of Europe. A series of wars occurred that might be termed world wars for the numbers of countries involved. Britain and France were competing for control of vast areas of North America and India. In North America, Britain made solid its holdings through several small wars, winning control of a large northern area around Hudson Bay in present-day New York and bases in Newfoundland and Nova Scotia in Canada.

British colonists of Virginia moved to open the Ohio Valley to

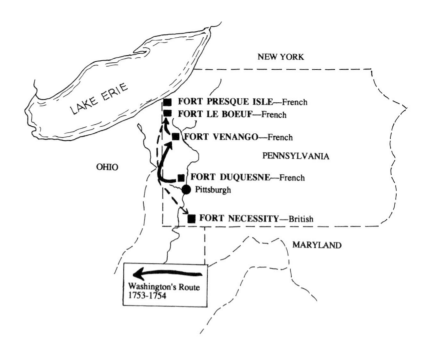

NEW YORK

LAKE ERIE

FORT PRESQUE ISLE—French
FORT LE BOEUF—French

FORT VENANGO—French

PENNSYLVANIA

OHIO

FORT DUQUESNE—French
Pittsburgh

FORT NECESSITY—British

MARYLAND

Washington's Route
1753-1754

▲ Major battle sites of the French and Indian War

colonial settlers in the mid-1700s. The French meanwhile built forts along the St. Lawrence River, Lake Erie, and the Ohio River. When, in 1753, the British attempted to clear the Ohio Valley of the French, a world war that was developing in Europe spilled over into the Americas. For the next nine years, Britain and France competed for control of North America. France had only 90,000 settlers there at the time, against 1.5 million settlers in the British colonies. Yet France claimed most of the continent, except for a section by the Eastern Seaboard. France's intention was to confine the British to this area of the continent. Britain's goal was to the drive the French off the continent altogether.

To Indians, the fighting among European powers offered special opportunities. Tribes of the Ohio River Valley, for example, were in sore need of an ally to supply firepower so they could keep the British from advancing onto their lands. The French had for years proved reliable trading partners. They had supplied the Indians with guns and ammunition in exchange for furs and corn without seizing their lands or attempting to change their lifestyle. By siding with the French, Chief **Pontiac** and other Indians hoped to make the conflict work to their advantage.

The British meanwhile attempted to win neutral Indian nations to their side. At the Albany Congress of June 1754 the colonies assembled in what was to become their first large cooperative meeting. Its main goal was to set up a common war fund, but they also tried to win over the Iroquois as allies. Deciding that staying neutral would benefit them best, these Indians had been playing the English and French off each other, extracting gifts and promises from both sides. The British offered the Iroquois gifts now too, but they would not be bribed. Better to wait awhile, they decided, to see which of the European powers was the likely winner. In 1758, when it was clear that Great Britain had begun to win the war, the Iroquois finally took her side.

Britain sent over thousands of soldiers in 1758, who were aided by the daring exploits of colonists such as **Robert Rogers.** The British attacked with success on three fronts that year—in Canada, New York, and the Ohio River Valley. Rogers, who formed his own company of rough-and-ready soldiers, led them on raids in New York. The following year the British met with more success in Canada. Battling at Quebec, both the British general James Wolfe and the French general Marquis de Montcalm would die in the fighting before France finally surrendered her claim to the city. A year later Montreal fell, too, and French power crumbled on the continent. The fighting stopped in North America, though it would continue for three years in Europe and the Caribbean.

World Wars of the 1600s and 1700s	
In Europe	**In America**
1688-1697 War of League of Augsburg	1689-1697 King William's War
1701-1713 War of Spanish Succession	1702-1713 Queen Anne's War
1740-1748 War of Austrian Succession	1744-1748 King George's War
1756-1763 Seven Years' War	1754-1763 French and Indian War

In 1763 the Peace of Paris brought an official end to the war. France gave up its claims to Canada and all territory east of the Mississippi River, except New Orleans (in present-day Louisiana).

▲ An Indian warrior

Britain now claimed North America from the Hudson Bay to the Mississippi, and the Indians as well as the French became the losers. No matter which side the various tribes had fought for, their bargaining power was gone. They could no longer gain strength by playing one European nation off the other. So how would they stem the tide of settlers?

The British, to preserve alliances with various Indian tribes, attempted to limit the movement of whites. Policymakers formed a boundary along the crest of the Appalachian Mountains, reserving land to the west for the Indians. The policy (called the Proclamation of 1763) ordered settlers who had already moved onto western lands to leave, but it was ignored. Indians of the Ohio Valley took matters into their own hands. Assembling tribes that had sided with the French in the war, Pontiac continued the fight. Pontiac's War failed to drive out the white settlers, but warriors of future generations continued fighting for the same cause. For the present, colonial settlers could remain in the Ohio Valley.

The colonists gained greatly from the French and Indian War, perhaps more than any other group involved. The conflict established Britain as the major European power in North America, giving British colonists more power than French ones. At the same time it weakened Indian tribes by robbing them of the French as an ally. Perhaps most important for the colonists, though, the war had sparked a new sense of unity among them. Forced to fight in a common cause, they had begun to gain the collective self-confidence that would carry them into the War for Independence.

Robert Rogers

1731-1795

Robert Rogers was born on November 18, 1731, in the town of Methuen, on the northeastern frontier of the Massachusetts Bay Colony. Just to the north lay a wilderness still largely unsettled by Europeans. Rogers's parents, James and Mary, moved there with some neighbors from Methuen in 1738, taking seven-year-old Robert, his three older brothers, younger brother, and sister. The Rogers family, Scotch-descended Presbyterian immigrants from northern Ireland, had not been warmly accepted by the Massachusetts Puritans. Along with other Scotch-Irish immigrants of the time, they hoped to carve out a more secure place for themselves to the north. They bought land and began farming near Rumford, along the Merrimack River.

Indian raids. Like other early immigrants, the Rogers's desire for land took them to the edge of white settlement, to lands that the Indians had occupied for centuries and were struggling to hold on to. During the 1740s the Indians, encouraged by their French allies, carried out raids on British settlements north of Massachusetts. In 1746 the fourteen-year-old Robert enlisted in the local militia, which helped guard the isolated farms but had no success in searching out Indian war parties. Two years later the militia guard proved to be no match for the raiding Indians, who destroyed the Rogers's farm, including crops and livestock, in an attack on Rumford.

Raiders on paper. Indians were not the only raiders that

▲ Robert Rogers

Event: Raids on French and Indian positions; capture of Montreal; Pontiac's Rebellion.

Role: A brilliant commando leader in the French and Indian war, Rogers led the 600-man force known as "Rogers' Rangers." Adapting Indian-based techniques of guerrilla warfare to European tactics, the Rangers contributed to British success in the wilderness of present-day northern New York, Montreal, and Michigan.

frontier settlers had to face. In 1740 the border of Massachusetts ran just north of Methuen, and the area that the Rogers family had settled in was officially created as a separate colony, called New Hampshire. Their claim to the land rested on its being part of Massachusetts, however, and in the same year that their farm was destroyed, Rogers's family lost their property to a group of rival claimants. They received a smaller amount of land in compensation. At the time, land clearly equalled wealth and opportunity. With the reduced acreage and with older brothers ahead of him, Rogers's prospects for sharing in the family holdings looked dim.

More militia service. Rogers did not seem cut out for farming anyway. When he was a boy his parents had given him a small farm south of Rumford, which he moved to in 1752. He soon gave up the situation, however, renting it out and joining the militia on another expedition. In March 1753 the twenty-one-year-old went north with a group to map and mark out a route for a road along the Connecticut River. One of the dangers they faced came from the Indians of St. Francis, who threatened any newcomers. They returned safely, and Rogers bought more land, this time in Merrimack, just north of the Massachusetts border. Further Indian raids in 1754 led to militia patrols, in which Rogers served. Once again, the Indians could not be found. The militiamen heard so much gunfire in the nearby hills, though, that they believed the Indians were making fun of their efforts.

Debt and counterfeiters. In buying the Merrimack land, Rogers had gone into debt, and he soon found himself unable to pay it off. He nearly joined a counterfeit ring that was passing false bills in the area. Apparently, on the advice of a friend, Rogers pulled away from the counterfeiters, but in 1755 he was listed among a group of suspects (along with his brother Richard). Some of the others went to jail, but the charges were dropped against the Rogers boys.

Restlessness. By this time Rogers had seen much of the northern wilderness, having served in military expeditions that faced winter conditions in mountainous and wooded terrain. He preferred the expeditions to a quiet farmer's life and took every opportunity to talk with hunters and Indians about areas that he had not been to himself. According to descriptions, Rogers was about

▲ An Indian raid

six-feet tall, "well proportioned and one of the most athletic men of his time—well known in all trials of strength … among the young men of his vicinity, and for many miles around" (Cuneo, p. 12). In 1755 the call went out for soldiers to serve in a new campaign against the French. Rogers, restless and eager to clear his reputation after the brush with the counterfeiters, enlisted immediately.

Participation: French and Indian War

World conflict. The British and French were fighting for control of North America, a struggle that was only a part of a larger, worldwide conflict between the two major European powers. The French controlled territory from Canada through the present-day midwestern United States all the way south to Louisiana. The British colonies meanwhile occupied a relatively narrow coastal strip. Yet the French had no colonial population, preferring to trap for furs (which were exported to France) rather than colonize. As a result, British colonists outnumbered French soldiers and trappers by a huge margin (1.5 million to about 90,000).

There was little interference from the French in Indian ways or with Indian territory. And faced with the threat of Europeans who refused to leave, many Indians preferred the French to the English. The French also opposed further settlement by the land-hungry colonists, but their manpower was limited. So they enlisted the aid of powerful Indian tribes, who shared the same goal: driving the British out of the area.

Meanwhile, the British decided to force the French from their forts deep in Indian territory. They opened what became known as the French and Indian War on four fronts: against forts near lakes Erie, Ontario, and Champlain, and against Quebec, the French capital of Canada. It was in the campaign against French positions on Lake Champlain and nearby Lake George, deep in the wilds of present-day northern New York, that Rogers would win fame.

Camp at Lake George. Rogers contacted a British recruiting office and offered to recruit men from New Hampshire to fight alongside the British regulars (soldiers). The recruiting officer accepted the offer, and Rogers gathered a group of about fifty men, including untrained farmers. He was named to command the group, which was called "Company One," and given the temporary rank of captain. His friend John Stark was appointed as his lieutenant. They marched the men to Albany, on New York's Hudson River, where they joined the army of General William Johnson. From Albany, in August 1755, Johnson's army marched north up the Hudson River, establishing a log fort near the southern tip of Lake George.

Intelligence mission. Johnson badly needed to know the strength of French forces at Fort St. Frédéric, on the southern end of Lake Champlain, and at Fort Carillon, located along the stream linking the more southerly Lake George to Lake Champlain. Johnson asked his officers for men who might be good scouts. Rogers's commanding officer recommended him for the dangerous job, and on September 14, 1755, Rogers set out at night in a small boat with four men. They rowed to Lake George's western shore; then, leaving two men to guard the boat, Rogers set out on foot with the two others.

Two-and-one-half days later, after slogging through gnat- and mosquito-infested woods and camping without fires so as not to alert the enemy, the three reached Crown Point, the site of Fort St. Frédéric. They spent the afternoon noting the numbers of French soldiers and Indians, watching the nearby encampments without being detected. Too hungry and tired to spy on Fort Carillon on their way back, they reached Lake George only to find that the two men they had left behind as guards had taken the boats and fled in fright. On September 23, exhausted and hungry, Rogers and his two remaining scouts finally stumbled back into camp with their valuable information.

"The most active Man in our Army." After resting for three days, Rogers led a similar scouting expedition to Fort Carillon with even greater success. This time he attacked a canoe with nine Indians and a Frenchman. Each time he went out, Rogers reported that the French and Indians made up a powerful force of several thousand men, many more than Johnson commanded. The British in Albany, eager to attack, refused to trust Rogers's reports, telling Johnson to send out other scouts. Yet the other scouts learned nothing. They went out a few miles, then simply returned and reported no sign of the enemy. Often the men refused to go farther, paralyzed by fear in the dark woods, where their imaginations put an Indian behind every tree. Johnson supported Rogers, saying, "His Bravery and Veracity stands very clear in my opinion" and calling him "the most active Man in our Army" (Cuneo, p. 26). Finally, in November, Rogers's information was confirmed, just in time to prevent a foolish British attack on the superior French and Indian forces.

"An Independent Company of Rangers." During the winter of 1755-56, Rogers was given larger groups of men to command, leading aggressive raids as well as spying missions. On the raids he would not only try to attack the enemy but to take prisoners. They were a valuable source of much-needed information about enemy plans and strengths. His leadership captured public attention because the winter usually meant a pause in military activity. He gained a reputation as a cool and resourceful commander who inspired courage and confidence in his men.

In May 1756, recognizing his abilities, the British decided to give him command of a new kind of military force. As "Captain of an Independent Company of Rangers" (Cuneo, p. 33), Rogers would be assigned the task of gathering information on the enemy. His job was to locate and attack small groups of French soldiers or their Indian allies and to interrupt French communications and supplies along lakes George and Champlain. The Rangers were to be recruited from the source Rogers knew best: the frontiersmen of New Hampshire.

Heroic deeds. By the summer of 1756, "Rogers' Rangers" had carried out several daring and dangerous raids on French boats traveling on Lake Champlain between the southern forts and Montreal. He was the toast of the colonies; to the Indian allies of the French he was "the white devil" whom they could not kill. His fame even reached England, where the Earl of Loudoun had just been appointed as new commander of the British forces in North America.

Warfare manual. In January 1757 the Rangers had their first serious defeat. Rogers himself was grazed in the head by a bullet. Ambushed on their way back to the fort, the party of seventy-four lost thirteen, with another nine wounded and seven taken prisoner. It was the first time Rogers had lost such a large number of men. The British did not criticize him, however; his superiors praised his handling of the ambush. By this time the force had grown to about 600 men in five companies of 120 each. Robert's brother Richard commanded one company; another brother also served. The missions continued throughout the year. During this time Rogers also wrote a book on his guerrilla warfare techniques, reportedly "the first written manual of warfare in the New World" (Cuneo, p. 55). Loudoun could use it, for he hoped to train British regulars to conduct similar missions.

Discipline problems. Toward the end of the year, while Rogers was laid up recovering from wounds, a scouting trip ended in failure because the men refused to follow orders. The incident led to criticism by the regulars who had led the mission. Soon after that, two Rangers who stole rum were whipped, a common punishment for minor offenses. This time, however, after the whipping a group of Rangers gathered around the whipping post. Suddenly one seized an ax, and with a few sharp blows chopped it down. Colonel Haviland, in charge of Fort Edward, wanted to put the offenders on trial. Rogers left the hospital to defend his men against the colonel. His superiors supported Rogers, but he and the Rangers had made an enemy.

A wilderness barbecue. A few weeks later came an episode that illustrates Rogers's popularity with his rowdy men and why they would follow orders only when they came from him. He was waiting with a group of Rangers outside Fort Carillon, hoping for a chance to capture a French prisoner or two. When no one left the fort all afternoon, Rogers tried to lure a party out by letting them see a small group of Rangers. When that trick did not work, Rogers had his men kill some cattle the French kept outside the fort and, using some of their wood supply, had a barbecue. Rogers then left the French a receipt for the cattle before heading back. He was using both armies' attention to red tape—the endless filling out of forms and receipts—to play a joke on the French. Rogers's scorn for red tape, however, would prove troublesome for him in the future.

> ## A Ranger's Battle Story
>
> The Ranger, Private Thomas Brown, has already been shot once "thro' the body" and attempts to escape: "As I was going to place myself behind a large Rock, there started up an Indian from the other Side; I threw myself backward into the Snow, it being very deep ... One Indian threw his Tomahawk at me, and another was just upon seizing me; but happily I escaped and got to the Centre of our Men, and fix'd myself behind a large Pine, where I loaded and fir'd at every Opportunity." (Cuneo, p. 48)

Battle on snowshoes. One of the Rangers' best-known battles came in February 1758. Haviland decided to send out one scouting party to Carillon under Israel Putnam (of Revolutionary War fame), followed by another one made up of Rangers led by Rogers, to St. Frédéric at Crown Point. Rogers knew that if a deserter or prisoner fell into French hands from Putnam's group, the French would be waiting for his own mission. In fact, that was exactly what happened. Putnam returned with the news that a prisoner had been taken. Rogers went out immediately with a few lightly armed men to recapture the prisoner but failed. There would be another attempt; 180 Rangers went out as dark fell the next evening.

The men wore special "ice creepers" so they could move on the frozen lake; the wind had cleared it of the deep snow that covered the land. On their backs, along with their packs, rifles, and blanket-rolls, the men carried homemade snowshoes fashioned of wood and rawhide thongs. They traveled at night and rested during the day. Still, Rogers was uneasy, so the following night he decided not to travel on the lake, where they could more easily be detected. Instead, they traveled through the woods on their snowshoes.

Late the next afternoon, as the men prepared to approach Fort St. Frédéric, they spied a group of about 100 Indians approaching. Rogers and his men attacked, but the group was only the advance guard of a much larger French expedition. In the battle that followed, the heavily outnumbered Rangers were severely defeated, and Rogers himself barely escaped. Of the original 180 men, only 54 returned, including the badly wounded Rogers, who earned the respect of his British commanders by searching for survivors after the long trek back, refusing to enter Fort William Henry until all possible surviving Rangers had returned.

Raid on St. Francis. The Rangers continued to prove their worth in campaigns throughout 1758 and 1759. In late summer of 1759 the Rangers helped in the capture of forts St. Frédéric and Carillon (which the British called by its Indian name, Ticonderoga). Soon after, Rogers's commanders agreed to a strike by the Rangers on the Indian village of St. Francis, northeast of Montreal. The Indians of St. Francis had carried out deadly raids on British settlements for years. (These were the same Indians who had raided New Hampshire when Rogers served in the militia there.)

▲ Elizabeth Browne Rogers

In striking so far north, 150 miles past Crown Point, the Rangers went deeper into enemy territory than ever before. The trip was exhausting. At one point they walked for nine days through the cold, muddy water of a seemingly endless swamp. All their clothes and bedding were thoroughly soaked. To escape being sighted, no fires were allowed, so nothing could be dried. They accomplished their mission, wiping out the village in what is now viewed as their most controversial raid. Two- to three-hundred men, women, and children died in the nighttime attack. Pursued by enemy forces on the month-long return trip back through the wilderness, the Rangers split up. Nearly fifty died trying to make it home.

French surrender. Rogers and his men participated in the taking of Montreal in 1760, after which the French forces officially surrendered. Rogers was sent west, his final duty as leader of the Rangers being to accept the surrender of France's forts at Detroit and Michilimackinac, in present-day Michigan. On this final assignment he proved as fine a leader as ever, guiding his men on the long, overland journey and conducting delicate business with both the French and the Indians. In 1763 Rogers was again sent west, where he participated in opposing Chief Pontiac's siege of Detroit (see **Pontiac**).

Aftermath

Marriage. In 1761 Rogers had married Elizabeth Browne, the pretty, twenty-year-old daughter of an acquaintance. He spent much of his time separated from her in the early years of their marriage, and there are many passionate letters to provide evidence of his love for her. In the difficult years to come, she offered him much support. However, Rogers's mounting personal problems proved overwhelming for Elizabeth, for, in 1778, she divorced him.

Debt and treason. From the moment the Rangers were disbanded following the end of the war, Rogers was plagued by huge debts. He had created the debts in paying, clothing, and arming his men, but when it came time to make his claims to the British army, accountants stubbornly disputed them. He had not kept enough records—because of his hatred of red tape, perhaps—and was unable to persuade the army to cover the debts.

In 1766 Rogers was appointed to command Fort Michilimackinac, but he was relieved of the command when enemies in the British army brought charges of treason against him. They claimed that he had plotted to hand the fort over to the French. At the trial Rogers was found not guilty. This affair, however, combined with his continuing debts, left a cloud over his name. Remaining loyal to Britain, Rogers fought on the British side in the American Revolution, leading "the Queen's American Rangers." He was removed from this command as well, and he left for England in 1780. He died there quietly on May 18, 1795.

For More Information

Bird, Harrison. *Battle for a Continent.* New York: Oxford University Press, 1965.

Cuneo, John R. *Robert Rogers of the Rangers.* New York: Oxford University Press, 1959.

Pontiac

c. 1720-1769

Personal Background

Pontiac was born about 1720 in the Great Lakes region, near the Maumee River in present-day northwestern Ohio. His mother was Chippewa and his father Ottawa. Little is known about Pontiac's childhood or family except that he grew up on what is now the Michigan peninsula, between Lake Michigan and Lake Huron. His tribe, the Ottawa—known as the "trade people" or "raised hairs"—hunted, fished, trapped, and farmed the lush land, which was rich in fish, game, and corn. Part of the year, while farming, the Ottawas lived in permanent houses in villages of 100 or so people. The rest of the year they lived in movable shelters, hunting big game and trapping valuable pelts such as beaver, otter, mink, and fox. At various times the Ottawa controlled all of Michigan and parts of Wisconsin. They lived close to the Chippewa, Potawatomi, Wyandot, Shawnee, Kickapoo, Menominee, Winnebagoe, Sac, Miami, Seneca, and Delaware—all of whom would become important allies in what has become known as "Pontiac's Conspiracy."

Warrior background. Pontiac's early years trained him for warfare. As a boy, he learned to shave his hair in back and on the sides and to cut it to a length of about an inch on top so that enemies could not grip him by the hair while stabbing him. Some of his youth was spent serving under the great Ottawa war chief Winniwok on the warpath against the Cherokee enemies of his people. In

▲ **Pontiac**

Event: Pontiac's Conspiracy, or the Great Indian Uprising of 1763.

Role: With other Native American leaders, Pontiac, an Ottawa chief, formed an alliance of forty-seven area tribes and villages (stretching from Canada to New Orleans, and from New York to Illinois) to make a military stand against the British. The Indians captured eight forts and killed more than 1,000 British. A leader in this action, Pontiac headed an alliance of tribes—Ottawa, Chippewa, and Potawatomi, known as the Confederacy of the Three Fires—in an attempt to capture Fort Detroit.

January 1746 he made a trip to Cherokee country with Winniwok and thirty-one warriors. The party returned to camp led by Pontiac: Winniwok and ten others had been killed in the battles. As repayment, the Ottawa had killed thirty-seven Cherokee, with Pontiac responsible for seven of the deaths.

Influence of the fur trade. Pontiac grew up in the midst of European competition for land and the resulting French and Indian War. The Old Northwest, as the Great Lakes region was then called, was becoming more than merely a center for hunting and fishing. Its waterways, which included the five Great Lakes, the mighty St. Lawrence, Ohio, and Mississippi rivers, and dozens of smaller tributaries, provided excellent trade routes. Stretching across the present-day United States and Canada, the region's ideal trade conditions and abundance of beaver pelts attracted the French.

The French coexisted well with most of the Old Northwest Indian tribes, especially with tribes such as the Ottawa. They paid fair prices for Indian goods and had little interest in farming Indian land. Rather, the French preferred to have the land in the hands of Indians, then trade with them for farm products and other goods. The Indians would exchange pelts, meat, and produce for French hardware, hunting and farming tools, ammunition, and liquor.

As with other tribes, this trading relationship became very important to Pontiac's Ottawa. Indian methods of farming and hunting had changed dramatically thanks to European tools and seeds, and the Ottawa had grown to depend upon a steady supply of such goods. When, around 1754, the French and English went to war over control of the territory and fur trade, most Northwest tribes sided with the French. Among them were Pontiac's Ottawa.

Respected chief. By the time he had reached his early thirties, Pontiac had become a respected chief among the Ottawa. An early historian described Pontiac, perhaps romantically, as he prepared to go to war against the oncoming British:

> With a flourish of his hatchet around his head, a chief leaped into the ring and began to chase an imaginary foe.... He was a muscular rather than a tall Indian, with high, striking features. His dark skin was colored by war paint, and he had stripped himself of everything but ornaments. (Tappan, p. 366)

▲ **An English settlement**

Other historians describe Pontiac as haughty and proud, with a quick, hot temper. Often, like other Ottawas, he wore no clothing at all; during times of conflict, as befitting a war chief, he would adorn his body with tattoos and paint. He was an able leader of his people, an interested learner, and loyal to his friends. During the battles to hold Quebec against the British, Pontiac steadfastly supported the French and swore allegiance to General Louis de Montcalm: "I, Pontiac, give you my word that I shall never desert you so long as the breath of life remains in one or the other of us" (Eckert, p. 83).

In hindsight, this stubborn allegiance to the French would help defeat him. Pontiac counted on more support from them than they would manage to give him. The French, though, valued the alliance and, around 1758, at the height of their friendship, Montcalm showed his respect by giving Pontiac a French army dress uniform.

From his dealings with the French, Pontiac gained firsthand knowledge of European war strategy and generalship. This knowl-

▲ Quebec, Canada

edge served him in the years right after the French and Indian War, when he organized the Ottawa Confederacy and sparked the episodes later known as Pontiac's War or Pontiac's Conspiracy.

Influence of the French and Indian War. During the height of the French and Indian War, Pontiac and the Ottawa fought with the French throughout the Old Northwest and along the East Coast. In the process, Pontiac became known for his strong mind and leadership abilities. He probably commanded the Ottawa on the Pennsylvania frontier at Monongahela on July 9, 1755, when British troops under General William Braddock suffered huge losses. Later that year and repeatedly from 1755 to 1760, Pontiac led his warriors in battle under General Montcalm. He learned all he could about strategy and weaponry from the French military. By war's end, Pontiac's speechmaking and commands were so masterful they earned him the nickname "Red Napoleon."

In 1760, despite a valiant effort, the French were forced to surrender at Montreal and Quebec, yielding their claim to northern America to the British. The French and Indian War had ended badly for the Ottawa. French trading posts and landholdings in the Great Lakes territory would be turned over to the British, leaving the Old Northwest tribes to fend for themselves. Adding to the difficulty, the Indians had little grasp of the concept of landownership. To the Native Americans, owning land was an unthinkable concept: "The Great Spirit had given the land to his children to live upon, to gain their subsistence from, and nothing could be sold except those things which could be carried away" (Hale, p. 2).

Even those French who had paid Indians for land had not occupied or attempted to colonize much of it. So the Northwest tribes were unprepared for British occupation of the territory. The sight of the British moving into the old French forts and erecting fences around farmland greatly disturbed Pontiac and other Indian leaders, such as Seneca chief Kyashuta and Delaware chief King Beaver.

Participation: Pontiac's Conspiracy

General Amherst. Not helping an already tense situation was the haughty attitude of British general Jeffrey Amherst, appointed to lead forces in the west. He refused to hear Indian complaints and considered their threats meaningless. Having just conquered the French army in America, the British viewed the Native Americans as nothing more than defeated savages. Further, Amherst insisted Northwest tribes return prisoners of war without offering payment for them. The Indians, particularly Pontiac, were greatly offended, for the promising councils between the English and French at the end of the French and Indian War determined that the Indians had a right to demand payment—in land and other concessions—for prisoners of war. The Indians were being greatly disrespected. These events heightened Pontiac's hatred and distrust of the British. During this time he also spent time with a psychic Delaware Indian called "The Prophet," who was predicting that the Indians would drive the white man from the west.

In the autumn of 1760 Amherst sent Robert Rogers to Fort Detroit to formally occupy the trading post there (see **Robert**

Rogers). When Rogers and his men rode through the Michigan area, they were greeted by some braves who warned the major that he was in Pontiac's territory and must receive permission from the chief to proceed. Rogers met with Pontiac, promising that Indian land rights would be respected and adding that the price of trade goods would be even lower now that the British were in control. Unconvinced, Pontiac agreed to let the British pass but warned Rogers that he would only keep the peace as long the British kept their word.

Pontiac suspected the true intentions of the British. He sent out war belts, notifying tribes of his plan to strike British forts on the Great Lakes. One by one, Northwest tribes took up Pontiac's cause:

> The messengers of the mighty Pontiac were welcomed everywhere, and their words were listened to with eager anticipation. The tribes thus leagued together comprised thousands of the bravest warriors. (Ellis, p. 53)

Pontiac's Giant Wampum Belt

To help spread the word of his plan for rebellion down the Mississippi, Pontiac had his squaws make a giant wampum belt. It was shell-beaded, six-feet long and four-inches wide. On it were symbols of forty-seven Indian groups Pontiac enlisted in the cause. The big belt was carried by Indians from village to village and by soldiers among the French as a symbol proclaiming Pontiac's plan to keep up the rebellion against the British.

British break their promises. By 1763 Pontiac had formed the Ottawa Confederacy, or the Confederacy of the Three Fires, which allied the Algonquian-speaking Ottawa, Chippewa, and Potawatomi tribes. Similar to but much smaller than the Iroquois Nation, Pontiac's Confederacy of the Three Fires was still very powerful, banding several hundred warriors together into one fierce fighting force. Pontiac worked to increase their numbers by enlisting the aid of some forty-seven area tribes and villages to make war on the British.

Just as the Northwest tribes were uniting and planning their attack, the British began to break all their promises. First they raised prices, making it nearly impossible for Indian farmers dependent on European tools and supplies to survive. The British government then dictated that the supply of liquor and

▲ **Pontiac denounces the English**

ammunition to the Indians be cut off, and British landowners started posting "No Trespassing" signs on all newly acquired land. Most disturbing, British settlers began pouring in from the east and occupying the Northwest territory in greater numbers than ever before. This was the time for Pontiac and the tribes of the Old Northwest to strike, before more English reinforcements arrived.

United Indian uprising. Proclaiming, "I mean to destroy the English and leave not one upon our lands" (Hale, p. 6), Pontiac led his Confederacy and some 1,200 Northwest Indian warriors into battle. In May and June 1763 Indian war parties from tribes throughout the Northwest struck a dozen British forts and captured eight of them. Almost universally, these groups used tactics that Pontiac seems to have originated with his warriors. Frequently, one or another pretense—game playing, gift bearing—gave the Indians entry into a fort and allowed them to carry hidden weapons with which they quickly killed the residents of the fort. Some of the forts were easily taken in this way, since they were poorly manned. Fort Michilimackinac, for example, was defended by just twenty-eight British soldiers. With these successes behind him, Pontiac then chose to lead his Confederacy of Three Fires against the strongly held Fort Detroit.

Fort Detroit. On May 7, 1763, with 300 of his own warriors and some 2,000 allied Indian forces spread throughout the area, Pontiac planned a sneak attack on the fort. The Indians were to gain entry to the fort by staging a peace council. They would carry guns under their blankets and, once inside, open fire and kill the British before they had a chance to fire back.

Major Henry Gladwyn, commanding officer of Detroit, however, was informed of Pontiac's plot. (An Indian woman is rumored to have informed him.) Prevented from entering the front gate, Pontiac began a siege of the fort, interrupting supply routes and staging surprise attacks. To make his forces more effective, he moved his village across the Detroit River so that he would be on the same side as the fort. The site he chose to build the new village was the farm of a Frenchman, Jean Baptiste Meloche. Forty years earlier this farm had been an Ottawa village and the birthplace of Pontiac.

> ## An Indian Woman Alerts Fort Detroit
>
> It is said that before Pontiac's attack a young Indian woman, a friend of the British commander of Fort Detroit, saw Pontiac's soldiers sawing the barrels off their shotguns. The plan was to hide them under their blankets when they entered the fort for a discussion about peace. Warned by the woman, Major Henry Gladwyn was able to ward off this attack. Pontiac afterwards surrounded the fort and began a siege. The Indian woman who betrayed his plan was captured and punished.

The British fought actively to withstand the siege. British ships sailed up and down the Detroit River and Lake Erie bringing new supplies. As they grew more confident, the British forces in the fort began to make sorties outside to remove outer buildings and trees from which the Indians carried out their attacks. There was even some trade and exchange between the fort and the Indians. For example, captured prisoners of each side were exchanged—at the rate of three British soldiers to one Indian warrior. Still, the Indians ambushed a ninety-six-man supply convoy led by Lieutenant Abraham Cuyler and killed more than half of them. In another instance, Indians wiped out an inexperienced captain (James Dalyell) along with twenty-three of his men and injured thirty-eight others. But the Indians were not accustomed to this lengthy sort of warfare. As they grew weary and the men in the fort grew more bold, the British attempted to attack Pontiac. In the famous battle of Bloody Run, Pontiac led 400 to 500 warriors as they trapped the British on a bridge at Parent's Creek. Pontiac's forces lost only six or seven men; the British were slaughtered.

Meanwhile, on July 28, 1763, the Delaware, Shawnee, Huron, Seneca, and some of Pontiac's warriors from Detroit took up positions on the banks surrounding the fort at the juncture of the Allegheny and Monongahela rivers, in present-day Pittsburgh, Pennsylvania. This fort had been called Fort Duquesne under the French but was now held by the British under the name Fort Pitt. The French allies had been unable to send ammunition and the Indians were forced to fight with only fire arrows. The attack was led by three Delaware chiefs, King Beaver, Shingas, and Turtle Heart (Pontiac was still at Fort Detroit). Though the Indians succeeded in wounding several British officers, they were forced to retreat after three days. These same Indians now joined the forces that were to fight the British at Bushy Run. They began this contest as victors, but after two days they were routed by the forces of General Bouquet, losing 120 men while the British lost 115. This battle thwarted the final Indian attempts to cut off and destroy Fort Pitt.

The siege of Fort Detroit lasted from May until September. Toward the end of September, Pontiac received word that the French had yielded Fort Pitt and that the expected help from them would not arrive. With his allies fading away to other ven-

British Forts Taken in the May-June 1763 Uprising of Indian Tribes in the Northwest

Location	Date	Tribes Involved
Ft. Sandusky Southern Lake Erie	May 16	Ottawa, Wyandot
Ft. St. Joseph Lake Michigan	May 25	Potawatomi
Ft. Miami Maumee River	May 27	Miami
Ft. Quiatenon Wabash River	May 27	Wea, Kickapoo, Mascouten
Ft. Michilimackinac Northern Michigan	June 4	Chippewa, Sac
Ft. Presque Isle Lake Erie	June 15-16	Shawnee, Ottawa, Potawatomi, Chippewa, Huron
Ft. Le Boeuf Lake Erie	June 19	Shawnee, Chippewa, Huron
Venango Lake Erie	June 20	Seneca, Shawnee, Huron, Potawatomi, Chippewa

tures, Pontiac was forced to abandon the siege and he returned to his homeland along the Maumee River. From there he continued to carry on occasional raids on British settlers. As late as 1763, his forces attacked British soldiers en route to Fort Detroit, killing hundreds of them at Devil's Hole. In another attack, twenty-five soldiers in a convoy from Niagara were attacked and killed. However, Pontiac's had been one of the most unsuccessful efforts in the Indian endeavor. Gradually his influence in the great Indian alliance faded, and when the Indians finally surrendered to William Johnson at Oswego, in present-day New York, Pontiac was one of the least significant chiefs there.

Aftermath

Pontiac's final days. In his last years Pontiac kept in contact with tribes from southern Louisiana to Illinois. His travels "caused uneasiness among the British" (Ellis, p. 121), but he gave them no real cause for alarm. When he was near fifty, the old chief settled in Cahokia, near present-day St. Louis, Missouri. There, in 1769, he was assassinated in the street. Just outside a prominent fur trading company (Baynton, Wharton and Morgan), a Kaskaskia Indian from Illinois drove a tomahawk into the back of his head. An English trader named Williamson is said to have paid the Indian with a keg of rum to kill Pontiac. Curiously, at the time none of the Ottawa, not even Pontiac's own sons, who were near the scene, made any move to retaliate for the killing. However, the assassination created ill feelings between the Ottawa and the Kaskaskia, which finally resulted in a war between the two groups and their allies that eventually wiped out the Kaskaskia.

The conspiracy. Pontiac's Conspiracy significantly slowed British progress and prevented the British from gaining more control in the Old Northwest. Frontiersmen, farmers, and other settlers in this region, angered by taxes, eventually did oust many British from this area and helped begin the American Revolution.

At the outset, outmanned and outsupplied by the British, the Northwest tribes were doomed to failure, but they put up a noble fight. Pontiac brilliantly promoted the alliance of forty-seven tribes and led a bloody and courageous siege that the French military could not match. He was a true leader and his effort was a gesture worthy of "a great race fighting for survival in its homeland" (Hale, p. 21).

"Pontiac's Conspiracy" is perhaps misnamed. Although he was one of the stronger Indian chiefs, Pontiac himself declared that he was not the leader of all the Indians who sought to drive the British from the west across a front that stretched from present-day Mississippi to the Great Lakes. In fact, Pontiac declared that he had done nothing in the affair without consulting and receiving direction from chiefs of other nations. Still, it was Pontiac who sent messages to Indians throughout the western river valleys, who planned well-timed attacks that ended in the British loss of eight forts, and who led several Indian tribes in the siege of Detroit.

For More Information

American Historical Images on File: The Native American Experience. Facts on File, Media Projects, Inc., 1991.

Ellis, Edward S. *The Indian Wars of the United States.* Chicago: J. D. Kenyon & Co., 1892.

Hale, Nathaniel C. *Pontiac's War.* Wynnewood: Hale House, 1973.

Tappan, Eva March. *The World Story,* Volume 2: *The United States.* Boston: Houghton Mifflin, 1914.

Declarations of Independence

1649-1696
▼
Navigation acts limit colonial trade.

1734
▼
John Peter Zenger arrested for printing critical comments about Governor William Cosby.

1770
▼
Samuel Adams protests "Boston Massacre."

1767
▼
Townshend Acts passed.

1765
▼
Stamp Act passed.

1764
▼
Sugar Act passed.

1773
▼
Boston Tea Party staged.

1774
▼
Intolerable Acts passed. **Patrick Henry** gives speech: "Give me liberty, or give me death."

1774
▼
First Continental Congress held; forms association to boycott British goods.

British and Minutemen fight at Lexington and Concord.
◄ **1775**

1776
▼
Thomas Paine publishes *Common Sense*.

1775
▼
Lord Dunmore, John Murray, promises freedom to slaves who will fight for British.

1775
▼
Second Continental Congress held; George Washington chosen to head army.

1776 ▶ **Thomas Jefferson** and committee write Declaration of Independence.

DECLARATIONS OF INDEPENDENCE

The American colonists declared their independence in several ways before the official Declaration of Independence was written. In this document, they announced and explained their decision to separate from Great Britain. The Americans, for the first time, stopped thinking of themselves as subjects within the British empire, as they had during all the earlier protests.

Rebels in Massachusetts and Virginia led most of the these earlier protests. The formal Declaration, however, was a joint effort by all the colonies. On July 2, 1776, the Continental Congress voted for independence and appointed a committee to prepare their official declaration to the world. **Thomas Jefferson** wrote the first draft.

Benjamin Franklin had, eight years earlier, questioned whether Britain had the right to make laws for its American colonies. However, he did not yet speak of separation. In fact, he and others envisioned America becoming the center of the British empire rather than a nation independent of it.

Franklin, who ran a newspaper, was outspoken about government and encouraged **John Peter Zenger** to speak his mind too. Zenger then wrote articles that criticized the behavior of his colony's governor. In doing so, Zenger disobeyed an English law. He did not, however, challenge the fairness of the law altogether, as other colonists after him would.

The British began a series of unpopular policies in America soon after the French and Indian War. Before 1763 Britain had, for the most part, left the colonies pretty much on their own. The colonists made their own laws, taxed themselves, and were responsible for their own defense. During the war, however, Britain spent large amounts of money sending soldiers to fight on American soil. The British government decided that the colonists should help pay the cost of the war. Beginning in 1764, the government started passing laws that increased colonial taxes.

From 1764 to 1776 a series of events took place that led the British colonists to begin thinking of themselves as Americans rather than as British subjects. It was a slow process, beginning with a few "radicals," such as Virginia's **Patrick Henry** and Boston's **Samuel Adams**, who led the way. While they resisted English policies, the idea of complete independence was hardly discussed at the time. It would become acceptable only in 1776, when **Thomas Paine**'s widely read pamphlet, *Common Sense*, won large numbers to the cause.

The first tax (Sugar Act, 1764) met little opposition, but the Stamp Act (1765) brought trouble right away. It required that each legal or business agreement be given a special stamp. Depending on the matter at hand, the fee might be a few pennies or a few dollars. In any case, the act meant high expenses for all businesses in the colonies. Samuel Adams organized demonstrations against it in Boston. In Virginia, Patrick Henry persuaded his colony's assembly to oppose the act.

Following the lead of Boston and Virginia, the rest of the colonies flatly refused to cooperate with the Stamp Act. In 1766 the British were forced to repeal it. Then came the Townshend Acts of 1767, which taxed imports such as glass, lead, paper, paint, and tea. This time Britain sent soldiers to enforce the taxes, a move that resulted in the "Boston Massacre."

The strain eased when the Townshend Acts were repealed in 1770 but then worsened with the Tea Act in 1772. The Tea Act actually cut the price of tea but made it impossible for the American merchants who sold this item to match the low English prices. The colonists supported the merchants and people refused to buy the

▲ Colonists rioting following the Stamp Act

tea (which was a sacrifice, because tea was a favorite drink). When the British attempted to land a cargo of tea by force, colonists protested by staging the Boston Tea Party (1773).

The colonies began to view all these hateful acts as part of Britain's scheme to crush their local self-government. They reacted by working more closely together. The colonies formed Committees of Correspondence to better communicate with each other, which led to the First Continental Congress in 1774. Local soldiers clashed with British troops at Lexington and Concord, Massachusetts, in 1775. So the Second Continental Congress began to organize a colonial army. Still, most of the colonists saw themselves as fighting not for independence but for their rights as British subjects.

Talk about liberty and human rights circulated through the colonies, and slaves began using it to justify their own quest for

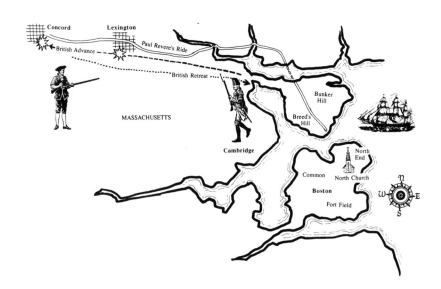

Concord Lexington
British Advance
Paul Revere's Ride
British Retreat
MASSACHUSETTS
Bunker Hill
Breed's Hill
Cambridge
North End
Common North Church
Boston
Fort Field

▲ **Early shots of the Revolutionary War took place at Lexington and Concord, Massachusetts**

The Declaration and Slavery

Congress struck out about 25 percent of Jefferson's first draft of the Declaration, including a passage that blamed the king for carrying innocent Africans into slavery in America. The king, Jefferson continued, was now exciting those slaves to rise up against the colonists to purchase the freedom that *he* has taken from them. In favor of the slave trade themselves, South Carolina and Georgia prompted Congress to strike out this passage on slavery, as did Massachusetts, whose shippers had carried slaves to America.

freedom. About 500 responded to a 1775 offer by the royal governor of Virginia, Lord Dunmore, or John Murray, to free all Virginia slaves willing to join the British military forces. Thousands more would join the British in the next few years—among them were many of Thomas Jefferson's slaves.

In 1776 after reading Thomas Paine's *Common Sense*, the North American colonists began to accept total separation from Great Britain as the most sensible path. When Congress met again in 1776 representatives from many of the colonies came with instructions to support the idea of independence.

The Declaration that followed was written in two parts. In the first part, Jefferson stated some general beliefs about human rights: that people are created equal, that they are born with certain rights, that government powers should come from the consent of the gov-

▲ **The signing of the Declaration of Independence**

erned, and that citizens may cast out a government that destroys their rights. In the second part, Jefferson listed charges against the British king that made independence from the empire necessary. With a few changes, Congress approved the document on July 4, 1776. Its words, adopted as the foundation of a nation, would soon raise disturbing questions about the existence of slavery.

John Peter Zenger

1697-1746

Personal Background

Childhood in Europe. John Peter Zenger was born in 1697 in Germany's Black Forest. At the time Germany was at war with France, and Zenger's parents, due to their Protestant religious beliefs, were not popular with either side. They hid in the forest and eventually fled to the Netherlands with thousands of their neighbors, working on farms along the Rhine River. However, danger followed them. Under the orders of French king Louis XIV armies began burning their houses and crops and many starved to death. Finally, England's Queen Anne sent a fleet of ships to Rotterdam, in the Netherlands, to rescue 30,000 and bring them to her country. Zenger, his parents, and his younger brother and sister, Johannes and Anna Catharina, all sailed to London, England. Like many others they were unable to find work there.

After two years the British offered free passage to America to families from Palatine, the German state where the Zengers and the other immigrants had been born, if they agreed to tap pine trees and make tar and turpentine for the British navy. The family readily accepted the offer and set sail for the colonies when Zenger was thirteen. They were hopeful about their future and eager to make a new life in America. But the boat trip was long and fever-ridden and Zenger's father died along the way. Zenger, barely a teenager, was now the man of the family. Not only did he face the challenges of

▲ **Andrew Hamilton defending John Peter Zenger**

Event: Battle for freedom of the press.

Role: As printer of the *New York Weekly Journal,* John Peter Zenger was jailed and tried for publishing what the English government called "seditious libel." That is, he attacked the actions and character of the governor of New York, William Cosby. Basing his defense on the fact that what he printed was the truth and therefore should not be against the law, Zenger won the first colonial victory for freedom of expression.

making a new home but he also had to find a way to support his widowed mother and brother and sister.

Immigrants in New York. Arriving in the colony of New York, Zenger's family moved into a tent-city called the Common along with 3,000 other newly arrived German immigrants. (The colony had been under Dutch control until it was seized by the English in 1664.) Rows of mildewed white tents were pitched in an open field just outside the city. There the Zengers shared a tent with four other families and received a small loan from the government for food.

During this period Zenger's eyes opened to the lively world of New York City. In the Commons people talked politics, discussing the governor's proclamation to lower the price of food or perhaps gossiping about the ex-governor's jail term. The corrupt former governor had been thrown in jail and had bribed his way out. Zenger was shocked: he never imagined that people could question the government, let alone jail an official.

Zenger befriended an older Palatine man his family had known in the Netherlands, who gave him books to read. From the books, written in Dutch, Zenger learned American geography and became fascinated by the printed word. His mind was also racing about ways to earn a living. Zenger hit upon the idea of mixing his two interests, reading and print, and decided to become an apprentice to a publisher.

While wandering along the muddy New York streets, Zenger came upon a print shop owned by William Bradford, the official printer of the king of England. Dressed in his tattered clothes and holey boots, Zenger boldly inquired about an apprenticeship. Bradford, impressed with Peter's knowledge of Dutch and seeing that he was strong and energetic, was interested, but said that Zenger would need to raise fifteen pounds to cover the apprentice fees. Zenger replied that even if he had the amount required, his mother would need the money for groceries. He then left the shop, thinking of a way to make the money.

Back in the Commons typhoid was spreading through the camp and the Zenger family was forced to flee to a temporary refuge. They, along with other Palatines, were sent to Nutten Island (now called Governor's Island) and were installed in a hut. The government had purchased 6,000 acres on the Hudson River for the Palatines to farm and occupy but, because Zenger was so young and his mother was a woman, the Zengers received none of this land. Hopes were dimming for the family. As all the others were moved off the island to their own plots, the Zengers remained behind with other widows and orphans. Winter was setting in and Peter and his brother were forced to tear down abandoned huts to gather enough firewood to keep the family warm.

Just as things looked the bleakest, a special order was passed to help the Palatine orphans. As a result, Andrew Bradford—son of the printer—arrived to see the young Zenger. He came to offer him an apprenticeship, working as a kind of indentured servant in lieu of paying the fifteen-pound fee. Zenger was overjoyed and his mother immediately agreed to let him go. He moved to New York and into the Bradford's house.

Fitting nicely into their daily scheme, Zenger soon regarded the Bradfords as second parents and their sons, Andrew and William, as brothers. The men worked together in the small shop all day and Zenger studied at night. Bradford tried to improve Peter's spelling; he felt that it was a printer's primary duty to make sure there was uniformity in spelling (especially because of all the different immigrant influences on American English at the time). Zenger, on the other hand, hoped there were more interesting things a printer could concentrate on. He never did learn to spell very well.

Changes at the press. When Zenger turned twenty-one, he set out on his own. He moved to Maryland, married, and opened his own print shop. During his three years there he and his wife had a son, John, but later his wife died and Zenger lost the shop. Forced to return to New York with his son, Zenger also returned to Bradford's press and within a few months married a Dutch woman, Anna Catherine Maulin. They moved into her mother and two sisters' small house in the city. Zenger returned to work with Bradford full-time, while Bradford's son Andrew was now in Philadelphia, Pennsylvania where he started his own newspaper, the *American Mercury*.

Benjamin Franklin. One day the future statesman and inventor Benjamin Franklin came by William Bradford's shop to inquire

▲ Benjamin Franklin

about a job. He was just seventeen but knew about printing and had already authored a book. Zenger said they regrettably had no work for him, but Franklin found out that Andrew, whom he knew of from his days in Philadelphia, was Bradford's son. Franklin told them how much he admired Andrew's work. On the pages of his newspaper, Andrew had been writing against the Massachusetts authorities, to whom Franklin was also opposed. Zenger was impressed with Franklin's interest in Andrew's newspaper and began to understand the power of the press.

Partners. Furthering Zenger's printing goals, Catherine one night introduced her husband to four Dutch immigrants who had written a book questioning some policies of the church. The men had been excommunicated, or expelled from the church, because of their views. Now they pleaded with Zenger to print the book so people could hear their side of the story. "How can people discuss the question intelligently if the book is not printed?" was the question they, along with Catherine, asked Zenger (Galt, p. 32). Zenger knew that Bradford did not want to upset the authorities, so he decided to publish the book himself. He bought some paper and approached Bradford about using his press and type. The two agreed to become partners and split the profits. This was a great risk for Zenger and Catherine, who were unsure how people would respond to the book yet were investing their life savings. How relieved they were by the project's success. When it was published, the book, called *Klagte,* quickly sold out.

Zenger next approached Bradford about their starting another newspaper. The fifty pounds a year the shop earned from printing for the king was not enough for the two of them, Zenger reasoned. They did not get many book orders, and besides, he had long wanted to follow in the footsteps of his "brother" Andrew. Bradford was easily convinced. He insisted, however, that the newspaper be tame and not at all radical like his son's. It certainly should contain "no criticisms against the governor" (Galt, p. 41).

With this proviso, the *New York Gazette* was born. On November 1, 1725, it became the first newspaper for this city of 6,000. The New York City paper was greeted with wild cheers from the community, and it sold well. Advertisers were anxious to support it and subscribers were signing up. Yet Zenger was unhappy. He considered the contents in the *Gazette* "useless drivel" and yearned to print the truth about the government, like Andrew did in Philadelphia (Galt, p. 44).

Though he felt dissatisfied, Zenger continued to work with Bradford and deliver the *Gazette* to potential advertisers. One journey led him to a warehouse on Broad Street that was run by a wealthy and influential woman, a Mrs. Alexander. Her husband, James, a well-known attorney, began to discuss the newspaper with Zenger. Alexander said the paper was "like a baby, without teeth" and Zenger agreed (Galt, p. 45). Zenger told Alexander his plan for starting his own press. Another man joined the conversation. Lewis Morris was a small but energetic colonist who served as chief justice of the Supreme Court. Like Alexander, he also thought the *Gazette* was without substance and wondered what held Zenger back from producing his own pamphlets or newspaper. Morris himself wrote many essays criticizing the corrupt government, and he had hoped the *Gazette* would print them. In response, Zenger explained that Bradford refused. Now Zenger and Morris discussed opening their own print shop.

Should the Constitution Provide for Freedom of the Press?

The writers of the constitution disagreed on whether to include freedom of the press. The statesman Alexander Hamilton was against it. But Thomas Jefferson made a strong argument for it: "The basis of our governments being the opinion of the people ... were it left to me to decide whether we should have a government without newspapers or newspapers without a government, I should not hesitate a moment to prefer the latter" (Malone, p. 158).

Together Alexander and Morris loaned Zenger half of the ninety-three pounds needed to start his own place. Once again, Zenger and Catherine took a gamble with their savings. By February they had their own shop on Smith Street, near city hall. Zenger's brother, Johannes, or "John," who was now an accomplished carpenter, helped build the shop. Zenger's first project was to set one of Morris's essays in type and issue it as a pamphlet. It was wildly successful and soon Catherine had to work with Zenger every day to keep up with the demand. But Zenger's success was short-lived. Few people brought their work to a new printer and Zenger's long-standing problem with spelling plagued his work. Only Morris continued to regularly send essays and legal opinions to him to print. For several years he printed less than one book a year. Now responsible for six children and a wife, he was forced to take a second job as a church organist.

Andrew Bradford's arrest prompts paper. In September 1729 Andrew Bradford's arrest for printing essays criticizing the government made front-page headlines. Zenger rushed to Andrew's father to inquire if there was anything he could do to help. Bradford replied that Andrew was already out of jail, and that Andrew knew what he was doing. While visiting his old friend's shop, Zenger noticed that Benjamin Franklin had bought a newspaper rivaling Andrew's, called the *Pennsylvania Gazette,* and on the front page was criticizing the *Mercury* for being too soft on the government. This example of two vibrant, political, and successful newspapers in the same city made Zenger realize he could and should start his own newspaper, which would challenge his friend William Bradford's *Weekly Gazette.* If Philadelphia had two newspapers, surely New York could support two. Besides, Zenger believed that the people of New York who disagreed with the government needed a voice. He and Catherine began to sell Franklin's *Gazette* in their shop. They would read and reread its pages to learn how to produce a successful opposition newspaper of their own.

> **First Amendment to the Constitution**
>
> Congress shall make no law respecting an establishment of religion, or prohibiting the free exercise thereof, or abridging the freedom of speech or of the press....

Participation: Freedom of the Press

The New York Weekly Journal. In 1732 New York Governor Rip Van Dam was replaced by the corrupt William Cosby. Sent from London, Cosby assumed control and immediately began collecting bribe money from local businesses, buying property all over New York with taxpayer money, and pestering former governor Van Dam for not paying Cosby half his salary. The political climate heated to the boiling point when Cosby took Van Dam to trial and then, abusing his power, had the jury dismissed and his own judges installed to try the case.

On November 5, 1733, just as the heat was rising, Zenger opened New York's first official opposition newspaper, the *New York Weekly Journal.* His old friends and partners Morris and Alexander

165

helped finance the venture. Zenger began printing articles attacking Governor Cosby. First he blamed Cosby for allowing French warships into New York harbor to spy on the colony's fortifications. Then he turned to the subject of Cosby's mistreatment of former Governor Van Dam. Zenger wrote:

> Deservedly therefore is this Tryal by Juries [of Van Dam's] ranked amongst the choicest of our fundamental Laws, which whosoever shall go openly to suppress, or craftily to undermine, does ipso facto, ATTACK THE GOVERNMENT AND BRING IN AN ARBITRARY POWER, AND IS AN ENEMY AND TRAYTOR TO HIS COUNTRY. (Smith, p. 31)

These articles enraged Cosby, who publicly burned the issues and vowed to arrest Zenger for treason.

Cosby tried to have Zenger convicted of treason but could not due to lack of evidence, so he had the attorney general of the colony file a "bill of information" against Zenger charging him with "raising sedition," or rising up against authority (Kobre, p. 40). Zenger was arrested on November 17, 1734, and bail was set so high he remained in jail for nine months.

During his stay behind bars, Zenger continued to publish the *Journal* with tremendous help from Catherine. Zenger would dictate essays through the bars of his cell and Catherine would return to the shop and print what they had discussed. In fact, during the whole nine months prior to Zenger's trial, they only missed one issue.

The trial. Before Zenger's arrest, Cosby dismissed Morris from the Supreme Court and replaced him with Judge James Delancey. Delancey was then assigned to Zenger's case. Zenger's lawyers, James Alexander and John Chambers, unsuccessfully tried to have Cosby's appointment to the Court removed. The upcoming trial did not look promising until Morris and other Zenger supporters hired the brilliant but aging attorney Andrew Hamilton to represent Zenger.

Andrew Hamilton. The eighty-one-year-old Hamilton was one of the most respected lawyers in the colonies. He practiced in Philadelphia, Pennsylvania, but was secretly brought to New York for this case. Hamilton worked magic on the jury and turned Zenger's persecution into an attack on the rights of every freeborn citizen, an attack on freedom itself: "The question before the Court and you is not of small or private concern … No! It may, on its consequences, affect every freeman" (Kobre, p. 41). Hamilton, arguing that Zenger's was the greatest cause, the cause of liberty, created an uproar. He called on the jury to defend the "cause of liberty both of exposing and opposing arbitrary power … by speaking and writing the truth" (Stephens, p. 186).

Libel had earlier been defined as any defamatory statement made against the government. Hamilton argued that if the content of the statement is true, it should not be against the law to print it. He admitted that Zenger printed statements attacking Cosby. However, he argued, they were true, and therefore Zenger could not be punished for printing them. The people had a right to know the truth about elected officials and newspapers had a right to print it. Hamilton's persuasive argument convinced the jury, who returned with a verdict of not guilty.

> ## American Press Reaches Europe
>
> Following his trial, Zenger wrote his memoirs of the experience. Four editions were published in London in 1738. Not only had the trial raised the issue of freedom of the press in America, it also helped the growth of its newspapers by spreading their story across the sea.

The crowd at the packed courthouse cheered when the decision was heard. The Zengers celebrated by treating Hamilton and all their supporters to a party at the Black Horse Tavern. Zenger had made his stand, had even gone to jail, and, with the help of family and friends, had won. More important, freedom of expression was upheld and the trial "had indirectly warned the governors of the colonies not to attempt to gag the press" (Kobre, p. 42).

Aftermath

Immediately following the trial, Zenger published *A Brief Narrative of the Case and Tryal of John Peter Zenger* concerning his recent experiences. Copies of his memoirs circulated throughout the East Coast and across the Atlantic to London and inspired many to begin their own newspapers. Zenger was a hero to the many immigrants of New York who had had enough of British tyranny

THE

Charter

OF THE

CITY

OF

NEW-YORK;

Printed by Order of the Mayor, Recorder, Aldermen and Commonalty of the City aforesaid.

TO WHICH IS ANNEXED,

The Act of the General Assembly Confirming the same.

NEW-YORK,
Printed by *John Peter Zenger*. 1735.

▲ The charter of the City of New York

and longed to form a government of their own. His example helped spark the American Revolution.

In 1737 Zenger was made public printer of New York and the following year was given the same honor in New Jersey. He also became a naturalized citizen in 1738 as a show of respect and gratitude from the city. He continued to run the *Journal* until his death in 1746. Catherine then took over operations until December 1748, when their oldest son, John, assumed control. He ran the newspaper for three more years until its publication ceased altogether.

Zenger's trial resulted in a new definition of damaging statements, or libel, and led the battle against censorship in the press. According to one author, it began a more basic fight too: "The trial of Zenger in 1735 was the germ of American freedom, the morning star of that liberty which subsequently revolutionized America" (Smith, p. 131).

For More Information

Galt, Tom. *Peter Zenger, Fighter for Freedom.* New York: Thomas Y. Crowell, 1951.

Kobre, Sidney. *Development of American Journalism.* Dubuque, Iowa: William C. Brown Company Publishers, 1969.

Malone, Dumas. *Jefferson and the Rights of Man.* Boston: Little, Brown & Company, 1951.

Smith, Peter. *John Peter Zenger.* New York: Dodd, Mead & Company, 1904.

Stephens, Mitchell. *The History of News.* New York: Viking/Penguin, 1988.

Samuel Adams

1722-1803

Personal Background

Samuel Adams (in his own day, only his enemies called him Sam) was born in Boston on September 27, 1722, to one of Massachusetts's leading families. The Adamses had settled in Braintree (later Quincy), just south of Boston, in the early 1600s. It was Samuel's father, also named Samuel, who moved from Braintree to Boston. There the elder Adams owned a brewery and led an active public life. As deacon of Boston's Old South Church, he oversaw the church's non-religious activities. Deacon Adams—as his friends called him—also belonged to the influential Caucus Club, an informal group of wealthy men who controlled local politics. He himself served in various offices. For example, Deacon Adams represented Boston in the Massachusetts House of Representatives.

Puritan upbringing. The children, Samuel, his older sister, Mary, and his younger brother, Joseph, rarely saw their busy father. They were raised instead by their mother, Mary, an old-fashioned New England Puritan and a follower of the Reverend Jonathan Edwards, who is commonly regarded as the strictest of Puritan churchmen. Samuel's Puritan values—especially his righteous, sometimes stubborn morality—would remain with him for the rest of his life.

Rambles along the waterfront. Another powerful influence

▲ Samuel Adams

Event: Stamp Act; Townshend Acts; Boston Tea Party.

Role: From 1764 to the signing of the Declaration of Independence in 1776, Samuel Adams worked—at first nearly alone and against the odds—to create and nurture the independence movement. A tireless politician with a sure sense of tactics and propaganda, Adams wrote endless attacks on British policy and organized the earliest American opposition to it.

was witnessing the lives of the sailors and dock workers who filled the ships, warehouses, and taverns of Boston's thriving waterfront. From the highest windows of his house, the young Adams would intently watch ships anchor and unload their cargoes in Boston's busy harbor. As an Adams, he was not supposed to mingle with the lower-class waterfront workers and their families. Yet from an early age, at least according to Adams's later accounts, he struck off on his own to explore the waterfront, becoming friends with the sailors, watching them handle the wares from far-off lands, and—most important—listening to their continual political discussions in the crowded, smoky waterfront taverns.

Harvard and the ideas of John Locke. In 1736, at the age of fourteen, Samuel entered Boston's Harvard College, where all the Adams males were educated. At Harvard, along with the other usual subjects for the time (Greek and Latin classics, philosophy, theology), Adams read the works of John Locke, a seventeenth-century English writer who had revolutionized political thinking. Locke believed that any government, to be legal, must take its power from the people, who will always maintain certain rights with which the government should not interfere. Adams filled his notebooks with Locke's ideas, underlining parts that he found especially important. Twenty years after Adams encountered Locke's works at Harvard, a young Thomas Jefferson would also be deeply impressed by the same ideas during his own education (see **Thomas Jefferson**). In many ways, the American Revolution can be seen as an attempt to put Locke's theories into practice.

Adams spent seven years at Harvard, receiving his Master of Arts degree in 1743, at age twenty-one. The title of the paper he wrote to earn his degree reveals the direction his own ideas were taking: "Whether It Be Lawful to Resist the Supreme Magistrate, if the Commonwealth Cannot Be Otherwise Preserved." In other words, was it ever lawful to resist the government if there was no other way to protect the common good? Unfortunately, the paper has been lost; we know only that Adams's answer was a definite "yes."

Attempts at a business career. Though it would be another twenty years before his political ideas began to see form, politics had established itself as Adams's only real interest. In the meantime, he made several attempts at a traditional career in business: at the bank of a close family friend; in an unknown personal venture, for which he borrowed 1,000 pounds from his father; and finally in the family brewery. But, money bored him. He spent his days in a relatively junior position at the brewery, looking forward to the evenings of lively political discussion he spent with his friends.

Early political activity. During the 1740s Adams supported his father's interest in anti-British politics and in the Land Bank, a scheme to aid farmers by creating a bank that issued paper money to farmers, using their land as security. Chief among Deacon Adams's opponents was Lieutenant Governor Thomas Hutchinson, who led the movement to dissolve the Land Bank in 1741. Also from one of Boston's wealthy and aristocratic families, Hutchinson sided politically with the aristocrats, viewing the Adamses as traitors to their class. Hutchinson, as lieutenant governor and, later, governor, would be the younger Adams's main opponent in the upcoming struggle. The two men were as opposite in appearance as in outlook. Hutchinson, slender and handsome, wore expensive and perfectly tailored suits. Adams, by contrast, was stocky, with rugged, square features, and he was well known for ignoring his clothes, which were generally sloppy and tattered.

Adams made little progress in politics at first. He wrote articles and essays for the *Public Advertiser,* an anti-British newspaper that he started with some friends. From 1756 to 1764 he was repeatedly elected as tax collector. In office he was popular but ineffective, piling up a debt of about 8,000 pounds in uncollected taxes. By 1764, at the age of forty-two, he seemed to be, if not quite a failure, certainly less than a success. Most saw him as an odd but harmless character, unable to handle money and obsessed with his opposition to the British. Yet in little more than a decade he would become, in British eyes, "the most dangerous man in the New World" (Lewis, p. x).

Participation: Boston Tea Party and More

End of "Salutary Neglect." Until the French and Indian War (1756-1763), Britain pursued a policy that generally left the colonies responsible for both their own rule and defense. The French and Indian War, during which British troops were used to protect colonial territory, interrupted this "salutary neglect," or healthy neglect, as the policy was called. British leaders now decided that if the colonies were going to receive royal protection, they ought to help pay for it. Without consulting the colonial assemblies, they began to pass laws that taxed the colonies, shocking the colonists, who were used to deciding such matters themselves. This shock soon gave way to anger and hostility, setting the stage for Samuel Adams's rise as, in Jefferson's words, "the patriarch of liberty" (Beach, p. 301).

Caucus Club. By the mid-1760s Adams and his friends had come to dominate the Caucus Club, the political group to which his father had also belonged. James Otis, a young Boston lawyer, was the recognized leader, with Adams as his assistant. Others included the handsome and wealthy John Hancock, whom Adams persuaded to join in 1765; Josiah Quincy, Jr., regarded as Boston's best public speaker; and Joseph Warren, who later sent Paul Revere on his midnight ride and died at the Battle of Bunker Hill. Otis and Adams both won seats in the state House of Representatives, in which Otis and then Adams himself led the "patriot" majority.

Behind the scenes. Adams's style was to work behind the scenes, writing articles under false names or organizing demonstrations during which he would quietly melt into the background so that they always appeared to be led by others. He often aimed to arouse the people, who at first—as after the Sugar Act of 1764—seemed indifferent to changes in the taxes. At other times the type of demonstrations inspired by Adams and others got out of control. After the unpopular Stamp Act of 1765, for example, an angry mob vandalized and set fire to Hutchinson's luxurious house in Boston. Adams also made use of and helped organize such groups as the Sons of Liberty, which sprang up in cities like Boston after the Stamp Act.

With his untidy clothes and a mild illness that often caused his head and hands to tremble, Adams did not fit the usual picture of a powerful leader. Yet his belief in the rightness of his ideas gave him a force that impressed those who saw him speak or read his articles.

Stronger position. With the repeal of the Stamp Act in 1766, Adams and his fellow radicals had won their first major victory. Adams remained busy, however, working to secure his position at home and strengthening his links with radicals in other colonies, especially in Virginia, where Patrick Henry had led the fight against the Stamp Act (see **Patrick Henry**). He also began to include his energetic second cousin John, thirteen years his junior, in his activities. John Adams, at this time a young lawyer from Braintree, would eventually take his own place in history, becoming the second president of the United States.

Adams's home life had improved as well. His first wife, Elizabeth Checkley, had died in 1757, leaving him to care for a young son and daughter. He remarried in late 1764, and his second wife, Elizabeth Wells, was attractive and practical. She was also a very patient woman and proved an ideal partner for her single-minded husband. Adams rarely spent time at home. Even when he sat down for dinner, he would sometimes lose patience if the conversation went off the topic of politics and would simply get up and leave. As John Adams recorded in his diary, his cousin was "stiff and strict and rigid and inflexible in the cause" of liberty, perhaps "too attentive to the public and not enough so to himself and his family" (Beach, p. 11).

Townshend Acts. The radical's next test came in 1767, as the English Parliament, stung by its retreat over the Stamp Act, moved to regain control with a new set of taxes. The Townshend Acts taxed imports such as glass, paper, lead, paint, and tea, all of which needed to be imported and required special customs officers to collect the taxes. The money would then be used to pay the salaries of royal officials in America, such as judges and governors, and the British troops protecting the colonies. Adams and the others argued that the colonies should control the salaries of the officials as well as be responsible for protecting themselves.

British troops arrive. In 1768, as the news reached Boston that the customs officers were on their way, accompanied by British soldiers, rioting erupted in Boston. Yet, despite Adams's efforts, when the soldiers arrived in October, they met no resistance. Adams at least won a victory by insisting that the troops be housed outside of the city center, but his attempts to create a boycott of the

▲ **The Boston Massacre**

taxed goods enjoyed only partial success as the colonies disagreed among themselves.

Boston Massacre. With Otis having fallen ill, Adams was now the undisputed leader of the Boston radicals. Though he had failed to organize armed resistance to the troops, the townspeople were bitter toward them, though not always openly. As time wore on, however, their hostility grew.

By early 1770, after more than a year of Adams campaigning to have the troops removed, small groups of townspeople had begun to harass them. Adams, writing furious newspaper articles, made the most of these "skirmishes," portraying the locals as innocent victims and the soldiers as bloodthirsty savages. The incidents accelerated, and in March 1770 a group of soldiers fired on a small crowd of townspeople, killing four. Adams immediately fired off his own articles, naming the incident the "Boston Massacre." Bostonians consequently elected a committee to confront Governor Hutchinson. As chairman, Adams forced Hutchinson to withdraw the troops from Boston and to surrender for trial the soldiers involved in the Boston Massacre. Ironically, the soldiers were successfully defended by John Adams.

Committees of Correspondence. For two years, as tension lessened in the wake of the "Massacre," a period of calm descended on the colonies. The Townshend Acts were repealed, and the people felt more friendly toward Britain. Talk of resistance ceased. Adams's grip on the House of Representatives—which he had come to control completely—also weakened. Even his cousin John retired temporarily from politics. Yet during this time Adams provided perhaps his most useful service: he refused to give up the fight, writing article after article condemning Britain, though fewer and fewer people read them.

In late 1772, Adams proposed that Boston create a "committee of correspondence" that would establish links with other Massachusetts towns. The colony would then be more unified in its policy toward Britain. These first committees provided a model for committees the colonies would later set up among themselves. These colonial committees, in turn, set the stage for the First Continental Congress. Adams thus sowed the first seeds of revolutionary government in America.

Tea Party. By early 1773 Adams had begun, for the first time, to call openly for complete independence from Britain and for the establishment of an American republic. Yet he lacked a cause to rally the people. In May 1773 Parliament and King George gave him one by passing the Tea Act. While the act actually cut the price of tea in half, it also hurt the American merchants who had previously made a profit from selling the tea. The atmosphere of calm was broken during the summer and fall as support for the American merchants grew, and people prepared to resist British attempts to unload the new tea. In Boston, on December 16, 1773, patriots disguised as Mohawk Indians spent three hours dumping the new tea into the harbor from the ships that had carried it. Called the Boston

Tea Party, this rough protest intensely angered King George and his prime minister, Lord Frederick North.

Throughout the colonies people celebrated the Boston Tea Party as a show of American determination and unity in resisting British policy. The "Mohawks" kept silent until years later, when several revealed that the scheme had been the work of Adams. Adams, behind the scenes as usual, did not actually take part, and of course had an alibi for the hours of the Tea Party.

British reaction. The Tea Party began a chain of events—actions and reactions—that hardened attitudes on both sides of the Atlantic. In response, Parliament passed a number of measures that Americans called "the Intolerable Acts." Among other punishments, Boston Harbor was closed until the Bostonians paid for the lost tea. Also, the Charter of Massachusetts, the governmental agreement between the king and the colonists, was canceled, thereby dismissing the legislature and giving all power to the governor. Other colonies came to the support of Massachusetts. Suddenly, Adams was no longer alone in calling for resistance to British policy, as leaders from Virginia to Philadelphia began discussing American options.

First Continental Congress. As tensions grew during 1773, Virginia radicals (see **Thomas Jefferson** and **Patrick Henry**) had taken Adams's idea for committees of correspondence and applied it on a large scale. They called for links among all the colonies rather than merely among towns within a single colony. Now, in early 1774, the Massachusetts committees, led by Adams, joined with others in calling for a meeting of representatives elected by the colonies to discuss their grievances and their aims. This First Continental Congress met in Philadelphia, Pennsylvania in September 1774, with both Samuel and John Adams among those elected to represent Massachusetts. With Boston the focus of tension between Britain and the colonies, the

Fit for a Congressman

Samuel Adams's tattered and stained clothes were one of his trademarks, but his friends thought his appearance should be improved if he was going to serve in the Continental Congress. The day before he left for Philadelphia, a trunk appeared on the Adams doorstep. It contained two new suits, new shoes with silver buckles, gold knee-buckles, a red cloak, a stylish cocked hat, and a gold-headed cane. The cane was decorated with the "Liberty Cap," the emblem of Adams's friends, the Sons of Liberty.

▲ The Boston Tea Party

Congress pledged to assist Massachusetts if armed resistance became necessary.

Lexington and Concord. On April 19, 1775, British soldiers marched from Boston toward Concord, twenty-one miles away, to arrest Samuel Adams and John Hancock. Warned by the Massachusetts Assembly's official courier, Paul Revere, who rode ahead of the soldiers, the two escaped. But fighting broke out at Lexington and nearby Concord between the soldiers and the American militia, or Minutemen. Adams immediately began writing pamphlets that turned the unwon battle into "the shot heard round the world" (Lewis, p. 237).

Second Continental Congress. Although the fighting sparked widespread hostility toward Britain, the idea of independence remained difficult for most leaders to accept. When the Second Continental Congress met in May 1775, Adams was nearly alone in calling for complete separation from Britain. Nevertheless,

▲ *The Massachusetts Sun* carried Benjamin Franklin's plea to "Join or Die"

the Congress quickly decided to create an army, appointing George Washington to command it. At the Battle of Bunker Hill on June 17, 1775, the Americans, though narrowly defeated, proved they could stand against British might. Washington spent the rest of the year trying to build up the American forces.

Independence. The momentum that Adams had started increased in early 1776, as events unfolded that brought the aim of complete independence into open discussion among American leaders. Previously, most had rejected Adams's position, believing instead that the colonies could reach a settlement that would keep them within the British empire. In January 1776, however, Thomas Paine's pamphlet *Common Sense* was published. Paine presented powerful arguments for independence that appealed to the general public, and for the first time the idea was widely discussed and accepted (see **Thomas Paine**). Working closely with his cousin John and such Virginians as Richard Henry Lee and Thomas Jefferson, Adams pressed hard for independence when the Congress met again in early 1776. The Congress approved the Declaration of Independence, formally separating America from Britain, on July 4, 1776.

Aftermath

"Man of the Revolution." Though Adams continued to serve in public life, he did not take much of a role in creating the new government. It has been said that when he signed the Declaration of Independence he signed away his position of leadership, and it is true that he was more of a revolutionary than a statesman. He continued to represent Massachusetts in the Congress until 1781, however, and was Massachusetts governor from 1793 until 1797. He died on October 2, 1803, at the age of eighty-one, secure in his place as one of America's founding fathers. In the words of Thomas Jefferson, who wrote the Declaration itself, Adams was "truly the Man of the Revolution" (Lewis, p. 273).

For More Information

Beach, Stewart. *Samuel Adams: The Fateful Years, 1764-1776*. New York: Dodd, Mead & Co., 1965.

Canfield, Cass. *Samuel Adams's Revolution: 1765-1776*. New York: Harper & Row, 1976.

Lewis, Paul. *The Grand Incendiary*. New York: Dial Press, 1973.

Patrick Henry

1736-1799

Personal Background

Patrick Henry was born on May 29, 1736, in the newly settled countryside of western Virginia's Hanover County. His father, John Henry, had immigrated to Virginia in 1727 from his native Aberdeen, Scotland. Making his way west, he joined the household of a fellow Scotsman named John Syme, also from Aberdeen. John Henry assisted the older man in running the Syme plantation until Syme's death in 1731. About a year later, John Henry married Syme's attractive and intelligent young widow, Sarah Winston Syme. He was soon granted several thousand acres of wilderness land next to Studley, the Syme plantation, adding to the family property. Patrick, born a few years later, was the couple's second son.

Up-country settlement. Life in western Virginia was very different from the elegant society of the older "Tidewater" settlements near the coast. The western frontier area, called the "up-country," was just beginning to be settled and mapped out in the 1730s. Large grants of wilderness land were given to men willing to work it, men such as John Henry and Peter Jefferson, father of future president Thomas (see **Thomas Jefferson**). Such men wore buckskin pants and homespun shirts, rather than the fine breeches and ruffled shirts found in the Tidewater. College educations were rare, and Patrick was fortunate that his father had more "book learning" than most, having attended Kings College in Aberdeen.

▲ **Patrick Henry**

Event: Stamp Act resolutions; speeches to Virginia assemblies.

Role: A powerful orator, Patrick Henry delivered stirring speeches against British policies. His speech against the Stamp Act (1765) persuaded the Virginia House of Burgesses to pass his Stamp Act Resolves, and put Virginia in the forefront of colonial resistance to Britain.

Frontier childhood. Hunting provided a large part of the up-country diet, and as a boy Henry enjoyed solitary hunting and fishing trips into the wilderness. The woods were filled with game (rabbit, partridge, squirrel, wild turkey, and deer, for example). Ducks, geese, and swans as well as fish could be found in the nearby rivers, the Pamunkey and the Totopotomoy. One of his teachers in the ways of the woods was his colorful uncle, William "Langloo" Winston. Langloo, a buckskin-clad frontiersman, spent half of every year hunting in the backwoods, camping on his own or with Indians. Henry's frontier ways stayed with him. Later in life, according to some of the many stories told about him, he would take time to hunt while riding into the courthouse to try a case. He would arrive with game slung over his saddle and march straight into the courtroom wearing his bloodstained leather hunting jacket.

Reluctant student. Other stories have portrayed young Patrick Henry as a poor student, impatient with books and always eager to get back to his beloved hunting rifle and the outdoors. Though probably exaggerated, these stories have some basis in fact. John Henry tutored his sons himself, giving them assignments in Greek, Latin, history, and mathematics. Yet the young Henry found plenty of time for climbing trees, fishing and swimming in the river, and canoeing. He would often tip the canoe over with himself and his friends in it. It would always seem to be an accident, but somehow Henry would manage to have his clothes off, ready for a swim, while his friends were still dressed.

Storekeeper, husband, planter. Despite his good start, John Henry proved to be a poor businessman, and when Patrick was about twelve the family moved to a smaller property. The new land, called Mount Brilliant, was twenty miles west of Studley, right at the western edge of Hanover County. By fifteen, Henry had finished his studies with his father. Too poor to pay for college, which boys began at fourteen or fifteen, John Henry instead borrowed enough money to set his two sons up with a small general store. William and Patrick had inherited their father's poor business sense, however, and the store quickly failed. Soon after, at eighteen and against the advice of his parents, Henry got married to a pretty, brown-haired sixteen-year-old named Sarah Shelton. Called Sallie, she lived near Studley and had known Henry all her life. As a dowry, Sarah's father offered Henry enough land to start a small tobacco farm, along with six black slaves.

Young father. In 1755, almost a year after being married, Henry and Sarah had their first child, a daughter they named Martha. Two hard years of tobacco farming passed, in which a second child, John, was added to the family. Then disaster struck when the farmhouse burned. The growing family moved in with the Sheltons, who ran a nearby tavern. Henry tended bar for his father-in-law and in 1758 opened a second general store. Times were difficult, with the economy based on tobacco sales. Since there was only a small amount of cash, such stores had to offer credit to their customers. Many customers traded things in, or simply went without paying for long periods of time. To add to their financial troubles, the couple continued to have children, with perhaps four altogether by 1760.

"Music, dancing, and pleasantry." Despite his discouraging situation, Henry remained lighthearted and hopeful. He was more interested in talking to his customers than wringing payments out of them. So the store became the scene of long conversations about politics and human behavior. Outside the store, Henry loved socializing, dancing, and playing the fiddle, especially at fancy parties in the homes of wealthy planters. Virginians loved such parties. In fact, seventeen-year-old Thomas Jefferson first met Henry, six years Jefferson's senior, at one in 1759. Already serious and hard-working, Jefferson observed Henry's popularity and "passion for music, dancing and pleasantry" (Mayer, p. 50). The two later became friends, although their differences would create rivalry between them as well (see **Thomas Jefferson**).

New career as a lawyer. Sometime around 1760, when he was about twenty-four, Henry decided to become a lawyer. With his ever-growing family, he needed a larger income than his badly managed store could provide. There are stories for every chapter in Henry's life, and those about his legal training claim that he only studied for six weeks before becoming a lawyer. Nevertheless, he was able to persuade four lawyers in Williamsburg, Virginia's capital, to approve him. With four signatures, he was allowed to set up his own legal practice.

He continued learning as he practiced law over the next few years, and his practice became modestly successful. He spent much of his time on horseback, riding from courthouse to courthouse, taking cases that covered different aspects of country life and business. Because cash was so scarce in the colonial economy, many of these cases involved suits to recover debts, in which he represented both debtors and creditors.

Participation: Declarations of Independence

The Parsons' cause. In 1763 one such case brought him sudden recognition. The case had begun five years earlier, when a bad tobacco harvest had led the Virginia legislature to pass temporary laws that, in effect, limited the payment that all creditors could collect on their debts. Though most creditors accepted this step, one group did not. The Church of England's ministers, called parsons, were paid by the government at a fixed salary, which was cut by one-third under the new temporary laws. The parsons sued, and government officials in London ruled in their favor. The law was repealed, and several parsons then began lawsuits to recover the salaries they had lost in the meantime.

One of these parsons was James Maury. The judge in the case was John Henry, Patrick Henry's father, who ruled in Maury's favor. (John Henry had gotten many of his ideas about the case from his brother, a parson also named Patrick Henry.) Judge Henry set a day for the jury to decide how much Maury was owed. At that point, with the case already lost, the lawyer arguing against Maury resigned. Patrick Henry took his place.

Crowded courthouse. On December 1, 1763, the court met to award Maury his back-pay. The Hanover Courthouse was crowded with Virginia parsons eager to hear the outcome and people who believed the parsons were wrong to oppose a law that had helped all Virginians. (When Parson Patrick Henry drove up in his carriage, Henry asked him not to attend the hearing. He was afraid he would have to say things that would be unpleasant for his uncle to hear. Agreeing, his uncle turned around and drove off.) Maury's lawyer spoke confidently, pointing out that the jury's duty was simple: to figure out exactly how much salary Maury had lost and award him that amount.

A larger cause. Then Henry got up to speak. He started hesitantly, nervous in front of the crowd and in front of his father. Gradually, however, as he grew absorbed in his arguments, his voice gained strength, his awkward movements became commanding, and the words began to roll easily and smoothly off his tongue. He supported the right of the Virginia legislature to make its own laws, and he attacked the parsons for thinking of themselves rather than helping to protect the common good. People nodded and even swayed as he spoke. Outraged, the parsons left the courtroom. Some people whispered "treason" because Henry questioned the right of the British government to overrule the Virginia legislature. Yet, when he finished, the courtroom erupted in cheers. The jury quickly awarded Maury the amount of one penny, and Henry had won his first major victory. More important, he had linked the parsons' case to a larger cause: the right of the colonists to govern themselves.

Popular leader. Overnight, Henry had become a public figure. The formerly unknown lawyer showed power to move an audience with his words that had been unsuspected. Furthermore, he had used that power on behalf of the people, against the unpopular parsons and the British government. In 1764 he was elected to the Virginia House of Burgesses, or the legislative assembly, which met in Williamsburg. He soon became the leader of what would become the Virginia independence movement, which was rooted in the up-country, where independence was a way of life. In Tidewater towns such as Williamsburg, by contrast, the general attitude was more conservative, and people felt stronger links with Britain. The conservatives held power in the assembly. With his next victory, however, Henry would break their grip on power and point the way toward revolution.

Stamp Act. Henry took his place when the burgesses met in Williamsburg in May 1765. On his third day he had already challenged the assembly's conservative leadership, giving a speech that attacked a proposal by the powerful speaker of the house, John Robinson, a Tidewater aristocrat. The speech by the new member won the House over, and Robinson's proposal was abandoned.

The House's attention then turned to the unpopular Stamp Act, a tax on colonial businesses that the British Parliament had put into effect in March 1765. The year before, while Parliament had been considering the Stamp Act taxes, the House (along with the other colonial assemblies) had sent letters to Britain protesting the idea. Now Parliament had approved the taxes, and Henry, leading the up-country burgesses, wanted to do something stronger than the previous year's mildly worded letter.

A lone voice. Leaders in Virginia and other colonies recognized that if Britain were able to take away the colonies' right to tax themselves, other rights might more easily be lost in the future. Yet it was one thing to oppose a plan and another to resist a law that had already gone into effect. Though popular demonstrations (see Samuel Adams) protested the Stamp Act in Massachusetts, the colonial governments seemed ready to accept it rather than openly oppose the British government. Seeing that no one else was prepared to lead the fight, Henry realized it was up to him. He wrote a list of resolutions that would set out, in clear and bold language, reasons for refusing to cooperate with the Stamp Act taxes. He then faced the challenge of persuading the House to adopt his "Resolves," making resistance the official—and rebellious—policy of the colony of Virginia.

> ## The Resolves in Henry's Words
>
> The ... resolutions passed the House of Burgesses in May, 1765. They formed the first Opposition to the Stamp Act and the scheme of taxing America by the British Parliament. All the colonies . . . had remained silent. I had been for the first time elected a Burgess a few days before, was young, inexperienced.... Finding ... that no person was likely to step forth, I determined to venture ... alone, unadvised, & unassisted. (From an account in Henry's handwriting, found with his copy of the Resolves; Meade, p. 167).

"Make the most of it." In presenting his case to the burgesses, Henry quickly gained the support of several important representatives from the up-country. Most notable were John Fleming and George Johnston, with whom he probably met at a nearby tavern before introducing the Resolves. Against them stood the Tidewater aristocrats, led by Robinson, who still dominated the House. Thomas Jefferson, training in Williamsburg as a lawyer, stood in the doorway as the debate began. Five of the seven resolves ultimately came under consideration. All five were passed after a rush of convincing arguments, or, in Jefferson's words, Henry's "torrents of sublime eloquence." The votes were extremely close, especially on the fifth and strongest resolve. It was then, according to tradition, that Speaker Robinson cried, "Treason!" and was echoed by others. "If this be treason," Henry is said to have replied, "make the most of it!" (Meade, p. 173). The next day, after Henry had gone home, the fifth resolve was rejected when some members changed their votes.

The Resolves. The first four resolves laid out the colony's reasons for claiming the right to tax themselves. That right rested on both the royal charter (the original agreement between the king and the colonists) and on history (the colony had always set its own taxes in the past). The fifth resolve claimed that only the elected assembly can tax the colony, and that any attempt to take that power away "has a Manifest tendency to destroy British as well as American Freedom." The sixth and seventh resolves went even further, stating that the colonists had no obligation to obey laws that their own legislature had not approved, and that anyone who said that the colony did not have the right to decide its own taxes "shall be deemed an enemy" to the colony (Meade, p. 171). Though not endorsed by the burgesses, these last three resolves were included with the others when the list was published throughout the colonies. With their publication, the young man who had championed them took his place with other radicals, such as Samuel Adams, at the forefront of American resistance to Britain.

Showdown. Few of Henry's words survive, except in tradition or in versions remembered by listeners like Jefferson. Yet all who heard the tall, thin, balding redhead agreed that Henry ranked with the greatest orators of all time. In persuading the reluctant burgesses to adopt his resolutions, he forced a showdown with the British government. Other colonies followed Virginia's example, and the Stamp Act was soon made impossible to enforce. It was repealed in 1766.

Famous Words by Patrick Henry

"If this be treason, make the most of it!"
"Give me liberty, or give me death!"
"The battle, sir, is not to the strong alone."
(Baker, pp. 75, 222, and 225)

"Spirit of the Revolution." Over the next decade Henry's family, like his fame, continued to grow. Eventually he would have twelve children and sixty grandchildren, many of whom lived with him. (His children were by two wives. Sallie had died in 1775, and

Henry remarried in 1777. His second wife, Dorothea, was the daughter of an old friend and a cousin of Martha Washington. Henry loved to surround himself with his numerous grandchildren. (One of his descendants joked that Henry, not George Washington, should be called the "father of his country.") Henry acquired land in frontier areas as far west as the Mississippi and explored the frontier with his brother William.

Mainly, however, Henry pursued his political career, remaining in the House of Burgesses until being selected to the first Continental Congress in 1774. In the House, he led the group of Virginia radicals who opposed Britain. Jefferson, elected as a burgess in 1769, wrote later about Henry's leadership and powers of persuasion:

> He was as well suited to the times as any man ever was, and it is not now easy to say what we should have done without Patrick Henry. He was far above all in maintaining the spirit of the Revolution.... His eloquence was peculiar, if indeed it should be called eloquence; for it was impressive and sublime, beyond what can be imagined. (Meade, p. 268)

Liberty or death. Henry's most famous speech came on March 23, 1775, before the Virginia Provincial Convention at St. John's Church in Richmond. Held to give the colony's approval to the Continental Congress, the convention included Virginia patriots such as Jefferson, Washington, and Richard Henry Lee. In his account of the speech, William Wirt, Henry's first biographer, used the reports of such witnesses. The speech's conclusion has gone down in history:

> Gentlemen may cry, peace, peace—but there is no peace. The war is actually begun! The next gale that sweeps from the north will bring to our ears the clash of resounding arms! Our brethren are already in the field! Why stand we here idle?... Is life so dear, or peace so sweet, as to be purchased at the price of chains and slavery? Forbid it, Almighty God! I know not what course others may take; but as for me, give me liberty or give me death! (Meade, p. 35)

The packed church remained silent for a long time after he finished. Outside, much of the crowd had heard the speech through the open windows, thanks to Henry's booming voice (his way of "sending" it, as his friends said). One man even sat in the window—and was so moved that he declared, "Let me be buried at this spot!" (Meade, p. 37). So he was, after his death in 1810, having witnessed one of the most effective revolutionary speeches in history.

Aftermath

Along with Samuel Adams, Henry was one of the earliest and most steadfast opponents of British rule in America. His speaking skills certainly added to his political achievements; indeed, the Stamp Act Resolves were probably approved only because of his persuasive words. But the Resolves' importance lay in their timing, when America was hovering between submission and resistance. Whichever course of action won the day was likely to shape the future. Henry tipped the balance toward resistance, when no one else had the will or courage to do so.

Life of service. Yet not all of Henry's achievements rested on his oratorical skills. He served as governor of Virginia for four one-year terms, including during much of the Revolutionary War. As in his earlier service in the House of Burgesses, he was a hard-working administrator who tirelessly performed numerous minor tasks less glamorous than the speech for which he is remembered. He opposed the Constitution, believing that it threatened individual rights, and was largely responsible for the adoption of the Bill of Rights (the first ten amendments to the Constitution). Heavily in debt from his long public career, he revived his law practice in 1788. His fame soon brought success and wealth, and in 1794 he bought an estate, Red Hill, in his beloved western Virginia. Coaxed out of retirement by George Washington, he ran for the state legislature; he won the election, but died, on June 6, 1799, before he could take office.

For More Information

Baker, Daniel B. *Political Quotations.* Detroit: Gale Research Inc., 1990.

Meade, Robert Douthat. *Patrick Henry: Practical Revolutionary.* Philadelphia: J. B. Lippincott Co., 1969.

Mayer, Henry. *A Son of Thunder.* New York: Franklin Watts, 1986.

Thomas Paine

1737-1809

Personal Background

Thomas Paine was born in the English village of Thetford on January 29, 1737. His parents did not have a happy marriage. In the garment business, his father, Joseph, barely made a living crafting whalebone stays, or ribs, for women's corsets. His mother, Frances, eleven-years older than her husband, was by all accounts a cold and irritable woman. Her husband was a Quaker, while she belonged to the Church of England. His family was poor; hers, though not wealthy, came from the village's upper class. Paine was their only child, except for a younger daughter who died in infancy.

"A sharp boy." Though poor, the Paines wanted their only son to have a good education. Typically, the boy would have gone to work for his father, but his parents made sacrifices so he could attend the village school. He did fairly well at subjects that caught his interest: science, which would continue to interest him throughout his life, math, and poetry. He did less well at Latin. Latin was then one of the most important subjects for anyone who wanted to go on to a professional career in medicine, the law, or the church, for example. Paine did not work at Latin because he did not like it. "A sharp boy," wrote one observer, "of unsettled application" (Hawke, p. 9). This charge of laziness would often be leveled at him in later years, despite the many influential writings Paine eventually produced.

▲ **Thomas Paine**

Event: The publication of *Common Sense*

Role: With his widely read pamphlet *Common Sense*, writer Thomas Paine made independence a household word in the colonies. Published in January 1776, the work crystallized the colonists' complaints against English rule. It also attacked the idea of rule by a king, supporting instead a republican form of government. Finally, it argued that independence was the colonists' best course. Before Paine, such ideas had been spread only by "radicals" such as Samuel Adams. Paine's achievement was to make them acceptable to the common man.

Sea tales. One of Paine's teachers, the Reverend William Knowler, had served as chaplain on a warship in the English navy. He entertained Paine and the other boys with tales of his exciting life at sea. Around the same time (when he was about twelve), Paine read a book about Virginia, one of the faraway American colonies. The restless boy developed a longing to see America that would finally be fulfilled twenty-five years later.

Apprentice, journeyman, runaway. By the age of thirteen Paine, refusing to learn Latin, seemed to have closed off any possibilities of a professional career. He left school, going to work for his father as apprentice and then journeyman staymaker (the three ranks of craftsman were apprentice, journeyman, and master). Three years later, inspired by his former teacher's exciting stories, he ran away and joined the crew of the privateer *Terrible,* commanded by the colorfully named Captain Death. His father persuaded him to return before the ship sailed, but from Thetford Paine followed the exploits of the *Terrible* at sea. Two weeks later, after several successes against enemy ships, the *Terrible* sank in a storm, with all hands lost. Undiscouraged, Paine ran off again about a year later, at the age of seventeen or eighteen. This time he succeeded, spending about a year aboard the privateer *King of Prussia.* Though he rarely spoke of it later, his time at sea seems to have satisfied—temporarily at least—his urge to see the world. In 1757, at the age of twenty, he resumed his father's trade, first as a journeyman in the port city of Dover, then as a master staymaker in London.

Years of failure. The years of Paine's early manhood were a time of repeated failures. In 1760, soon after Paine married, his staymaking shop failed. His young wife died less than a year later. He gave up staymaking in 1761 and returned to Thetford, where he spent a year studying to become an excise officer, which had been his maternal grandfather's career. Excise officers, who inspected and taxed goods such as alcohol, tobacco, and other common items, were unpopular and poorly paid.

Less than a year after Paine became an excise officer (1764), he was dismissed for passing goods that he had not fully inspected. (This was a common practice, apparently, because the workload was very heavy.) He returned to staymaking, working in several towns, then tried his hand at teaching. He even became a preacher for a short time. In 1768, at thirty-one, he managed to get back his old job as excise officer. He was posted in the town of Lewes, south of London.

Taking up the pen. In Lewes, where Paine lived for six years, things finally seemed to look up. He moved in with a family, the Ollives, who ran a small grocery. When Mr. Ollive died, Paine married the daughter, Elizabeth, and took over the grocery. The marriage, however, was one of convenience. Though friendly, Paine and Elizabeth were never in love. Instead, Paine's life centered around a growing circle of friends, some of whom also worked for the excise and some of whom he met in long evenings of drink and discussion at local taverns. Paine acquired a reputation as a skilled arguer. In 1772, a year after his marriage, a group of his superiors in the excise asked him to write a pamphlet supporting their attempt to gain a pay raise for British excise officers. Though the pamphlet had little effect on Parliament, it was clear and well argued, drawing wide recognition for its author.

Benjamin Franklin. In the fall and winter of 1772-73, Paine moved to London to promote the excise officers' cause, which had become a small-scale rebellion. Though it failed, his involvement in it led to his meeting Benjamin Franklin, who represented the colonies' interests in London. It also caused him to be dismissed a second time, for ignoring his excise duties while pleading the officers' case. The grocery failed, he and Elizabeth separated soon after, and he had to sell his belongings at public auction. At thirty-seven, with both his marriage and career having failed, he saw nothing to keep him in England. He discussed with Franklin the idea of emigrating to America, and Franklin wrote him several letters of introduction. In October 1774 Paine set sail for the colonies.

Participation: Declaration of Independence

"On fire about my ears." Paine arrived in Philadelphia, Pennsylvania, the colonies' leading city, at a time of great political tension and excitement. The atmosphere infected Paine immediately. He later said: "When the country, into which I had just set my foot, was set on fire about my ears, it was time to stir" (Hawke, p. 35). The colonists' hostility toward England, born in the 1760s out of English measures such as the Stamp Act (1765) and the Declaratory Act (1766), had solidified in the early 1770s. The Boston Tea Party had occurred in December 1773, a year before Paine's arrival, resulting in the closing of the port of Boston by the English government.

In the fall of 1774, just before Paine came to Philadelphia, the city hosted the first Continental Congress, which brought together leaders from twelve of the colonies. Clashes between British troops and American militia men took place at Lexington and Concord, Massachusetts, in April 1775; the second Continental Congress met in May. It brought to Philadelphia, among others, the Massachusetts cousins John and Samuel Adams, George Washington, Thomas Jefferson, Richard Henry Lee, and Patrick Henry. Revolt was in the air, yet the colonists aim remained unfocused.

Sharpening the pen. Though Paine had initially intended to establish himself as a teacher, one of Franklin's letters brought him a job at *Pennsylvania Magazine,* just started by publisher Robert Aitken. From February to September 1775, Paine edited the magazine—and also wrote many articles himself. His clear, everyday language and forceful arguments brought the magazine quick success. He penned essays attacking slavery, promoting women's rights, condemning British social institutions such as the aristocracy, and opposing practices such as dueling.

Pamphlets

In an age without television or radio, the printed word played the central role in the spread of information and ideas. Philadelphia, as the colonies' cultural center, was also the center of American printing.

When Tom Paine arrived in Philadelphia, the city of perhaps 30,000 people boasted seven newspapers. It also enjoyed a large bookstore, Bradford's, which sold not only books but also the latest British magazines. Bradford's also sold pamphlets, opinions written in essay form, like *Common Sense,* which were longer than a magazine article but shorter than a book.

Writers often used not their real names but pen names. When *Common Sense* was first published, its author was listed as "an Englishman," leading to speculation that it had been written by John Adams, Benjamin Franklin, or others. William Smith, who attacked *Common Sense,* did so under the name Cato (a famous Roman), but insiders knew Smith's identity, as they did that of "an Englishman."

The job led to friendships with other writers and activists, many of whom could be counted among the few but increasing supporters of independence from Britain. One was Benjamin Rush, a doctor who had written a pamphlet against slavery. Rush believed in independence but was hesitant to endanger his social position by advocating it publicly. A newcomer like Paine, Rush suggested in late 1775, would have less to lose.

Common Sense. Paine took up the challenge with enthusiasm. He wrote *Common Sense* (the title was suggested by Rush) in November and December 1775 and published it on January 10, 1776. The pamphlet condemned the English constitution, called for a republican system of government, and put forward convincing arguments for American independence. Although the ideas were not original—John Adams complained that he had been supporting them for some time—Paine linked them together in a single, powerful argument that spoke of the everyday world of the common American colonist. He thus appealed to a wider audience than other writers. His language, as in earlier works, was simple and direct, aimed at the artisan, merchant, and farmer. By contrast, other writers (Adams and Rush, for example) had written in flowery language directed at only the most educated levels of society.

> ### Excerpt from
> ### *Common Sense*
>
> But Britain is the parent country, say some. Then the more shame upon her conduct. Even brutes do not devour their young, nor savages make war upon their families.... Europe and not England is the parent country of America. This new world hath been the asylum for the persecuted lovers of civil and religious liberty from *every part* of Europe. Hither have they fled, not from the tender embraces of the mother but from the cruelty of the monster; and it is so far true of England, that the same tyranny which drove the first emigrants from home, pursues their descendants still. (Paine, pp. 84-85)

A new political language. Paine's use of language changed political thought forever. One of the first writers to use the words "republic" and "democracy" in a positive rather than negative sense, Paine also helped give "revolution" its modern meaning. (It had earlier been used mostly to describe the motions of the planets.) In forging a new political language and making it understandable to all levels of society, Paine pointed the way to a system of government in which all of society might take part.

"A powerful change." The public reaction to *Common Sense* shows the power of Paine's broad appeal. The pamphlet's success was immediate and spectacular. Where other pamphlets were lucky to sell 5,000 copies, *Common Sense* sold probably over 150,000. The pamphlet was read and discussed throughout the colonies. For those who could not read, it was read aloud in public meeting places. An article in an English newspaper reported that *Common Sense* "is read to all ranks; and as many as read, so many become converted; tho' perhaps the hour *before were most violent against the least idea of independence*" (Aldridge, p. 42).

Washington himself saw the pamphlet "working a powerful change … in the minds of many men" (Aldridge, p. 42). It was said that without the pen of Paine, the gun of George Washington would have been shot in vain. Singlehandedly Paine put desire for independence in the minds of common Americans and switched their allegiance from the English crown to the colonies. *Common Sense* has been called "the most brilliant pamphlet written during the American Revolution, and one of the most brilliant pamphlets ever written in the English language" (Bailyn, p. 67).

Voice of revolution. *Common Sense* brought Paine to the forefront of revolutionary activity both in America as a whole and within Pennsylvania itself. During the coming months he wrote further essays defending his ideas from attacks by loyalist writers. He also became involved in supporting the fledgling army under Washington's command. *Common Sense* had raised the army's morale, inspiring enthusiasm both in the army itself and among the public. On July 4, 1776, largely as a result of this new enthusiasm, the Continental Congress adopted the Declaration of Independence.

Paine's eccentric personal habits, however, led to charges of laziness and drunkenness. A confirmed bachelor (though officially he remained married), Paine usually woke up late, enjoyed a large lunch, and went for a long walk in the afternoon. He would then nap in a comfortable armchair, and only afterward write for an hour or two. He often drank a glass or two (or three) of brandy while writing. In the evenings, as in England, he loved to go to a tavern for long hours of drink and political discussion.

Nonetheless, Paine was determined to continue his efforts in the struggle facing the new nation. Marching with the army, he wrote accounts of its early retreats, as Washington continually withdrew rather than face the superior British forces. His reports emphasized the wisdom of Washington's strategy, doing much to maintain the general's popularity and reputation despite the frustration of constant retreat. By winter of 1776, however, morale had sunk to a new low in the face of the seemingly unstoppable British advance.

"The times that try men's souls." Paine rose to the occasion with a series of brilliant pamphlets designed to rally the army's and the public's flagging spirits. As Washington's troops, discouraged and poorly equipped, waited out of range on the Delaware River's west bank, the British occupied Trenton, on the east bank, and prepared to march on Philadelphia. Outraged by the sense of defeat in the air, Paine composed the piece that opens with his most famous lines:

> These are the times that try men's souls. The summer soldier and the sunshine patriot will, in this crisis, shrink from the service of their country; but he that stands it now, deserves the love and thanks of man and woman. Tyranny, like hell, is not easily conquered; yet we have this consolation with us, that the harder the conflict, the more glorious the triumph. What we obtain too cheap, we esteem too lightly; it is dearness only that gives every thing its value. (Hawke, p. 60)

Published on December 19, 1776, the work was bought and read eagerly throughout the former colonies. Tradition has it that Washington read it aloud to his troops on Christmas Day, before the battle of Trenton. Combined with the victory at Trenton, it succeeded in renewing confidence that the war might indeed be won after all. Paine called it *American Crisis No. 1,* and followed it with a number of *Crisis* pamphlets designed to maintain the spirits of army and public alike.

Aftermath

Public service. While the *Crisis* pamphlets appeared throughout the rest of the war, Paine's greatest usefulness had come in the early, uncertain days. After *Crisis No. 1,* Paine was given a series of jobs in both the national and Pennsylvania governments. Yet he was not entirely at home as a government official; the American Revolution had turned him into a revolutionary voice, a rouser of the people. The rough edges that made his writing so effective seemed to create only friction when it came to working with others.

After his job at *Pennsylvania Magazine,* Paine had published all his works, including *Common Sense,* at his own expense and had never tried to make any profit from them. As a result he had very little money until after the end of war, when he persuaded Congress to reward him for his services. Yet the difficulty of doing so made him bitter, adding to the enemies he had made in his political wrangles.

Further career in Europe. Paine left America in 1787 for Europe, where he lived for the next fifteen years. Continuing as a revolutionary writer in England and then France, he wrote two other works that rank alongside *Common Sense* in importance.

> ## Major Works
>
> *Common Sense* (America, 1776)
>
> *Rights of Man* (England, 1791-92)
>
> *The Age of Reason* (France, 1795)

In *Rights of Man* (1791-92), Paine vigorously defended the French Revolution of 1789 against the attacks of the English conservative writer Edmund Burke. Of the many such pamphlets published at the time, Paine's (with about 100,000 sold) had by far the greatest impact, contributing much to the growing movement for democratic reform in England. As the government attempted to silence him, Paine wrote further essays denouncing their attempts at censorship and attacking the British political system. He left England in September 1792. A British court outlawed him and, with the government's encouragement, loyalist groups made and burned stuffed likenesses of Paine.

During visits to France, where his writings had made him a popular hero, Paine had become deeply involved in the ongoing French Revolution. In the atmosphere of violence and distrust that consumed France in the 1790s, as his friends were being led to the guillotine and executed, Paine wrote his last major work, *The Age of Reason* (1795). In it he ridicules the Bible and rejects traditional Christianity, arguing that God can be properly worshiped only in a private and personal way, without the social trappings of organized religion.

Return to America. Paine returned to America in 1802, at the age of sixty-five. His health had declined, owing partly to his having spent nearly a year in a French jail, a victim of political power struggles. He continued to write from his cottage in rural New York state. His last years were lonely ones, as his radical religious views and eccentric character had driven away many of his former friends. Partly disabled by a stroke in 1806, he died on June 8, 1809.

For More Information

Aldridge, Alfred Owen. *Man of Reason: The Life of Thomas Paine.* New York: J. B. Lippincott & Co., 1959.

Bailyn, Bernard. *Faces of Revolution.* New York: Alfred A. Knopf, 1990.

Hawke, David Freeman. *Paine.* New York: Harper & Row, 1974.

Paine, Thomas. *Common Sense.* New York: Penguin Books, 1986.

Philp, Mark. *Paine.* New York: Oxford University Press, 1989.

Thomas Jefferson

1743-1826

Personal Background

Thomas Jefferson was born at Shadwell, the Jefferson family home in western Virginia, on April 13, 1743. His mother, Jane Randolph Jefferson, came from one of Virginia's largest and most influential families. His father, Peter Jefferson, was from a well-established but less prominent line. A tall man of legendary strength and a planter and surveyor who helped map the boundaries of Virginia's western wilderness, Peter Jefferson worked hard to contribute to Virginia society. In 1754 he was elected to serve in the colonial assembly, the Virginia House of Burgesses. Though not one of the area's largest landowners, by the time he died in 1757 (when Thomas was fourteen), Peter Jefferson was regarded as the county's leading citizen.

Up-country childhood. Thomas Jefferson had three younger brothers and six sisters, two older and four younger. Their home lay on Jefferson land in Albemarle County, along the hills east of the Blue Ridge Mountains. Even for wealthy plantation owners like the Jeffersons, life in this relatively unpopulated "up-country" region was simpler and more rough-and-ready than in the older settlements of coastal "Tidewater" Virginia. As a child, Jefferson learned to hunt and to ride and became an excellent horseman. He grew to love the freedom, simplicity, and self-sufficiency of up-country life and would later bring these values to his public career.

▲ Thomas Jefferson

Event: Declaration of Independence.

Role: Statesman, scientist, farmer, lawyer, engineer, architect, and writer, Thomas Jefferson is widely regarded as the most accomplished individual America has ever produced. His best-known accomplishment came early in his long career: authorship of the Declaration of Independence. Adopted by the Continental Congress on July 4, 1776, the Declaration made formal the American colonies' separation from Britain. It officially began the American Revolution, though armed clashes had occurred the previous year.

Classical education. Though not formally educated, Peter Jefferson had a deep curiosity about life and a love of books, both of which he passed on to his son. Young Jefferson received the best education his father could obtain for him. But good teachers were scarce in the up-country, and it was not until after his father's death that Thomas met the first of several superb teachers who would guide his education. Under the Reverend James Maury, who ran a small school near Shadwell, Jefferson mastered the Greek and Latin "classics" while reading widely in English literature.

College in Williamsburg. An even greater influence in Jefferson's education, however, was Dr. William Small. Jefferson met Small when he ventured into the Tidewater to attend William and Mary College at Williamsburg, the Virginia capital. Small, eventually a close friend as well as a mentor, introduced Jefferson to science, which became his major interest. (Jefferson always felt he was meant to be a scientist, but the lack of careers in science in colonial Virginia prevented him from becoming one.) Small also introduced Jefferson to the philosophic movement known as the Enlightenment. The Enlightment rejected traditional social, political, and religious ideals and emphasized rationalism and scientific learning. While in Williamsburg, Jefferson also became friends with Patrick Henry (see **Patrick Henry**), who was about to begin practicing law.

Law student. Jefferson graduated from William and Mary in March 1762, and shortly after his nineteenth birthday began studying law under George Wythe, a friend of Small's and one of Williamsburg's leading lawyers. The following year he joined Small, Wythe, and Virginia's royal governor, Francis Fauquier, in meeting regularly for dinner and discussion of ideas. In his later years these stimulating dinners would stand as one of Jefferson's brightest memories. In May 1765, at the House of Burgesses, Jefferson heard the speech in which his friend Henry denounced British policy toward the colonies, supposedly declaring, "If this be treason, make the most of it!" (Bishop, p. 2).

Law practice and Virginia politics. After five years of hard study, Jefferson began practicing law in Albemarle County in 1767. He gained a reputation as a thorough, painstaking lawyer and a quietly impressive speaker, though without the fiery oratorical skills of a Henry. "Mr. Jefferson drew ... from the depths of the law, Mr.

Henry from the recesses of the human heart" (Cunningham, p. 12), observed one of Jefferson's Randolph relatives. In 1769 Jefferson began his political career after Albemarle's "freeholders" elected him to the Virginia House of Burgesses. (Freeholders, white males who owned a minimum amount of property, were the only people allowed to vote.)

Participation: Declaration of Independence

The Virginia Radicals. Once in the House of Burgesses, Jefferson became associated with a group of young radicals led by Henry that pushed for stronger opposition to Britain. Just over a week into its session, because of unfair taxes levied on the colonists by the Townshend Act, the burgesses unanimously passed a series of measures that went against British policy. The regulations, among other things, claimed that only the burgesses could tax the colony, that they had the right to speak directly to the king, and that Virginians accused of crimes could not be sent to England for trial. The new royal governor, the Baron of Botetourt, dissolved the House, but the burgesses continued to meet, choosing a local tavern as their meeting place. There they continued to pass measures directly opposed to British laws.

Committees of Correspondence. The English Parliament repealed the Townshend duties in early 1770, which brought about a two-year period of relative calm in colonial politics. During this time Jefferson pursued reading about politics, pushed ahead with building his home, Monticello, near Shadwell, and married a young widow, Martha Wayles Skelton.

The political quiet was brief, however. In early 1773 the Virginia radicals drew up a plan to unify the colonies against the British. Under the plan, each colony would create a Committee of Correspondence, which would plan and act together with the committees in other colonies. All the burgesses adopted the plan, and Jefferson and the other radicals were named to be on Virginia's committee. Their first task was to set up links with the other colonies. This was the first time the colonies cooperated systematically, setting the stage for the First Continental Congress, which met in Philadelphia, Pennsylvania, in September 1774.

"The Rights of British America." Jefferson and his associates began pushing for such a Congress after Britain closed the port of Boston in June 1774, following the Boston Tea Party. Jefferson spent the summer of 1774 writing bills for local and state leaders to vote on. While some were adopted, the boldest one was rejected as too radical. Jefferson instead had it published under the title *A Summary View of the Rights of British America.* In it, he argues that Americans possess a natural right to govern themselves, basing his argument on English legal and political traditions. Although the House of Burgesses did not adopt the resolution, the piece established Jefferson as a major revolutionary voice. Its list of complaints against the British government would be expanded and included in the Declaration of Independence.

Richmond Convention. In March 1775 the burgesses, again prevented by the royal governor from legally meeting in Williamsburg, met in Richmond. Although Jefferson attended and participated, it was Patrick Henry who captivated the burgesses with the dramatic proclamation, "Give me liberty or give me death!" (Cunningham, p. 32). Jefferson's contribution to the convention was to draft a plan for Virginia's defense against British troops. The convention also named Jefferson as an alternate delegate to the second Continental Congress. He would substitute for his older relative Peyton Randolph in case Randolph could not serve. That May the royal governor, having stopped the burgesses from meeting in Williamsburg, decided to call them to assembly after all. As Speaker of the House, Randolph was required to attend this assembly and would have to miss the second Continental Congress. The Congress began meeting in Philadelphia on May 10, 1775; in early June, Jefferson hurried from Virginia to join the meeting in Philadelphia.

Second Continental Congress. Events had moved quickly. First the British government had made a proposal to ease the colonists' concerns over taxation. Soon after, in April 1775, fighting between British troops and American militia had broken out at Lexington and Concord, Massachusetts. Tensions were running high, and one of the Congress's first actions had been to see that the colonies' were well protected. It named George Washington commander in chief of the American forces.

Jefferson came to Congress with his own draft of Virginia's

▲ Independence Hall, Philadelphia, where the Declaration of Independence
was accepted

response to the British proposal that had been made to quiet the
colonist's concerns over taxation. His response rejected the British
proposition in stinging and dramatic terms. Now, having arrived in
Philadelphia, Jefferson for the first time met such leaders as Benjamin Franklin, Samuel Adams, John Adams, and others. He had
brought, as John Adams put it, "a reputation for literature, science,
and a happy talent" for precise, graceful, and stirring writing (Cunningham, p. 36). Jefferson was thirty-two; it was only his second trip
away from Virginia.

"Necessity of taking up arms." The Congress soon put the impressive Virginian's talents to use. In July Jefferson was named, with John Dickinson, to help write a speech Washington could publish as he took command of the American troops. The resulting statement, to which both men made important contributions, was titled "Declaration of the Causes and Necessity of Taking up Arms."

Later that month Jefferson was chosen to draft the Congress's reply to the British "conciliatory proposal" to quiet the colonists' anger over taxation. Using the draft that had been approved by the Virginia burgesses, he composed a strong rejection of the proposal, which Congress adopted (with minor alterations) on July 31. Within six weeks of arriving in Philadelphia, Jefferson had written two major proclamations for the Congress and had won a place among its leaders.

Concerns at home. Congress recessed during August, and Jefferson returned to Virginia, where he and six other delegates were elected to represent the colony at the next Congress. (Jefferson came in third in the election; Peyton Randolph placed first.) Delayed by the death of his second daughter, Jefferson did not arrive in Philadelphia until October 1, two weeks after the meeting had begun. He stayed for three months, working hard on various committees and growing increasingly concerned about events at home. Coastal Virginia had been attacked by the British, and Jefferson had heard nothing from his family. With no urgent business before Congress, he returned to Virginia in December 1775, where he would remain until the following May.

Then, as always, domestic matters ranked high in importance to him. Jefferson loved his family deeply and seemed always to prefer the country life of a gentleman farmer to the stress of politics.

Jefferson and the Enlightenment

By the time Jefferson drafted the Declaration of Independence, the principles introduced to him by Dr. William Small had come to shape Jefferson's thoughts deeply. Called the Enlightenment, a movement grew up around these principles that stressed the power of human reason. One of its strongest advocates was a British thinker, John Locke (1632-1704).

Locke reasoned that "since governments exist for men, not men for governments, all governments derive their just powers from the consent of the governed." Further, Locke wrote, "Reason ... teaches all mankind ... that all being equal and independent, no one ought to harm another in his Life, Health, Liberty, or Possessions" (Bober, p. 28-29). Jefferson adopted these ideals in his personal life and in his politics. (Compare Locke's words with the opening of the Declaration of Independence.)

Yet even with his family he was slightly reserved, with the same coolness also noticed by his closest friends. When separated from his daughters, he wrote them long letters, for example, warning them to work hard if they wanted to earn his love. His daughters worshiped him, but it could not have been easy having a father with such high standards for himself and others.

Spirit of independence. While Jefferson tended to affairs in Virginia, events unfolded that focused the aims of the rebellious colonists. So far, only a few "radicals" (for example, Samuel Adams) had called for outright independence from England. Most still believed that remaining part of Britain's empire was not only possible but desirable. In short, the colonists still considered themselves British and viewed their fight as one to secure their rights as British subjects.

In January 1776, however, news reached America that the British king and Parliament had formally decided to wage war on the colonies, and would hire German mercenaries—Hessians—to fight there. These events, combined with the January 10 publication of Thomas Paine's pamphlet *Common Sense,* produced a change in the colonists outlook. *Common Sense,* which argued powerfully for independence, took the colonies by storm. It was read and discussed by almost the entire population (see **Thomas Paine**). By the time Jefferson returned to Philadelphia, on May 14, the word "independence" was on everyone's lips.

July 4, 1776. Soon after his arrival in Philadelphia, the Virginia delegates received instructions from the House of Burgesses to propose independence to the Congress. At the same time, Congress recommended to the colonies that they form new state governments. Jefferson threw himself into drafting a new constitution for Virginia. On June 7, Richard Henry Lee of the Virginia delegation fulfilled his instructions, reading out to Congress a resolution "that these United Colonies are, and of right ought to be, free and independent States" (Cunningham, p. 46).

On June 11 the Congress appointed Jefferson to a committee with John Adams and Benjamin Franklin that would write the document declaring independence. The committee chose Jefferson to write the first draft. He did so alone in his apartment, using a

portable lap-desk that he had designed himself. When he was finished, he showed it to Franklin and Adams, who made some changes. The committee then passed it to the Congress, which made further changes. After debating it for three days, the Congress adopted the Declaration of Independence on July 4, 1776.

"An expression of the American mind." Congress had made significant changes to Jefferson's document, including shortening it by about twenty-five percent. Much of what was cut was a strong condemnation of the British for allowing the slave trade, which Jefferson called "a cruel war against human nature itself" (Cunningham, p. 47). Other revisions shortened or improved the wording of various passages.

Despite the changes, Jefferson could rightly take credit for the Declaration's authorship. He has been criticized for not being original in the ideas it contained. Yet he never intended the Declaration to state original ideas—rather, the reverse. He aimed instead to capture the essence of America's political goals and to present them to the world, in his own words, "to place before mankind the common sense of the subject in terms so plain and firm" that all would understand. "Neither aiming at originality of principle or sentiment, nor yet copied from any particular and previous writing, it was intended to be an expression of the American mind" (Cunningham, p. 48).

Opening of the Declaration of Independence

When in the course of human events, it becomes necessary for one people to dissolve the political bands which have connected them with another, and to assume among the powers of the earth the separate and equal station to which the laws of nature and of nature's God entitle them, a decent respect to the opinions of mankind requires that they should declare the causes which impel them to the separation.

We hold these truths to be self-evident: that all men are created equal; that they are endowed by their Creator with certain inalienable rights; that among these are life, liberty, and the pursuit of happiness; that to secure these rights, governments are instituted among men, deriving their just power from the consent of the governed; that whenever any form of government becomes destructive of these ends, it is the right of people to alter or abolish it, and to institute new government.... (Donovan, pp. 80-81)

Aftermath

The Declaration's influence. Jefferson's Declaration is perhaps the most influential state document in history. In presenting

◀

America's case to the world, it relates the colonies' specific complaints to concerns that people anywhere would share. This universal tone has combined with the power of Jefferson's literary genius—his simple but majestic writing—to serve for over two centuries as an inspiration for people struggling for human rights. It inspired popular leaders in England, fueled the French Revolution, whose beginning Jefferson would witness in 1789, and helped encourage liberal movements in nearly every other European country during the 1800s.

Service to Virginia. Jefferson returned to Virginia in September 1776, where he spent the rest of the Revolutionary War organizing and running the state. He drafted a monumental law code, only parts of which he was able to get the state legislature to adopt. His Virginia Statute for Religious Freedom, for example, took ten years before being passed. Other bills, such as one banning capital punishment, or the death penalty, were rejected. From 1779 to 1781 he served as governor, overseeing the state's shaky military operations. Stung by criticism of his performance, he retired to Monticello after the war, vowing to end his public life and devote himself to his family and land.

Years in France. With the death of his wife in 1782, however, Jefferson grew depressed and restless. He served in Congress again, and in 1784 Congress appointed him to join John Adams and Benjamin Franklin in France to negotiate commercial and political treaties with European states. Jefferson spent five happy and fruitful years in France, in 1785 taking over from Franklin as minister to that country.

Jefferson and Slavery

No topic about Jefferson's life and work is as controversial today as his attitude toward slavery. Jefferson claimed to hate slavery, calling it a "blot" and a "stain" upon America, yet he held slaves himself. He argued for abolishing slavery and attacked it in the original version of the Declaration of Independence, yet failed to press his views as far as he might have. He proclaimed that "all men are created equal" yet believed that whites had superior intelligence. While in so many other areas Jefferson was ahead of his time, his attitude toward the slaves seems to have been colored by beliefs of his time.

Presidency. Jefferson returned to America in 1789, becoming President Washington's secretary of state in 1790. In 1796 John Adams narrowly defeated him to win the presidency. According to the law of the day, Jefferson then became vice-president. Jefferson headed the Republican Party, against Adams's Federalists, who supported laws limiting the freedom of speech. Agreeing with the public's opposition to such laws, Jefferson and the Republicans swept to power. They won the presidential election of 1800, which is commonly seen as the first national election fought between organized political parties. Jefferson served two terms as president, during which he restored freedom of the press, reduced the army, and shrank the swollen national debt. Looking westward, he made the Louisiana Purchase (1803), which added nearly one-million square miles to the United States.

Retirement. In 1809 Jefferson retired to his beloved Monticello, where he remained as busy and productive as ever. Surrounded by grandchildren, the offspring of his two daughters, he kept up a constant stream of letters to his many friends as well as to various admirers. His major focus was public education, and in 1819 he founded the University of Virginia, designing the buildings, selecting the faculty, and compiling and setting up the school's library himself. After the Declaration of Independence and the Virginia Statute for Religious Freedom, the University was his proudest achievement. He asked for these three accomplishments to be listed on his gravestone, which he designed himself. Jefferson died on the Declaration's fiftieth anniversary, July 4, 1826, within a few hours of his friend and rival John Adams.

For More Information

Bishop, Arthur. *Thomas Jefferson, 1743-1826*. Dobbs Ferry, New York: Oceana Publications, 1971.

Bober, Natalie. *Thomas Jefferson: Man on a Mountain*. New York: Atheneum, 1988.

Cunningham, Noble. *In Pursuit of Reason: The Life of Thomas Jefferson*. Baton Rouge: Louisiana State University Press, 1987.

Donovan, Frank. *Mr. Jefferson's Declaration*. New York: Dodd, Mead and Co., 1968.

Revolutionary War

1775
Fighting breaks out between the British and Americans at Lexington and Concord, Massachusetts. Colonists attempt to invade Canada.

1776
Congress declares independence, names **George Washington** chief commander of the colonial army.

1777-1778
Washington's army survives winter at Valley Forge.

1777
Washington loses at Brandywine Creek and Germantown. John Burgoyne surrenders to Americans at Saratoga.

1776
Washington's army wins the Battle of Trenton.

1778
War moves south. British take Savannah, win thousands of slaves to their side. France enters the war on rebel side.

1779
Colonial forces burn Iroquois villages.

1780
Benedict Arnold betrays Americans at West Point. Charleston surrenders to the British.

1783
Treaty of Paris ends war.

1782
Deborah Sampson enlists in the American army.

1781
Marquis de Lafayette traps Charles Cornwallis at Yorktown. Cornwallis surrenders.

REVOLUTIONARY WAR

The first shots of the Revolutionary War were fired at Lexington and Concord, Massachusetts, on April 19, 1775. A few months later Congress appointed **George Washington** commander of the troops at Boston and the next year leader of the colonial army in a war for independence from Britain. Lasting nearly eight years, it was a struggle fought by a large, well-trained British army and navy against a far smaller assortment of inexperienced and ill-equipped American soldiers and sailors.

On one side were the British and their hired German troops; on the other were the Patriots, colonists who favored independence. But the colonists were far from united. Besides the Patriots, there were Loyalists, or Tories, who preferred to remain part of Britain. The Loyalists made up about 20 percent of the colonial population. Other colonists, **Benedict Arnold,** for example, switched sides during the war.

A number of Europeans who were in sympathy with the ideals of the rebels lent their desperately needed talents to their cause. The German volunteer General Friedrich von Steuben drilled and redrilled Washington's soldiers. Coming from Poland, Thaddeus Kosciuszko positioned the Americans and built fortifications for them in New York at Saratoga (a battle they won). He then designed the military post West Point. Leading Virginia's troops, the Frenchman **Marquis de Lafayette** kept the British at bay in Yorktown before their final surrender.

▲ **American troops secured the Ohio Valley on a march from Fort Pitt to Fort Vincennes**

The War for Independence was fought in two main stages: from 1776 to 1778 in the North, and from 1778 to 1781 in the South. In 1778, France, encouraged by the American victory at Saratoga, joined the war and persuaded Holland and Spain to take an active role against England. Most other European countries quietly resisted the British, and the war took on worldwide overtones.

By 1779, the British had turned their attention toward the South, where there were more Loyalists. The Americans learned early in the war they would lose to the British in head-on attacks. So they fought small, defensive battles against the British for much of the war. In 1780, British forces seized all of Georgia and took Charleston, South Carolina, capturing 5,000 colonists and 400 cannons. Lord Charles Cornwallis began a long march through the South before losing to American forces under General Nathanael Greene at Kings Mountain and Cowpens, in present-day South Carolina. Cornwallis then retreated to Yorktown, Virginia, to await supplies by sea.

Meanwhile, France sent a strong fleet to help the Americans trap the British at Yorktown and block them from getting supplies. By the time Washington's troops joined the battle, there was a Patriot force of 16,000 around Yorktown; more than half of them were French. The British, with only 8,000 men, many of them ill, were sorely outnumbered. On October 19, 1781, Cornwallis surrendered. Though now the war was basically over, with this last major battle being lost by the British, fighting would drag on for several months, with new volunteers engaging in minor battles. The surrender at Yorktown meant that Britain finally accepted American independence.

At first all types of colonists did the fighting, but later the middle and upper classes hired poor men to fight in their places. The poor gave their blood for a country that would represent the interests of all citizens, rather than just the wealthy upper class. In fact, after the war government was more democratic. The old colonies, for example, increased the size of their assemblies, giving farmers and craftsmen more voice than before.

Not allowed into the army at the time, women managed nevertheless to take active roles in the Revolution. Molly Pitcher followed her husband to war, then took his place in battle when he fell. She was probably one of many women who traveled with their husband-soldiers and at some point joined in the fighting. **Deborah Sampson** went so far as to disguise herself as a male soldier. Other women took over family businesses—jobs they had never handled before—while fathers or brothers went off to war.

Many more blacks fought for the British than for the Americans in the Revolution. It was apparent that when the colonists spoke of liberty from England, they did not mean to extend that freedom to their slaves. But General Henry Clinton, commander of the British forces, promised the slaves liberty if they deserted their masters. So, in 1778, when the war moved southward, tens of thousands of colonial slaves fled to the British side.

After the war, white Patriots themselves began questioning the practice of owning slaves. If all men were in fact created equal, some asked, why should some still be slaves? George Washington, for one, grew uneasy about keeping slaves at his estate. State by

217

▲ Dress and discipline of professional British soldiers

state the North abolished slavery or began taking steps to do so. In the South, Virginia and Maryland passed new laws making it easier for owners to free their slaves.

The outcome was less fortunate for Native American tribes. As in earlier conflicts, they had analyzed the war to see which side would benefit them most. Iroquois Indians, for example, anxious to save their lands, sided with the British. For this they were punished. In 1779, colonial forces swept through Iroquois country, killing families, burning villages, and destroying crops. After the war, in 1784, they were forced in the Treaty of Stanwix to forfeit most of their lands.

But farther west, in the Ohio River Valley, the outcome of the war between the Indians and the colonists was less clear. Tribes here claimed they did not lose the Revolution and entered into a dispute that would continue until the War of 1812.

George Washington

1732-1799

Personal Background

Family and early years. George Washington was born February 22, 1732, in rural Virginia. His forebears had arrived from England to the American colonies nearly a century before. George's mother, Mary Ball Washington, was Augustine Washington's second wife, and George was the first son and the oldest of six children born to the couple. From his father's first marriage George also had two half-brothers and a half-sister, who was to die in childhood. In George's early years his parents moved several times to farms along the Rappanhannock River before settling on a 260-acre farm near Fredericksburg.

Unlike many others of his era, Washington did not belong to the aristocratic, wealthy upper class. Augustine Washington was "land-poor"—he owned a great deal of land but did not have sufficient capital to productively work it. He died when his son was only eleven, leaving him under the guidance of his mother, a demanding and unhappy woman. Lack of money prevented George from following in the footsteps of his two half-brothers, Lawrence and Augustine, who went to England to receive a formal education. Instead, he learned what he could locally, studying math, geography, and spelling. He also taught himself rules of social conduct by copying into his notebook maxims from a book called *Rules of Civility and Decent Behavior.* Included were such sayings as: "Sleep not when

ARMIES OF THE U.S. OF AMERICA & PRESIDENT OF THE CONVENTION 1787

HIS EXCEL. G. WASHINGTON ESQ. LLD. LATE COMMANDER IN CHIEF OF THE

Painted Engraved by C.W.Peale 1787

▲ George Washington

Event: The American Revolution, which gave the thirteen colonies independence from Britain and self-rule.

Role: As commander in chief of the Continental Army, George Washington provided the leadership needed to bring the American colonies to victory in their fight for independence from Britain. Later, his strength and popularity helped unite the thirteen colonies into a single nation: the United States of America.

others Speak"; "Talk not with meat in your mouth"; "Wear not your clothes foul, unript, or dusty" (Osborne, p. 8).

Further training and influences. For the young man from the rural farmland, education and social standing were very important. Without these he could barely hope to get ahead in the world in which he lived. Washington was fortunate to have had guidance from his half-brother Lawrence, who cared a great deal about his young brother's future and welfare. George had always looked up to Lawrence, who was fourteen years his senior. As a boy he had played at being a soldier, copying Lawrence, who served as an officer in the British army. When George was thirteen he began the first of many extended visits to Mount Vernon in Virginia, the plantation that Lawrence had inherited from Augustine. Lawrence's wife, Anne Fairfax Washington, came from a distinguished and wealthy family who lived on a nearby plantation.

Washington's lengthy visits to Mount Vernon marked his entry into a world of wealth and social advantage. He gladly left behind his life in rural Virginia among mostly uneducated and rough-and-tumble frontiersmen for this new life of sophisticated parties, social card games, and lively talk among some of the most notable members of society. At Mount Vernon, mingling with the Fairfaxes and their guests at their Belvoir plantation, Washington established important connections while developing his social graces and furthering his limited education through reading and discussion.

During these years Washington began earning money surveying land for Lawrence and his friends. At the time, Virginia was a sprawling mass of forests, wilderness, and other unclaimed land. Farmers were anxious to settle this land, but first it had to be measured and charted. Washington, who had always shown a strong ability in math, traveled out into this wilderness with surveying parties. In the few years he spent as a surveyor, Washington learned about the American wilderness—including how to live in it and travel through it. This knowledge would serve him well in his later years as an officer and then a general.

Washington the man. The years that Washington spent in the wilderness molded him into a strapping, sturdy young man.

Over six-feet tall, long-limbed, and solidly built, Washington presented a fine and commanding figure. He had brown hair, blue eyes, a broad nose, and pale skin scarred by pockmarks left from his bout with smallpox.

His physical strength was legendary: he is said to have been able to throw a stone across the Potomac River. Known for his excellent skills on horseback, he could ride for six days without rest. In later years he supposedly could bend a horseshoe using only his hands and open the hard shells of nuts with his fingers. His constitution enabled him to withstand illnesses that would have killed a weaker person. While still a young man, Washington suffered malaria, smallpox, typhoid, dysentery, and lung disease—and he survived them all.

Those who knew him described Washington as reserved, somewhat humorless, humble, and very gracious, with a commanding and calm presence. His bearing and person inspired great respect and trust in his soldiers as well as his peers. Thomas Jefferson described him as "a wise, a good, and a great man" (Marrin, p. 78). Washington's powerful presence may have inspired some fear; apparently, many of his friends did not feel comfortable addressing him in familiar terms, and Washington himself probably discouraged it. One story relates how he bristled into an icy reserve when a friend slapped him on the back and greeted him with, "Good morning, George!" Although he always retained a reserved graciousness, Washington could relax among close friends and converse in an engaging and lively manner. In essence, Washington was a man whom others liked, respected, and admired—one to whom they turned for leadership and guidance in times of crisis and need.

French and Indian War. While still in his early twenties, Washington began to show his mettle as a military officer. He served in the French and Indian War, which broke out in the colonies in 1754. This struggle was just one of many going on in various parts of the globe as Britain and France competed for power.

In the colonies Washington became directly involved in the war at its beginning. Robert Dinwiddie, governor of Virginia, sent Washington on a two-month journey across rough wilderness to carry a message to the French fort in Pennsylvania. His mission was to tell the French commander that he and his troops must leave the fort immediately, that they were on British territory. When the French officer refused, Washington ventured back, braving icy conditions and attacks by Indians, to alert the governor that the French were indeed pushing their way into British territory.

Soon afterward, Washington led 400 men to begin fighting the French. From his post, called Fort Necessity, Lieutenant Colonel Washington ordered some of the first gunfire in the French and Indian War. This was his introduction to warfare, and he wrote about the impression it made on him: "I heard the bullets whistle, and believe me, there is something charming in the sound" (Osborne, p. 23).

Later, however, he would not speak so glowingly of war. In one bloody wilderness attack by the French on General Edward Braddock's troops, Washington was the only officer to escape injury. Incredibly, Washington remained unharmed, though two horses were shot from beneath him and four bullets passed through his coat. All around him, men lay dead and wounded in the aftermath of the brutal and bloody fight. Washington never forgot the horror. He wrote, "The shocking scenes which presented themselves in this night march are not to be described. The dead, the dying, the groans ... and cries along the road of the wounded for help" (Osborne, p. 29).

Washington distinguished himself as a superior military leader in this war. In 1759, after the French had finally surrendered their major fort, Washington retired from the army and returned to his beloved Mount Vernon, which he had inherited when Lawrence died.

Married life at Mount Vernon. Soon after the war, Washington met and married Martha Custis, a wealthy young widow with two toddlers. Short, plump, talkative, and engaging, Martha was a direct contrast to George. The marriage not only made Washington a wealthy man, he also became a member of one of the first families of Virginia. At Mount Vernon the newlyweds set up a home with Martha's two young children, Jack and Patsy.

Like many plantations of the day, Mount Vernon was a thriving, self-sufficient, and productive community within itself. Black-

▲ The Washington family

smiths on the grounds forged iron into the tools needed for the plantation's operation while shoemakers crafted shoes and clothesmakers wove, spun, and sewed clothing. A miller ground the wheat grown on the farm into flour, and in the surrounding woods, workers chopped trees into timber that carpenters used for building. Cows, pigs, and sheep provided the meat and dairy products as well as such goods as wool and leather.

Washington was happiest living at Mount Vernon. Each morning he mounted his horse and rode through his vast acreage, studying the land and marking the plantation's progress and productivity. If the weather was bad, he would stay inside writing letters and settling his accounts. Evenings found him enjoying fine dinners with friends and family as well as the many guests who passed through the country. It was a peaceful, pleasant existence. When duty once again called him to the frontlines of war, Washington left Mount Vernon with great reluctance.

Participation: The American Revolution

The eve of the American Revolution. Washington lived the life of a wealthy country gentlemen for nearly sixteen years, before the stirrings of war again called him to serve his country. The French and Indian War had taken its toll on the treasury of the British Empire, and the Crown struggled to regain its losses. Under the rule of King George III, Britain began to impose a series of unpopular taxes on the colonies. The Stamp Act, in 1765, required colonists to pay taxes on various documents, including marriage certificates, college diplomas, land deeds, mortgages, wills, and newspapers. The act enraged many colonists, who resented being taxed by lawmakers whom they had not elected and who did not represent their interests. Angry colonists under such leaders as Patrick Henry rose up in rebellion, crying, "No taxation without representation!"

Although Parliament repealed the Stamp Act within months, it had stirred colonists to action. When the British Parliament set new taxes on British imports such as glass, lead, paper, paints, and tea, the colonists again opposed it. Rebel leaders encouraged boycotts of the goods. Although Parliament again repealed the taxes, tensions mounted in the colonies.

The conflict came to a head in 1773 when Britain passed the Tea Act, which gave one tea company—the East India Company—control over the American tea market. Colonists expressed their outrage at this act, which made it impossible for American tea to compete with the cheap English product. Disguised as Indians, they climbed aboard ships and dumped 342 chests of tea into Boston Harbor in Massachusetts. This famous tea riot became known as the Boston Tea Party. Britain punished the colonists with the Intolerable Acts. Troops were sent to Boston and the port closed; the city became an armed camp.

Commander in Chief of the Continental Army. With this latest show of oppression, the mood began to change in the colonies. Influential colonists met to discuss in earnest the problems. Washington, John Adams, Patrick Henry, and other representatives gathered in Philadelphia, Pennsylvania, in 1774 at the First Continental Congress. The delegates agreed to meet the British with force if necessary. They decided also to meet again the following May to see how matters then stood.

By May, when the delegates met again, much had changed. "The shot heard round the world" had been fired in Lexington/Concord, Massachusetts, by New England minutemen against British redcoats. A month later, at the Second Continental Congress, a grave set of delegates prepared for war.

The colonial army would need a strong leader to guide the colonies through the struggle. Who better than the tall, commanding, and upright Virginian who sat quietly in his red and blue military uniform observing the proceedings? The tremendous respect that the delegates felt for this patriot showed itself in the words of John Adams: "Colonel Washington appears at Congress in his Uniform, and by his great Experience and Abilities in military Matters is of much Service to us" (Emery, p. 175). The Congress unanimously elected the popular colonel to the post of "General and Commander in Chief of the entire army of the United Colonies." Showing his characteristic modesty, Washington accepted the command humbly and reluctantly, saying, "I beg it may be remembered by every gentleman in this room I do not think myself equal to the command I am honored with" (Kent, p. 33). He promised to do his best to meet the responsibility demanded of him, but insisted that he be paid for no more than his expenses during the war. In haste, he wrote a letter to Martha, telling her he would return to her and Mount Vernon by fall. Traveling to Boston to assume his command, Washington could not know that it would be six long years before he returned to his Virginia home.

> ### Minutemen
>
> The War for Independence could not have been won without ordinary citizens becoming soldiers almost overnight to fight the British. Around Boston, as troubles grew, local farmers and merchants organized into fighting forces that could be called to action at a minute's notice. When British soldiers confronted the local rebels at Lexington, killing or wounding eighteen, minutemen sprang to attack. As the British militia marched toward Concord, minutemen shot at them from behind walls, fences, and farmhouses.

Organizing the troops. Arriving in Boston in the fall of 1775,

Washington looked over the men who had come from all corners of the northeast to volunteer for the war. Most of them were farmers and merchants and had no training as soldiers. The colonists did not have enough money to pay the volunteer army, so spirits were low. Adding to this, there were barely enough supplies to feed, cloth, and arm the makeshift army. And their heavy, unreliable muskets were hardly a match for the British army's sophisticated rifles with bayonets.

That winter, as he and his men camped out in tents outside Boston, Washington began to realize the difficulty of the task he had undertaken. He struggled to obtain food, medicine, clothing, blankets, weapons, and other supplies for his cold and hungry men. He also worked to teach the untrained men the fine points of warfare. Later, he was to write about this time: "Could I have foreseen what I have, and am likely to experience, no consideration upon earth should have induced me to accept this command" (Cunliffe, p. 65).

Washington's skills are evident in the fact that he did manage to keep this ragtag army together through the winter of 1775-76. The following spring he and his men took Dorchester Heights, above Boston. British general William Howe was scared off by the taking of this powerful position. In retreat, Howe loaded his troops onto ships and sailed to Canada. Washington's military strategy had freed Boston from the grip of British command.

The commander in chief's next move was to push on to New York with an army of about 20,000 men. Anticipating the worst, he wrote to his brother: "We expect a very bloody Summer of it in New York" (Cunliffe, p. 70). There Washington spent weeks dodging his opponent, who had more men and training behind him. Washington soon realized that he and his soldiers would be no match for Howe if they stayed on the island of Manhattan. He guessed that Howe planned to trap the Americans on the island and decided it would be best to abandon New York. While giving the impression that he was reinforcing, or strengthening, his troops, he managed to withdraw his forces. By late fall, he had retreated with his troops, which now numbered around 5,000 (many had been captured), into New Jersey. He and the rapidly dwindling army readied themselves for one of the most masterful battles of the war, one that turned the tide of the revolution.

▲ **Washington crossing the Delaware River**

Battle of Trenton. On Christmas night 1776, while Howe's unsuspecting men drank and celebrated, Washington and about 2,400 soldiers marched through snow along the edge of the Delaware River. They then climbed into waiting boats. As they pushed these boats through the block ice that filled the river, a fierce winter storm began, slowing their journey even more. Hours later, they landed about eight miles north of Trenton. Now, in the early hours before dawn, they divided into two groups and started their march toward the British camp. Although the storm had eased, the men still struggled through blinding snow, slipping and sliding on rough, icy roads. Some wore no shoes, just rags wrapped around their feet. However, the weather worked to their advantage, for the enemy could not see their approach.

Meanwhile, in Trenton, about 1,600 Hessians—German soldiers hired by Britain—slept off the excesses of the previous night. They had celebrated the Christmas holiday with food, drink, and

Major Battles of the War for Independence

Site and Date	American Casualties	British Casualties
Lexington and Concord April 19, 1775	49 killed 41 wounded 9 missing	73 killed 74 wounded 26 missing
Bunker Hill June 17, 1775	145 killed 304 wounded 30 captured	226 killed 828 wounded
Trenton and Princeton December 26, 1776 and January 3, 1777	4 wounded	22 killed 83 wounded 891 captured
Germantown October 4, 1777	152 killed 521 wounded 400 miss./capt.	70 killed 450 wounded 14 miss./capt.
Monmouth June 28, 1778	69 killed 161 wounded 132 missing	294 kill./wound. 64 missing 600 deserted
Cowpens January 17, 1781	12 killed 60 wounded	110 killed 702 wounded
Yorktown Sept. 28-Oct. 19, 1781	75 killed 199 wounded	156 killed 326 wounded 70 missing

cheer. None suspected they would soon be under attack, even though someone had tried to warn their leader, Colonel Rall. The night before, an American farmer had sought out Rall at the house where the colonel celebrated Christmas. When Rall refused to see him, the farmer left a note warning him of the upcoming attack. Rall, who could not read English, had slipped the note into his pocket without even looking at it.

So Rall and his men were unprepared when the American army struck the next morning. In little over an hour, Washington's troops managed to overtake Rall's command—killing 22, wounding 83, and taking nearly 900 as prisoners. Only four Americans were wounded in the battle, although two more would freeze to death on the return journey.

Washington's victory was decisive and complete. The bold and successful strike lifted American spirits. The tide had turned: now Americans realized that they really did have a chance to win this war, and the British understood that this would not be the easy fight they had anticipated.

Valley Forge. As the war trudged on, however, the Battle of Trenton soon became just a memory. By the next winter Washington and his army were fighting not only the enemy but also the ongoing hardships of cold and hunger. The general struggled to get pay for his men as well as clothing and food. During the winter of 1777-78, while the British ate well and lived comfortably in their winter camps, Wash-

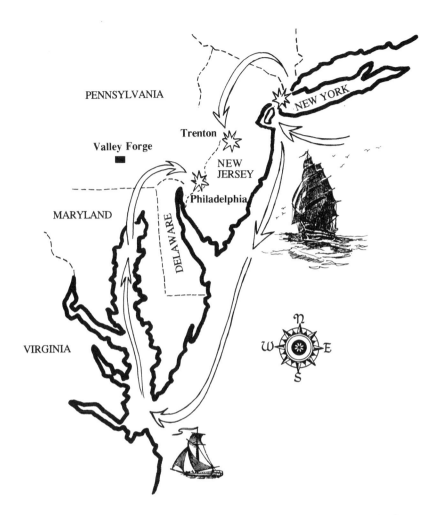

▲ From his base in New York, British General William Howe attacked Washington's forces by land and sea

ington and his men were holed up at Valley Forge, Pennsylvania, living under wretched and bitterly cold conditions.

At this hilltop site just twenty miles outside Philadelphia, the troops worked hard to build a camp on the muddy ground. They chopped trees and, within a few weeks, had constructed nearly 1,000 log cabins. Although they had shelter, the conditions proved miserable. Rain leaked through the roofs, turning the dirt floors into pools of mud. In the windowless cabins, smoke from the fires blinded the men and scorched their lungs. Worse, there was barely

231

enough food or clothing for the starving and bedraggled soldiers. They survived on firecake, a bread of flour and water, and faced the cold winter in rags. Many had no shoes. By winter's end, more than 2,500 of the men had died, killed by disease, starvation, and cold.

A doctor at Valley Forge, Albigence Waldo, described the horrifying existence in grim detail:

> It snows. I'm sick. Eat nothing.... Cold and uncomfortable. I am sick, discontented, and out of humor. Poor food. Hard lodging. Cold weather. Fatigue. Nasty clothes. Nasty cookery. Vomit half my time. Smoked out of my senses. The Devil's in it. I can't endure it. Why are we sent here to starve and freeze? (Marrin, p. 144)

All was not misery and hardship at Valley Forge, however. A Prussian lieutenant general named Baron von Steuben came to the camp to teach soldiers military techniques. The drillmaster taught the untrained men battle tactics that would later serve them well. At the same time, Washington did his part by sharing in the men's hardships. Although he could have eaten better and lived more comfortably, he chose not to. This earned him the respect and admiration of his men and, as a result, their morale rose. Good news the following spring lifted their spirits even further: the French had signed a treaty of support for the American cause (see **Marquis de Lafayette**). With France as an ally, the revolutionaries grew more confident of victory. Washington was elated and wrote, "I believe no event was ever received with more heartfelt joy" (Osborne, p. 69).

Aftermath

Forging a new nation. Three years after Valley Forge the war would finally be won. Peace talks began after the Battle of Yorktown in October 1781, and a treaty was signed two years later, in September 1783. Washington journeyed to Maryland, where Congress now met, to resign his commission. Along the way guns boomed, music played, and churchbells rang; the joyous Americans celebrated their hard-won victory and cheered the patriotic general. After resigning, Washington retired to Mount Vernon to spend Christmas Eve, and his retirement, with his wife and family.

Washington's life as a country gentleman would not last long, however. In the years after the war, the new nation struggled to form itself. It soon became increasingly clear that the states would need a firm central government to "make thirteen clocks strike as one," as Benjamin Franklin described it (Cunliffe, p. 114).

In 1787 delegates met at the Constitutional Convention to establish a government. They drafted a set of laws and guidelines for the new nation. Written primarily by James Madison, the Constitution outlined a federal government with three branches: a congressional branch, a judicial branch, and an executive branch. The last branch would be the office of president. Once again, Washington would be elected to a position that required a strong, steady, respected leader.

Presidency. Washington accepted the presidency, though he hated to give up his life as a private citizen: "My movements to the chair of government will be accomplished by feelings not unlike those of a culprit who is going to the place of his execution" (Osborne, p. 88). He stepped into his new position with his usual humility, insisting that he be called only "Mr. President" and not pompous, royal-sounding titles like "His Majesty" or "His Highness." As president, Washington provided the firm guidance that the young country needed. He made sure that he had able, intelligent men advising him. He learned as much as he could about the country by visiting shipyards, farms, plantations, and cities around the new nation.

Elected to a second term in 1793, Washington faced conflict and some criticism in his final years as president. Two political parties—Federalists and Democratic-Republicans—had formed, and they fought for their interests. In Europe, the French Revolution began, and Washington, against popular opinion, chose to remain neutral. He did not think that the developing American nation could survive another war with Britain. He insisted that the United States must now focus only on its own growth: "If we are permitted to improve without interruption," he maintained, Americans had the chance to be "among the happiest people on this globe" (Kent, p. 79).

After serving as president for two terms, Washington finally retired to Mount Vernon in 1797. He spent the time left him making

▲ Lord Charles Cornwallis surrenders to Washington at Yorktown

repairs on the neglected plantation and receiving the throngs of visitors who traveled there to meet him.

One winter morning, when he was riding on the plantation grounds, Washington got caught in a storm of snow and cold rain. The next day he came down with a sore throat, which grew into a severe infection. Doctors were called, but their decision to "bleed" the ailing former president only weakened him. On December 14, 1799, Washington died.

Washington left behind a saddened but grateful nation. His secretary, Tobias Lear, who ate and drank with Washington and on most evenings played cards with him, said of the statesman: "A complete knowledge of his honesty, uprightness, and candor … have sometimes led one to think him more than a man" (Flexner, p.188).

Still, Washington was a man of his times and, like most of his peers, owned several hundred slaves. The contradiction between this and his own hard-won struggle for liberty troubled him greatly as he grew older. So in his will, he ordered that all his slaves be freed after Martha's death. Mount Vernon fell into decay after his own passing, though, and the majority of the slaves were freed in 1800 before her death.

For More Information

Cunliffe, Marcus. *George Washington and the Making of a Nation.* New York: American Heritage Publishing Co., 1966.

Emery, Noemie. *Washington, A Biography.* New York: G. P. Putnam's Sons, 1976.

Flexner, James Thomas. *Washington: The Indispensable Man.* New York: New American Library, 1969.

Kent, Zachary. *Encyclopedia of Presidents: George Washington.* Chicago: Childrens Press, 1986.

Marrin, Albert. *The War for Independence: The Story of the American Revolution.* New York: Macmillan Publishing Company, 1988.

Osborne, Mary Pope. *George Washington: Leader of a New Nation.* New York: Dial Books for Young Readers, 1991.

Benedict Arnold

1741-1801

Personal Background

Family life. Benedict Arnold's great-grandfather was governor of Rhode Island four times. The Benedict name passed from this great-grandfather to Arnold's grandfather and father. Born January 14, 1741, Benedict Arnold became the fourth man in the family with this name.

In his early years Benedict Arnold was a prankster. He tried to impress his friends by making running jumps over loaded wagons on the main street of Norwich Town, Connecticut, where he was born. He also made friends with the local Indians. At age eleven, Arnold's parents sent him to a private school in Canterbury, Connecticut, where he studied history, mathematics, theology, Latin, and Greek. This taste of formal education was brief, for two years later the family business collapsed and Arnold was forced to drop out of school. His father, once a wealthy trader and now suddenly poor, took to drinking heavily, and Arnold's mother was forced to shoulder the burden of raising their children. Unable to afford her son's education, Hannah Arnold decided young Benedict should learn a trade. She arranged for him to serve as apprentice to one of her relatives, Dr. Daniel Lathrop, a wealthy druggist. For the next eight years, Arnold worked in Norwich Town as Lathrop's apprentice, learning the pharmacy business. Lathrop owned several ships

▲ **Benedict Arnold**

Event: American Revolution.

Role: Benedict Arnold was one of America's boldest and most brilliant military leaders during the early years of the American Revolution. However, soon after leading a daring assault that turned the tide of battle at Saratoga, Arnold switched sides. He nearly succeeded in delivering West Point to the British.

used for business, so Arnold also learned how to sail and trade. In time, he became the doctor's chief clerk.

When Arnold turned twenty-one, Lathrop provided him with money to start his own drugstore business. Arnold set up shop in New Haven, Connecticut, selling drugs, stationery, wine, surgical instruments, and books to students at nearby Yale University. When his father died in 1762, Arnold sold the house he had inherited to buy a ship. In a few years, he owned three ships in addition to his drugstore.

As a trader, Arnold protested royal tax and trade policies by writing newspaper articles against the British and by joining the Sons of Liberty, a collection of outraged colonists who favored military action against the British.

Arnold married Margaret Mansfield in 1767. Because he spent much of his time away from home on sea voyages, his sister Hannah helped Margaret raise the couple's three sons. Margaret died in 1775, when the boys were three, six, and seven years old. Afterward, Hannah stepped in to run the household and raise Arnold's sons.

Participation: Revolutionary War

From New Haven to Cambridge. In the weeks preceding the revolution, a group of leading citizens of New Haven formed a militia. They selected Arnold to lead it. When war broke out on April 19, 1775, New Haven's town council chose to stay neutral. Arnold, however, eager to fight for independence, forced the council to hand over the town's supply of gunpowder to the militia. Armed and ready, he and his men marched to Cambridge, Massachusetts, and joined the Massachusetts militia in the fighting.

Crown Point and Ticonderoga. At the start of the war, the American patriots faced shortages of supplies, especially cannon. Arnold pointed out to Colonel Parsons, leader of the militia from nearby New London, that hundreds of cannon sat at the undermanned British forts, Crown Point and Ticonderoga, on Lake Champlain in northern New York. Sam Adams and other Massachusetts rebels made Arnold a colonel with orders to recruit a force to seize the forts.

On their way to the British forts, Arnold and his men learned that the Connecticut government had given similar orders to Ethan Allen, a Vermont revolutionary. Arnold and Allen met in Vermont, where they agreed to join forces, each leading his own men in a combined attack on Fort Ticonderoga.

On May 10, 1775, while a smaller unit took the Crown Point fort, which was guarded by only twelve men, the two larger forces stormed Fort Ticonderoga. Attacking at four o'clock in the morning, they quickly overpowered the sleeping garrison. In the chaos, many of Allen's men started looting the belongings of the British soldiers and their families. Arnold tried to stop the looting, and he and Allen quarreled. Later, when filing reports of the battle, Allen, who claimed chief command of the enterprise, gave Arnold little credit for the victory.

Shortly afterward, Arnold seized a small schooner belonging to a British sympathizer on Lake Champlain. The schooner, together with two small, flat-bottomed boats, became the first ships in the United States Navy. Leading this small naval force of about fifty men, Arnold sailed up Lake Champlain and captured the British outpost at St. John, Quebec. He returned to Ticonderoga with hopes of leading an even larger raid into Canada.

Lake Champlain. During his six weeks on Lake Champlain, Captain Arnold had proven himself to be an unusually capable officer. He helped seize two of Britain's most valuable fortresses, capture a flotilla, wrest control of a vast frontier region from the British, and reduce the threat posed by Indian enemies. He returned to Ticonderoga to find his command in question.

On June 22, he received orders from the Massachusetts government to turn the Lake Champlain command over to a Connecticut officer appointed by Colonel David Wooster. Wooster was the man who had been forced by Arnold at the start of the war to turn over New Haven's gunpowder to him. In addition, the Massachusetts government ordered Arnold to appear before the state legislature and give an accounting of his expenses. Refusing to turn over the command, he resigned and disbanded his troops.

Quebec. The conquest of Canada was high on the list of goals set down by the Continental Congress. Battles in Canada would

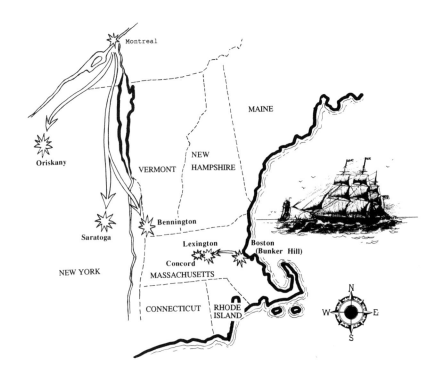

▲ **After the British attacked at Lexington and Concord, they planned assaults from Montreal**

divert attention from action around Boston, Massachusetts, and a victory in Canada would remove a central base from which the British attacked the colonies. With these goals in mind, shortly after arriving in Massachusetts, Captain Arnold arranged to meet George Washington, the commander in chief under whom the American forces had now been united. Arnold convinced Washington to let him lead an invasion of Quebec City, which he believed to be held by only a few hundred British troops. This, along with an already planned attack on Montreal, would destroy British plans to use these bases in a drive down the Hudson Valley. The British planned to move south from Montreal and Quebec and north from a base in New York to cut off New England from the southern states.

Receiving the go-ahead from Washington, Arnold took less than a month to recruit troops for the invasion. They would reach Canada by water and by foot. Boarding ships in September 1775, his force slipped through a British blockade of Massachusetts and sailed to Maine. Once landed, they began a march across nearly 300 miles of rivers, forests, and swampland. Food ran short, and rain and snow slowed the troops. By October, when Arnold reached the first French settlement in Quebec, 40 percent of his force had died or deserted. His men had grown too weak to take Quebec City directly. Instead, Arnold aligned his troops outside the walls of Quebec to wait for reinforcements from those who had already taken Montreal. The combined forces attacked on New Year's Eve, under cover of a snowstorm. Quebec's garrison held off the attack, taking 400 prisoners. In the fighting, Arnold was wounded in the leg. Defeated, but refusing to give up the attempt, Arnold maintained a four-month siege on Quebec City. In May 1776 British reinforcements and warships finally drove off the Americans. Arnold's actions won him a promotion to the rank of brigadier general by action of the Continental Congress.

British attacks soon forced the Americans to abandon Canada. As he and his men retreated, Arnold pursued a "scorched earth" policy, taking anything that could be of use to the enemy—boats, wagons, horses, and food—and burning what they could not take. He even shot his own horse to prevent British soldiers from seizing it before he boarded a bateau (a small, flat boat) to leave Canada.

Back at Lake Champlain. Later that year, British General Guy Carleton gathered a large fleet and sailed up Lake Champlain intending to strike down the Hudson River. Meanwhile, General Howe would take New York City and move up the Hudson to isolate New England. Arnold's slow retreat had already disturbed the British timetable. Now he gathered a small fleet and lay in wait for Carleton's forces. At Valcour Island, the two navies met and fought to a draw. At night, surrounded by the enemy, Arnold took his ships through the British fleet and retreated to Fort Ticonderoga. The British plans had been so upset that General Carleton returned to Canada.

By setting siege to Quebec and in his retreat, Arnold had forced the British to use up much of the ammunition and supplies that had been stored there. This and the scorched earth policy used in retreat created supply shortages for the British in their Hudson Valley campaigns of 1776 and 1777.

Promotions and pass overs. General Arnold went home to New Haven and then to Boston to recruit troops. While in Boston, Arnold learned that on February 19, 1777, Congress had promoted five officers with less seniority to the rank of major general. Arnold, a brigadier general, had been next in line for promotion by military custom. Fearful of losing one of his finest generals, Washington pleaded with Arnold not to resign. A disheartened Arnold agreed to stay in the service.

In the spring of 1777, hearing that a British force had attacked Danbury, Connecticut, Arnold gathered a force and harassed the intruders into returning to their base at Norwalk. For this action, Arnold was finally promoted to major general, but was not given his rightful position of seniority over those previously promoted. Again Arnold resigned his command, and once more General Washington persuaded him to stay.

Attack on Rome. Later that year, the British planned a two-pronged attack to take control of western New York and the Hudson Valley. General John Burgoyne would follow Lake Champlain while Lieutenant Colonel Barry St. Leger would cut across the state from Oswego to meet him at Albany. St. Leger had already set siege to Fort Schuyler near present-day Rome, New York. Major General Arnold was sent to relieve the fort. If it fell, the British would have a clearer path down the Hudson to New York. Badly outnumbered, Arnold resorted to a ruse to win the fort. He sent a mentally retarded man, whom the Indians regarded as divine, to spread a rumor among them that thousands of Americans were approaching. The Indians, and then the British soldiers, panicked and fled.

Battle of Saratoga. When the British finally began their New York offensive on September 13, 1777, General Gates was in charge of the Americans. British and American soldiers met at Freeman's Farm, an abandoned farm north of the American stronghold at Bemis Heights, three miles north of the spot where the Hudson joined the Mohawk River. With the help of Polish general Thaddeus Kosciuszko, Arnold planned a battlefield that gave the Americans the advantage. He afterward led a bold, brilliant, orderly attack, but the fighting was indecisive. Arnold returned to headquarters and persuaded Gates to send reinforcements. This General Gates did, but he refused to allow Arnold to lead them. Instead, Arnold was

▲ **General Horatio Gates**

relieved of his command and had no choice but to sit in camp while the fighting continued. Impatient as the battle roared on in the distance, Arnold rode around camp. Suddenly, shouting "victory or death," he galloped toward the battlefield. Again, Gates sent a rider after him, but this time Arnold was too far ahead.

Later, General Arnold led some men to a small fort, entering it through an opening in the rear. Although his horse was shot from underneath him and he was shot in the leg, Arnold's men took the fort and turned the tide of battle. Without enough supplies to retreat to Fort Ticonderoga, which was now in their hands, the British surrendered. Thus, the Battle of Saratoga ended the threat of British invasion from Canada. In his report of the action, General Gates did not mention Major General Arnold.

First court-martial. Meanwhile, Arnold faced a court-martial. An old enemy, John Brown, had pressed charges, accusing the general of looting Montreal during the retreat from Canada, starving his men at Quebec, and more. General Gates ordered a trial, held in Philadelphia, Pennsylvania. After a week, Arnold denounced the court-martial and challenged each officer on it to a duel. Gates, however, saved the day by disbanding the court.

Congress also held hearings on the Canadian defeats. Arnold's enemies seemed intent on trying to ruin his reputation. Even General Gates, his superior, criticized him in letters to the Congress. Arnold had been a brilliant military leader but had made enemies both in and out of the service by his position of wealth and his impulsiveness. Some rebels feared that generals such as Arnold aimed to put themselves in power and remain there as a privileged group. They came to identify Benedict Arnold with wealth and privilege.

Philadelphia. After recovering from his injury, Arnold returned to duty in May 1778. His wound had not completely healed, however, and he was unable to ride a horse, a requirement for a field officer. Washington, therefore, appointed him military commander of Philadelphia when that city was abandoned by the British. Although he was a strong leader in combat, Arnold had neither the patience nor the diplomatic skills to deal with the politicians in America's new capital. This weakness, combined with his desire to make money and live in luxury, led him into trouble.

Arnold soon came under attack from Pennsylvania's revolutionary government, which was dominated by Joseph Reed. In particular, he was charged with the use of army wagons to unload cargo from a ship that had been seized, not by the government but by privateers. The ship had been taken to New Jersey. From there the wagons brought the cargo to Philadelphia to be sold and the profits split with Arnold. Explaining himself, Arnold claimed he intended to pay for the use of the wagons, and the quartermaster supported his claim. A congressional committee then cleared Arnold of all charges of misconduct except misusing the wagons.

Second marriage. While in Philadelphia, Arnold met his second wife, Margaret Shippen, the daughter of a judge loyal to Britain. Peggy, as she was called, hated the revolutionary effort. Arnold was soon neglecting his duties as military governor in order to spend time with her. On April 8, 1779, they were married. The early months of their marriage proved stormy for Arnold, who was under attack from the citizens and the government.

Court-martial. Under pressure from some politicians, Congress resolved that Arnold should be court-martialed on several charges his enemies in the service had brought against him. The charges were many, and included misuse of the wagons to haul goods for Arnold's own trading business. Added to this charge were accusations that Arnold made purchases from stores in Philadelphia when they were closed to the public, then resold the goods for his own profit, and that he helped protect the pro-British Loyalists. Arnold wanted an immediate court-martial, but Reed wanted it delayed so that he could gather more evidence. Washington agreed to the delay, whereupon Arnold wrote him a letter of protest. In this letter, he complained about the thanklessness of his fellow Americans and pleaded for an early trial. "For heaven's sake," Arnold wrote, "let me be immediately tried and, if found guilty, executed. I want no favor. I only want justice." He concluded by saying, "Delay in the present case is worse than death" (Randall, p. 452).

Arnold's letter had some effect, for when his trial finally got under way in December 1779, he was cleared of the charges made against him except for misuse of the army wagons and another minor charge. The court sentenced him to be reprimanded by Washington. By this time being cleared of charges meant little to

Benedict Arnold, however, for around the same time he had written his plea to Washington, he had already begun to contact the British about changing sides.

Beginning to defect. Arnold had begun negotiating with the British by contacting the British high command through Joseph Stansbury, a Philadelphia glass and china merchant who was serving the British as a "stay-behind" agent after the British had abandoned Philadelphia. Arnold told Stansbury that he thought American independence could bring ruin to both Great Britain and America and that he intended to offer his services to the British commander in chief, Sir Henry Clinton, in order to restore British rule. Stansbury then left for British headquarters in New York City, where he met Clinton and his aide, Captain John André.

In a letter to Stansbury dated May 10, 1779, André wrote that the British command accepted Arnold's offer of service and promised to reward him if he would bring a band of men over to the British or give the British the advantage in a military campaign.

André and Stansbury set up a system by which Arnold could secretly communicate with the British high command. The messages would be written in code or with invisible ink, and the writers would use false names. Agents would smuggle the letters between Philadelphia and New York.

To show his good faith, Arnold sent André information about troop movements and diplomatic moves. He demanded 10,000 pounds for his services and compensation for the loss of his property in America should he defect. The British refused to guarantee this fee until they had seen what Arnold could bring to them. Then André suggested that the British were interested in information about West Point, New York.

The fortification at West Point prevented the British from sailing up the Hudson River from New York City. Washington considered West Point to be a key strategic location for Americans. While André struggled to get more information about West Point, his plans with Arnold remained stalled. During this time, until 1780, Arnold continued to live the lifestyle of the rich, riding around Philadelphia in a fancy coach. Still, he claimed without success that the army owed him four years' pay as a Continental officer and for meals provided at his own expense for his staff.

West Point. Now Arnold used the influence of his friend in Congress and old military commander Philip Schuyler to ask for a command at West Point. Washington, however, had other plans. The commander in chief wanted to make Arnold one of his top divisional commanders, but Arnold argued that he was still not well enough to ride a horse. Washington relented and gave him the command at West Point. Soon word came from British headquarters that General Clinton would pay Arnold 20,000 pounds if he would surrender the fort.

Arnold began to weaken West Point. Over the protests of his officers, he scattered the fort's troops, sending hundreds of soldiers out to chop wood or to escort prisoners. At the same time he pestered Washington for supplies, possibly to reduce Washington's own store of them, then sold the supplies on the black market.

Major André. General Arnold found it difficult to communicate with British headquarters from West Point. Finally a meeting was arranged. A British warship, the *Vulture,* sat anchored below West Point with Major André on it. The night of September 21, 1780, Arnold's messenger, Joshua Hett Smith, along with two oarsmen, the Colquhoun brothers, took André

> ## André Reacts to Being Caught
>
> "You never saw such an alteration in any man's face. Only a few moments before, he was uncommonly gay in his looks, but after we made him prisoner, you could read in his face that he thought it was all over with him. After travelling one or two miles, he said, 'I would to God you had blown my brains out when you stopped me!'" (Randall, pp. 554-555)

ashore aboard a rowboat. Arnold was waiting for him. When the meeting was concluded, the Colquhoun brothers, protesting that they were too tired, refused to row André back to the ship. This seemingly minor act changed the course of American history.

Blocked from a speedy return to his ship, André was forced to spend the day at the home of the messenger, Joshua Smith, and to try to return to his ship at night. However, American cannon on shore that day forced the *Vulture* to move downstream. Now Smith encouraged André (acting as a merchant named Anderson) to return to the British lines by land, walking part of the way with him.

Within sight of the British lines, André was stopped by three absent-without-leave American militiamen. Assuming the deserters were pro-British, André told them he was a British officer and showed them a pass given him by Arnold. Suspicious, they searched him and found documents hidden in his sock and written in Arnold's handwriting. Among them were the plans for West Point.

Washington Reacts to Arnold's Treason

Washington doubted that Arnold was torn by regrets about having committed treason. "He wants feeling!" Washington wrote. He thought Arnold "so hackneyed in villainy" that he was "lost to all sense of honor and shame" (Randall p.564).

Escape. American spies in New York City learned that André had been captured and turned over to an officer. The spies insisted the officer send the captured papers directly to Washington but the unsuspecting officer also sent Arnold a message about what had happened. Minutes before Washington arrived at West Point, Arnold boarded a boat and fled to the British *Vulture*.

Aftermath

Benedict Arnold, traitor. After Arnold defected, André was tried and convicted of spying. He was sentenced to hang. Washington offered to substitute Benedict Arnold, whom he considered to be the true villain. Such a trade was unthinkable to General Clinton, though, who hoped to encourage more rebels to join the British. André was executed on October 2, 1780.

In Philadelphia a mob bounced a dummy of Arnold in a wagon over cobblestone streets, jeering as it went. In New York, though, Arnold was rewarded with 6,000 pounds and a commission in the British army. He was soon back in combat, leading British forces on a raid into Virginia. In September 1781 he led a force in an attack on New London, Connecticut. Much of the town was burned, but his troops also suffered heavy losses.

England. After the fall of Yorktown, Virginia, Arnold left for England. He refused to give up on the British cause in America. He even saw King George III and urged him to pursue a stronger policy for the British. By this time, however, they had lost their enthusiasm for the war and the new prime minister was committed to peace.

In England, Arnold and his wife, Peggy, received a kind welcome at first but, as enthusiasm for the war dwindled, the two grew unpopular. Attacked as traitors in the press and shunned by old friends, they moved to St. John, Canada, and then to the West Indies, setting up a trading business and investing in real estate. When their business failed, the Arnolds moved back to London.

Final years. A series of tragedies dominated Arnold's last years. His oldest son was killed in Jamaica in 1796 while fighting as a soldier there. Afterward, Peggy's health began to decline, as did Arnold's. His business suffered and his debts increased.

In the summer of 1801, Arnold's health worsened, and he developed a cough and asthma. He died on June 14, 1801. His wife, who died a few years later, managed to pay off all his debts.

Because of his treason, Arnold is considered one of the great villains in American history. But for the stubbornness of two tired boatmen, he might have given the British a victory that could have defeated the cause of American independence. However, his feats early in the war may have saved this very same cause. Because of this paradox, Benedict Arnold remains one of the most complex and curious figures in American history.

For More Information

Ameringer, Charles D. *United States Foreign Intelligence: The Secret Side of American History.* Lexington, Mass.: Lexington Books, 1990.

Bylan, Brian Richard. *Benedict Arnold, The Dark Eagle.* New York: Norton, 1973.

Randall, Willard Sterne. *Benedict Arnold: Patriot and Traitor.* New York: William Morrow and Co., 1973, 1990.

Marquis de Lafayette
(Marie-Joseph-Paul-Yves-Roch-Gilbert du Motier)
1757-1834

Personal Background

Family life. Marie-Joseph-Paul-Yves-Roch-Gilbert du Motier, or the Marquis de Lafayette, was born in Auvergne, France, on September 6, 1767. Both of his parents descended from noble families, and there was a long family tradition of military service. In fact, Lafayette's father was killed at the Battle of Minden in the Seven Years' War (known in America as the French and Indian War) before the young Lafayette's second birthday. His mother died by the time he reached thirteen, and his grandfather passed away just a few weeks later. Heir to a great fortune and title, Lafayette was raised by his grandmother and aunts. They hired private tutors to educate him, and later enrolled him in the College du Plessis. His ambition for a military career led him to the military academy in Versailles. There, in 1771, he became a member of the king's Musketeers, the French royal bodyguard.

Lafayette's great wealth and noble title made him a much sought-after marriage prospect. At the age of only sixteen he married Marie Adrienne Francoise de Noailles, a daughter of one of the wealthiest, most powerful families in France. The great wealth at his disposal would later enable Lafayette to spend lavishly in support of the American Revolution. Not long after his marriage, Lafayette became a captain in the cavalry (he had proved himself a

▲ The Marquis de Lafayette

Event: American Revolution, Battle of Yorktown.

Role: Marquis de Lafayette, a French soldier and statesman, risked imprisonment to join the American rebels. He agreed to serve without pay and, in fact, spent 200,000 dollars of his own money on the American cause. He was a devoted supporter of George Washington and played an important role in the decisive victory at the Battle of Yorktown. Perhaps his greatest contribution was persuading the French government to send a French army to aid Washington's forces.

highly skilled horseman). His military duties allowed him to participate, unwillingly, in the court life at Versailles. Shy and awkward, he despised this court life and suffered great embarrassment when the French queen, Marie-Antoinette, laughed at his dancing.

Decision to go to America. Eager to escape the shallow ways and underhanded schemes at court, Lafayette returned to his military duties at Metz. While stationed there, in August 1775, he attended a dinner given in honor of the Duke of Gloucester, a brother to King George II of Great Britain. Surprisingly, the Duke expressed sympathy for the colonies in America and praised their leaders. Lafayette immediately began planning to enlist in the ranks of the American rebels.

His biographers list many reasons for Lafayette's decision to leave a life of ease and comfort so he could support the "glorious cause" of the American colonists. Foremost is that he sought revenge against Great Britain for defeating France in the Seven Years' War, the war in which his own father was killed. Next is the belief, inspired by the French philosopher Jean Jacques Rousseau, that America was a reborn world free from corruption and loss of faith that plagued governments in Europe. Lafayette also felt sympathy for the American colonists, whom he thought stood for the same republican ideals as his heroes of ancient Republican Rome. And he was seeking personal fame and glory, fed by the feeling that he was not respected at the French Court.

Lafayette's critics, perhaps because of his reluctant, half-hearted support of the commoners who sparked the French Revolution when they arose up against the monarchy and aristocracy, do not think he believed in the ideals of the American Revolution when he first committed himself to go to America. But the men he fought alongside never doubted his commitment to their cause, and even Lafayette's harshest critics believe he eventually made America's cause of liberty his own. He unswervingly supported that cause the rest of his life.

When the news of Lexington and Concord, Massachusetts, reached France, it raised hopes that the hated English might be humbled. The French government authorized secret aid to the American colonies in the form of loans and supplies but avoided open opposition to Great Britain in the conflict at this time. Lafayette decided to go to America a full two years before France openly allied herself with the American rebels. He met Silas Deane, an American representative in France, who promised him and his friend Baron de Kalb commissions as major generals in the Continental Army. Lafayette purchased a ship (the *Victoria*), escaped some authorities who attempted to keep him in France, and set sail for America. The date was April 20, 1777.

Lafayette meets Washington. Lafayette's vessel reached the American colonies on June 13. He and his companions landed near Georgetown, South Carolina. There they were greeted by a hail of bullets (fortunately very poorly aimed), because they were mistaken for a party of Hessians, German soldiers hired to fight for the British. Once Lafayette and his party were correctly identified, they were entertained by Major Benjamin Huger. He helped outfit the Frenchmen for the difficult six-week journey to Philadelphia, Pennsylvania, where Lafayette presented his qualifications to the Continental Congress.

> ## "Lafayette, We Are Here"
>
> During World War I American forces arrived in France on June 23, 1917. A few days later, July 4, 1917, a grateful French people enthusiastically joined in the celebration of American Independence Day. An American battalion marched to the Paris cemetery where Lafayette was buried. By his grave an American colonel, Charles E. Stanton, delivered these historic words, "Lafayette, nous voilà" (Lafayette, we are here). At the time many Americans believed their aid to France in World War I was, at least in part, repayment of the debt owed to the French for their assistance in the American Revolution.

The representatives of Congress who received Lafayette gave him a cool reception. They told him that Deane had exceeded his authority in offering Lafayette a commission. (By this time a host of foreign adventurers had come to Congress, demanding both appointments as officers and generous pay.) It was politely suggested that Lafayette and his companions return to France. But the young Frenchman persisted. He wrote a letter to the Congress, offering to serve without pay and to begin his service as a volunteer rather than an officer. This modest request, coupled with Lafayette's charm and enthusiasm for American liberty, prompted Congress to reconsider. They made him a major general but gave him no troops to command. The next day he was introduced to George Washington, commander in chief of the Continental Army.

Lafayette's meeting with Washington was perhaps the great turning point in his life. Orphaned at an early age and not yet twenty, the young Marquis came to regard Washington, who had no children of his own, as his adopted father. The commander, usually very reserved in his personal relationships, returned the affection and accepted the role. Lafayette became a member of Washington's staff. In time this would allow him to acquire the military experience he needed before he was given command of his own forces.

Lafayette showed an immediate and lasting admiration for Washington. He was quick to defend Washington against any criticism. Early in the war, when some of the rebels tried to replace Washington as commander in chief (the Conway Cabal incident), Lafayette served as his strongest defender. Meanwhile, Washington felt growing respect for Lafayette. Perhaps the clearest sign of Washington's regard for the Marquis was the growing responsibility he placed upon him. Washington would give Lafayette a real command and key roles in some of the Revolutionary Army's most ambitious campaigns.

Lafayette and Slavery

In the fight against slavery, Lafayette was far ahead of his American friends. He wrote George Washington proposing the purchase of property to be farmed by free blacks so the world could see that slavery was not necessary for landowners to prosper. Also, he encouraged France's government to help end the slave trade. Using his own wealth, he bought two plantations that were dedicated to fair treatment and preparation for freedom from slavery. An engraving of the time shows Lafayette as the "Friend of the Black Man."

Participation: The American Revolution

Battle of Brandywine. Lafayette saw his first military action at Brandywine Creek, a tributary of the Delaware River in Pennsylvania. The Battle of Brandywine turned into a British victory and a near disaster for the Americans, who suffered great losses (mostly in prisoners taken). Lafayette courageously exposed himself to enemy fire while trying to prevent the American withdrawal from turning into a disorderly rout. In the retreat his leg was wounded. Washington instructed his own surgeon to treat the Marquis like a son, because "I love him as if he were" (Smith, p. 976). Lafayette recovered for several weeks at a religious community of Moravians in Bethlehem, Pennsylvania. In fact, the wound he suffered at

▲ **Soldiers suffering at Valley Forge**

Brandywine worked very much in his favor. His friend the Baron de Kalb called it a piece of good luck, proof that Lafayette was willing to risk life and limb for the American cause.

Plan to invade Canada. After recovering from his wound, the Marquis rejoined Washington's army. Almost immediately he won praise again for his courage and skill in leading a successful raid against a party of Hessians at Gloucester. His personal conduct at Brandywine and Gloucester, coupled with a desire to win further French aid, persuaded the Congress to give Lafayette command of a Virginia division. His rank as major general was no longer a honorary title without men to command; he would remain a leader of troops to the war's end.

Lafayette's popularity in America grew steadily. He wintered at Valley Forge, Pennsylvania, with Washington's forces. Enduring the same hardships as the common soldiers, they called him "the soldier's friend." He lived up to the title, spending his own money on shoes and clothing for the men he led.

Controversy in Lafayette's military career occurred when the Board of War, a committee including some of Washington's harshest critics, selected the popular young Marquis to lead an invasion of Canada. The prospect excited Lafayette, who dreamed of restoring the empire France had lost in America due to the French and Indian War. He hastily accepted command without consulting Washington, who was against both the invasion and France's gaining a foothold in North America. Lafayette hurried north from Valley Forge to Albany, New York, where he found neither the men nor the supplies promised to him by the Board of War for the invasion. Consulting some experienced commanders in the region, he learned that such an invasion was likely to fail. Distressed, Lafayette wrote to Washington (who was secretly pleased that the enterprise was being abandoned). The letter conveyed his disappointment and his feeling of having been deceived.

French-American alliance. When Lafayette returned to Valley Forge he quickly forgot his bitterness with the news that the French government had signed a treaty of alliance with the American colonists and had declared war on Great Britain.

Many historians believe that the French alliance may have been the great turning point in the Revolutionary War. The French had long been secretly sending aid to the rebel forces but had avoided any open support. Only after the British General Burgoyne surrendered to American forces at the Battle of Saratoga did the French agree to the alliance. Also a strong showing of Washington's troops at Germantown had impressed them. These events gave support to the argument Benjamin Franklin kept making to France's government: American forces could defeat British forces in open battle. In the end, the French government agreed to an alliance because she sought revenge for the defeat she had suffered at the hands of Great Britain in the Seven Years' War (1756-63) and to protect her holdings in the Western Hemisphere.

The alliance between France and the Americans raised Lafayette's spirits and his stock with colonial leaders. His performance on the battlefield cemented his popularity. In May 1778, through skillful maneuvers, he avoided capture by a much larger British force at Barren Hill in Pennsylvania. The British had been so sure of victory that their commander, General Howe, had planned a dinner party to meet the Marquis de Lafayette. Giving the Americans a "good laugh," his dinner guest managed to artfully escape the trap Howe had laid. Lafayette also demonstrated skill and courage at the Battle of Monmouth, in which for "the first time … American regulars fought on equal terms with British regulars on an open field" (Dupui, p. 169). The British commander, General Henry Clinton, yielded the win to Washington, slipping away with his forces after dark.

The arrival of French forces in America made Lafayette even more valuable to the American cause. He helped prepare a joint naval and land attack against Newport, Rhode Island. The plan badly misfired, but Lafayette proved invaluable as a go-between and "did much to calm the jealousies … of both French and Americans" (Malone, p. 537).

Success in France. Following events at Newport (and two near duels—one with an American general who questioned French courage and another with a British peace commissioner to the colonies), Lafayette asked for a furlough, or leave. He wanted to return to France for a while. Washington thought the trip a good idea; the Marquis might bring back more aid. So Lafayette set sail for France. He carried two letters. One, written by Washington to Ambassador Benjamin Franklin, praised Lafayette for the "generous motives" that first brought him to the colonies, for his "gallantry at the Brandywine," and for other "such proofs of his zeal, military ardor, and talents, as have endeared him to America" (Criss, p. 57). The second letter, from the American Congress to King Louis XVI of France, recommended the Marquis to the king "as one whom we know to be wise in council, gallant in the field, and patient under the hardships of war" (Criss, p. 57). Lafayette was returning home in glory, something he had longed for and achieved.

The ship on which Lafayette sailed back to France was manned by British prisoners (many of them deserters). Lafayette succeeded in putting down a mutiny and arrived safely in France. After being held under house arrest for a week (his punishment for having originally left France against the king's wishes), Lafayette presented himself to the French court at Versailles: "He was welcomed and acclaimed, received by the King and Queen, consulted by all the ministers, and kissed by all the ladies. He was discussed, toasted, entertained" (Malone, p. 537).

Full of bold projects, Lafayette proposed invading England, Ireland, or Canada to help America. He also advocated hiring part of the Swedish navy to aid the colonies. None of these schemes were carried out. It was then that Lafayette performed his greatest service for America: he won approval for a French military force, combined with a large naval detachment, to serve under Washington.

Washington meets Rochambeau. Lafayette proposed himself as commander of this force, but his youth and the jealousy many French officers felt toward him resulted in the command being awarded to the Comte de Rochambeau. Lafayette complained but adjusted to this turn of events. He rushed back to America to prepare the way for the French force. After outlining to Congress how to prepare for the French navy, his old command was restored to him. When Rochambeau and a French fleet arrived in America, he needed to confer with Washington. Lafayette served as a go-between for the two commanders, who discussed possible plans for joint campaigns against British forces. Washington favored driving the British out of New York. The French leader believed the war might be won in the South, where French naval power could have the greatest impact.

Lafayette and Benedict Arnold. At this point Lafayette and Washington visited West Point, New York. Benedict Arnold, an American commander of great skill who was disappointed at being passed over for promotion, had committed treason against the American forces there. Washington and Lafayette served on the military court that tried and sentenced to death Major John André, the British officer who had accepted Arnold's offer to turn the fortress at West Point over to the British (see **Benedict Arnold**). Lafayette felt so sorry for André, who the court convicted as a spy, that he sent a message to the British proposing to trade André for Arnold, the truly guilty party. British general Clinton refused (although Arnold seemed willing to go). So André was hanged. Neither Washington nor Lafayette could bring themselves to witness the event.

Washington, eager to capture Arnold, sent Lafayette, with 1,200 New England soldiers, south to the Chesapeake region to snag the traitor. But the French fleet, which was supposed to assist Lafayette, did not arrive on schedule. Arnold managed to escape and eventually settled in England.

Yorktown. Lafayette's last great military service to America occurred in the critical Yorktown, Virginia, campaign, where he displayed great patience and skill. He fought opposite perhaps the finest English general of the Revolutionary War, Charles Cornwallis, who commanded a much larger force than Lafayette could gather in Virginia. As the British advanced northward the Marquis slowly retreated, managing to do some damage to the enemy while avoiding a major engagement. Lafayette thus imitated Washington's pattern of skillful, successful retreats.

In the present campaign the main American and French armies were threatening the British hold on New York City. Washington was expecting a French fleet to supply needed aid in the Chesapeake region. Meanwhile, he sent word to Lafayette not to let Cornwallis leave Yorktown, located on the Virginia coast, before Washington's army, joined by a French force led by Rochambeau, could hurry south to help trap the enemy. Lafayette cornered Cornwallis, who thought he could escape by sea, at Yorktown.

The British commander finally realized the danger he was in when the expected French fleet drove off some British ships that were attempting to help his trapped force. When Washington and his French allies arrived, they successfully attacked the British. Lafayette's forces played a leading role in this attack. Cornwallis surrendered. At first he tried to surrender to the French, but they insisted the Americans, not they, be given the defeated general's sword. Although two years passed before the Treaty of Paris was signed, American independence had clearly been won at Yorktown, the last major battle of the American Revolution.

Aftermath

United States citizen. After Yorktown, Lafayette returned to France. He received a hero's welcome from both the French people

▲ Queen Marie-Antoinette of France was beheaded during the
French Revolution

and the royal court. The Marquis was helping to prepare an army to invade Britain when the Treaty of Paris brought an official end to the American Revolution.

The bond between Lafayette and Washington continued long after American independence was won. Washington was godfather to Lafayette's son (named George Washington de Lafayette). Also, Lafayette worked to persuade a reluctant Washington to become the first President.

At Washington's invitation Lafayette returned to America in 1784. During this visit Maryland's General Assembly awarded him and his heirs citizenship, making him a United States citizen when the states became a union (1787).

French Revolution. Lafayette played a major role in European as well as American events. The French Revolution found him in favor of a constitutional monarchy, a king with very limited power ruling along with a popularly elected national assembly. He lent his support to the French Declaration of the Rights of Man and the Citizen, a document based partly on the American Declaration of Independence. The French named him commander of the National Guard. When a Paris mob stormed the royal prison, or Bastille (a hated symbol of oppression), Lafayette ordered the destruction of the prison. He then sent the key to its main entrance to Washington, acknowledging him as the inspiration for the revolutionary movement in France. (The key can be seen today by visitors to Washington's home at Mount Vernon, alongside a drawing of the destroyed Bastille.)

The rebels in France, however, were disappointed in Lafayette: he was more moderate and conservative than they would have liked. Indeed, he saved the king and queen from a mob in Paris. Also, in the view of some historians, he hesitated when he might have seized the opportunity to become leader. Those who did seize power condemned him.

Afterward, he left the army, which he had been commanding due to Austria's invasion of France. He fell into the hands of the enemy and was imprisoned for five years. Meanwhile, the French king and queen, Louis XVI and Marie-Antoinette, were beheaded, a reign of terror erupted, and Napoleon Bonaparte became dictator of France. It was Napoleon who secured Lafayette's release from prison. (Washington tried but failed, and a dramatic rescue attempt involving the son of Major Huger, the man who had first welcomed Lafayette to America, also misfired.)

Last days. Following his release from prison, Lafayette returned to France. He could not bring himself to support Napoleon, so he declined all offers to serve in the French government. He also turned down President Thomas Jefferson's offer to appoint him governor of Louisiana, the vast territory the United States purchased from France in 1803.

Accepting an invitation from President James Monroe, Lafayette made one last visit to the United States in 1824. He received perhaps the warmest welcome ever tendered a foreign visitor. The sixteen months he spent in America visiting every state marked the happiest period in his life. After his return to France, he allowed himself to be drawn back into political life. Revolution swept the country again in 1830. Had Lafayette acted more forcefully at this time, perhaps he would have become its democratic leader. As before, though, Lafayette hesitated, and Louis Philippe was crowned the new king of France.

The Marquis de Lafayette died on May 20, 1834. He was buried near his wife in a Paris cemetery in earth that was brought over from Bunker Hill in his beloved America. Many in France grieved for him, but perhaps even more grieved in America, where a national period of mourning was proclaimed and flags were flown at half-mast for a full thirty days.

Later, some historians looked more closely at what Lafayette did not achieve in the French Revolution than at what he did accomplish for the earlier revolution in America. Washington, for one, never doubted Lafayette's immense contribution to the success of the American Revolution. When news of the alliance between France and America reached Washington, he told Lafayette that he had done more than anybody else to bring about this fortunate event. Certainly Lafayette's strong support for Washington was a major factor in France's decision to put its forces in America under Washington's command after this alliance. It is hard to imagine American victory against the forces of Britain without the aid of the

French. The actions of Lafayette, Rochambeau, and the fleet from France were critical to success at Yorktown, the climax in the American Revolution.

For More Information

Dos Passos, John. "Lafayette's Two Revolutions." *American Heritage,* December 1956, pp. 4-9.

Criss, Mildred. *LaFayette on the Heights of Freedom.* New York: Dodd, Mead & Co., 1954.

Dupui, Trevor N., and Hammerman, Gay M., eds. *Events of the American Revolution.* New York: R. R. Bowker, 1974.

Holbrook, Sabra. *Lafayette: Man in the Middle.* New York: Atheneum, 1977.

Horn, Pierre. *Marquis de Lafayette.* New York: Chelsea House, 1988.

Loth, David. *Lafayette.* London: Cassell and Co., Ltd., 1952.

Malone, Dumas, ed. *Dictionary of American Biography,* Vol. 5, Part 2. New York: Charles Scribner's Sons, 1960-61.

Smith, Page. *A New Age Now Begins.* People's History of the American Revolution, Vol. 2. New York: McGraw-Hill, 1976.

Deborah Sampson

1760-1827

Personal Background

Early years. Deborah Sampson was born December 17, 1760, in Plympton, Massachusetts, near Plymouth. Her parents, who were very poor, did not want their daughter to grow up in poverty or face hardship. So, when Deborah was eight years old, they sent her to live with another family as an indentured servant. This was a common arrangement in colonial America, in which people worked for families in exchange for food, clothing, and shelter. Deborah signed on for ten years with the family of Jeremiah Thomas, a farmer living in Middleborough. At the Thomas home she tended farm animals, plowed fields, and cared for the young Thomas children. Her daily duties included sewing, cooking, and making deliveries on horseback around the village. In between duties she took lessons in handling guns from the older Thomas boys.

The Thomases, like many people in the 1700s, did not believe it was important for women to learn to read and write, so they chose not to send Deborah to school. Still, she managed to educate herself. Every night, after everyone in the house had gone to bed, Deborah studied the other children's schoolbooks. She fashioned a pen out of goose feathers and, using homemade ink, copied each day's lessons on pieces of bark from a nearby birch tree. Soon she was reading and writing, and she even began teaching the younger Thomas children to do the same.

▲ **Deborah Sampson, like Molly Pitcher pictured here, fought alongside the American troops**

Event: The American Revolution.

Role: Deborah Sampson was the first woman to enlist in the American Army. Disguised as a man, she fought in several battles of the Revolutionary War.

Helping the war cause. By the time she was thirteen, Sampson was becoming aware of the American struggle with England. After the Boston Tea Party, King George III of England cut off all import ships to the Boston Harbor so the colonists could not get any food or supplies. The king demanded payment for all the tea that had been dumped overboard, and the people of Boston, Massachusetts, refused; they would not be taxed on English tea without having any of their own representatives in Parliament. Deborah read about the event in the newspapers and heard people talking about it at the inn where she made deliveries. Knowing the rebels needed assistance, she planted extra corn on the farm and, with the help of the Thomas family, sent it to the people of Boston.

As Sampson grew older her desire to help in the quest for independence increased. When she turned eighteen she was free to leave the Thomas farm. Many schoolteachers had joined the army, which gave Sampson the opportunity to teach summer school to the local children. Though she had never been to school herself, Sampson was prepared for the job because of the time she had spent helping the Thomas children do their lessons. She moved into a room in a house next to the school and taught for three summers. During the winter she spun wool into clothes for families in Middleborough, living with them until she had finished making the clothes they required.

Meanwhile, during these years, Sampson saw men all around her going off to war. The young woman watched with curiosity and wonder as they left their homes to fight in battles far away. Seeing the soldiers in the uniforms and hearing of the revolutionary battles, a plan began to take root in Sampson's head. While her mother urged her to marry and raise a family like other women her age, the free-thinking young woman, uninterested in taking this conventional path, concentrated instead on how to achieve her newly formed goal: to join the fight for independence from Britain. After much thought, she came up with a plan. She would enlist in the American army, dressed as a young man.

Dressing up. When Sampson was moving from house to house as a seamstress, she once stayed with Sam Leonard and his family. Leonard, leaving a worried but supportive wife and children behind, had joined the Revolutionary Army. One night during her stay, Deborah sneaked into Leonard's closet and found an old suit of his tucked away in the back. She hurriedly rolled it up and stuffed it under her arm, then hid it away with her belongings. When she eventually left the Leonard home, the borrowed suit went with her.

When she returned to her room next to the schoolhouse, Deborah tried on the suit. It fit perfectly, so she went right to work making her own suit out of an extra piece of homespun wool, matching it against Leonard's suit exactly. In a couple days she finished the suit. Then, with the little money she had, she went to a cobbler to get a pair of men's boots made, pretending they were for her sister's husband, who had the same size foot as she did.

Her outfit complete, Sampson was now ready to try it out in public to see if she could fool anybody into thinking she was a young man. She cut off her long hair to shoulder length, the fashionable style for men in those days. When she put on the suit, she bound her breasts with linen tied tightly around her chest. No one knew her secret, except a slave girl named Jenny, who also worked for the Leonard family. The two had become good friends, and Jenny promised not to tell anybody about the daring plan.

Sampson adventured out of the house—as a man—to the inn where she had made so many deliveries for the Thomases. She visited a fortune-teller there to have her palm read. The fortune-teller studied her palm and her face. He didn't seem to suspect a thing. He told her that she was a strong, hard-working young man who would like to appear older. He also guessed that she was planning an adventure, and that this adventure would succeed. He advised her to join the army, for such a strong young man would make a terrific soldier. He told this to many men who came to have their fortunes told, for the war was on, and soldiers were needed. Overjoyed, Sampson took the fortune-teller's words as a positive sign that she should continue with her plan. She had easily passed for a young man at the place where she would most likely be recognized. Soon after, Sampson enlisted in the war for independence.

Participation: American Revolution

Enlisting in the cause. There are two different accounts of what happened when Sampson first tried to enlist in the Continental

Army under the name Timothy Thayer. The first story is that she enlisted at the Middleborough recruiting office, easily passing as a young man in the recruiting officer's eyes. However, she had a distinctive characteristic—a bone felon on her right forefinger. Felons were caused by sprains that did not heal correctly, making the bones around the sprain stiffen. This, in turn, caused her finger to be completely stiff, making it difficult to write.

A local woman named Mistress Woods happened to be in the recruiting office at the time and noticed that the young stranger's stiff finger resembled exactly that of a woman she knew. She commented to the officer that this young soldier held a pen just like her grandchildren's old summer school teacher, Deborah Sampson. Thinking quickly, the disguised Sampson said to the officer that the felon was the result of shooting too much, back on the farm where she grew up. Since girls were rarely taught to handle guns, the officer thought nothing of the coincidence and signed his new recruit on as a soldier and handed her the bounty money she needed to proceed. (Bounty money was given to new soldiers to cover their expenses during wartime.) Sampson left the office with her money, her new identity, and a promise that the army would soon send for her.

But in the meantime, through Mrs. Woods, the news spread like wildfire that a strange young man resembling Deborah Sampson had enlisted in the army. Fearing she would be found out, Sampson hurriedly gave the bounty money to her friend Jenny, asking her to return it to the recruiting officer. Jenny did this, telling the officer that the money was from Timothy Thayer, and that he had decided not to join the army after all. Sampson then left Middleborough and headed toward Boston, determined to take another try at joining the army.

The second version of the story does not include her being recognized by Mrs. Woods. Excited to have fooled the recruiting officer, the story says, Sampson ran to a local tavern, where she celebrated so noisily that someone recognized her. She then fled the tavern and ran to the house where Jenny was staying, giving her the bounty money and the same instructions on returning it. This story ends the same as the other, however, with Sampson heading for Boston for another try at enlisting.

The journey. On her way to Boston, Sampson stopped at an inn in the port-city of New Bedford. The port, which sits along Buzzards Bay, an inlet from the Atlantic Ocean, harbored many warships. There Sampson met a ship's captain, who offered her work as a cabin boy, doing odd jobs aboard the ship. She accepted, following the captain to the ship to sign the agreement papers for the job.

On board, the first mate showed her around the ship as the captain put together the papers. As Sampson was exploring the vessel alone with the first mate, he warned her not to work for this captain. The first mate said that the captain had a reputation for treating his shipmates horribly, and told her stories of his beating and starving the crew. One cabin boy had even disappeared—he went out on a voyage and never returned. The first mate told Sampson that a young, promising boy had no business on any vessel run by this man. She heeded his words and, before the captain returned to the ship's deck, ran straight back to the inn from which she came. The barmaid was glad to see her, agreeing the ship was no place for a young boy—the captain could not be trusted.

Sampson traveled through cities and towns around Boston, stopping along the way to work as a stable boy for families whose fathers and sons were already off at war. She remained in disguise, claiming she was an orphan trying to make it to Bellingham, Massachusetts, where she would enlist. She worked her way slowly, earning just enough to get her to the next town, where she would easily find work again. Finally, she reached Bellingham, one year after she wisely left New Bedford.

In the army. The day she arrived in Bellingham, Sampson went straight to the recruiting office. An army captain was there to interview potential soldiers. Thinking she must be quite young, he noticed she lacked facial hair. This did not seem to concern him, though, for many soldiers were needed, even young boys. To her advantage, she was quite tall for a woman, about five feet

Deborah Sampson and Paul Revere

When she was fifteen, Deborah Sampson vowed that someday she would meet her war hero Paul Revere. They met twenty-nine years later, in 1804. Revere opened a copper manufacturing plant not far from Sharon, Massachusetts, where Sampson eventually settled with her family. The two became friends and began to meet regularly at taverns to exchange conversation, praise, and war stories.

eight inches, almost a foot taller than most women of the time, and several inches taller than most men. She was also noticeably muscular and strong. The recruiting officer signed her up for three years or until the end of the war in the Fourth Massachusetts Regiment under the command of General Paterson. Sampson gave her name as Robert Shurtliff, the first and middle name of her oldest brother, who had died shortly before her birth. The date was May 20, 1782. Deborah Sampson was going to war.

Her first assignment was a twelve-day march to West Point, New York. Ten days into the march, the troop stopped to rest at a tavern. Sampson, unaccustomed to hiking such a long distance fainted in front of the fireplace. When she came to, she found friendly soldiers and workers from the tavern gathered around her. Her first thought was that her true identity might be discovered. Fortunately this was not the case; the innkeeper's wife even insisted that Sampson lie down in bed with her husband for the night. Reluctantly, she accepted the offer, but refused to take off her uniform before lying down. She slept in peace that night, regaining her strength.

The next morning Sampson set on the last two miles of the journey to West Point, where she was given a new uniform, stockings, breeches, boots, a knapsack, a small rifle with a bayonet, and a set of thirty cartridges of ammunition. She sneaked off into the forest to change clothes. By now she had become accustomed to sneaking to take care of normal tasks like changing clothes and going to the bathroom. Most of the other soldiers assumed she was shy because of her youth and did not suspect anything abnormal. They even called her nicknames like "Bloomin' Bobby" and "Molly" because of her beardless face. When the time came to bathe, she usually limited herself to using washcloths to clean her face and hands. Once every week or two, the soldiers had the opportunity to bathe in the restrooms at local inns or taverns along their path. On these occasions, Sampson would quickly rinse her body, making sure to keep herself well hidden, should some man walk into the restroom.

The Battle of Tarrytown. At West Point she and her fellow soldiers were ordered to divide in half and meet again in Tarrytown the next day, then wait for more instructions from the commanding officer. Her division arrived the next morning. Suddenly from out of the distance a shower of bullets flew all around the soldiers. Before

Sampson knew what was happening, she saw a soldier she had be-friended shot in the chest. He slumped over and lay still.

Reacting quickly in spite of her shock, Sampson began shooting rounds of fire back at the British. A musket ball whizzed past her head. Another followed, this time tearing through her hat and grazing her scalp. As blood started to flow from her wound, she began feeling dizzy. But still she fought, wounded and with her eyes stinging from gunpowder, firing round after round at the enemy. Minutes seemed like an eternity until finally she heard the sound of American drums and a hail of gunfire erupted from behind her on the hill.

Another American battalion, led by Colonel Ebenezer Sproat, had come to the rescue. In a strange coincidence, Sampson recognized the colonel as a man from her hometown of Middleborough. He ordered her and the others in her group to retreat immediately. They did, and Sproat's men, who outnumbered the British, finished the battle. The Americans emerged in victory from what came to be known as the Battle of Tarrytown. After the battle, Sampson's wound was treated; luckily, it was only a flesh wound and would heal easily. Without recognizing her, Sproat congratulated Sampson for her bravery and asked her to join a special mission to repay the British for those lives lost at the Battle of Tarrytown. She readily accepted.

Sampson's mission was to accompany a new group of soldiers to the neutral territory of East Chester, where they were to wait for the approaching British army and ambush them. As scheduled, the British arrived that night in the village, and her division was ordered to fire. A battle instantly broke out. A British officer came after her with a sword and slashed her head. She knocked him unconscious with the butt of her musket, and continued fighting against the other British soldiers. Suddenly, she felt a sharp, stinging pain in her inner thigh. She had been shot. A fellow soldier saw her stagger and fall, and insisted on carrying her to safety. She begged him to leave her there to die. He refused, slumping her over the back of his horse and carrying her to the nearby military hospital. Later, the army commended her for her bravery.

At the hospital, the doctor who treated her head wound noticed that her pants were torn and that blood was running down her legs. He ordered her to remove her trousers so that he could treat the wound. Fearing she would be found out if she removed her pants, Sampson insisted she had simply caught a nail in the thigh from the horse's saddle, and she just needed to go into the other room and change. Since other soldiers were near death and needed assistance, the doctor allowed her to do so. Sampson limped into the other room and, taking brandy as an anesthetic, quickly used a surgical knife she had taken from the doctor's table to remove the musket ball. Some accounts say there were in fact two musket balls in her leg, and she could only remove one. In any case, she did operate on herself, narrowly escaping being found out.

News of the young Robert Shurtliff's heroism soon traveled to Paterson. He asked for Shurtliff to be sent to his quarters immediately. Since there were no major battles being fought, and she certainly was not being sent away, Sampson assumed that she had finally been discovered. When she arrived at the general's Pennsylvania office, he praised her bravery and courage and asked her to be his personal orderly. He, like so many others, still did not suspect her true identity. Breathing a sigh of relief, she went right to work for Paterson. She cleaned his boots, polished his swords, prepared his meals, and ran errands for him daily. Not only was her secret still safe, she had even succeeded in being promoted for her heroism. She stayed with Paterson until she received word that she might be needed again in battle, then returned to join the troops in their camp.

The truth discovered. Everything was running smoothly until an epidemic of malignant brain fever spread through Pennsylvania while Sampson was back with her troops. She fell extremely ill. While she was near death at the hospital she heard soldiers arguing over her clothes. They thought she was already dead. She gathered enough strength to ask for help, and before she knew it, Doctor Barnabus Binney was at her side. He began unbuttoning her shirt to feel for a heartbeat, and this time she did not have enough strength to stop any doctor from examining her. The linen cloth she used to bind her breasts was now exposed. Puzzled, the doctor unwrapped it and discovered her secret. He appeared shocked, but said nothing. He pulled off her britches, discovered her gunshot wound, and treated it. He ordered the nurse at the hospital to send for a carriage and bring the young soldier to his home immediately.

At the Binney home, the kind doctor's wife nursed Sampson slowly back to health. She was addressed by Mrs. Binney and a visiting niece as Robert Shurtliff. Doctor Binney had told no one. The niece sat by her bedside for hours on end, bringing her flowers, medicine, and new shirts. Sampson feared the doctor's niece was romantically interested in Robert Shurtliff, the young, heroic, male soldier. As soon as she was able, she decided to leave the Binney home and return to the company of Paterson. The war was over, but she desperately wanted to contact the man who had been so generous toward her. Binney handed her a sealed envelope, addressed to Paterson, asking her to deliver it. She knew that the letter inside told the truth, but she could not betray the doctor's trust in her to deliver the letter, for he had saved her life and kept her secret for so long.

Aftermath

Returning to Paterson's office, Sampson promptly presented him with the letter. The general was happy to see his former orderly. He had assumed that she, like so many other young soldiers, had died of brain fever. As Sampson had expected, the letter revealed that she was a woman; it further advised that she be treated like a heroine. The general read the letter right away and asked her to speak honestly with him.

He reminded her that he thought she was a very brave and faithful soldier, and that he must now ask for the truth. Was she—under the concealing uniform—a woman? Sampson confessed that yes, she was a woman, and pleaded for him not to punish her; she was only trying to serve her country. In response, the general assured her of an honorable discharge and money to travel back to her family, who had no idea where she was. He still could not believe what he had just learned. So Sampson convinced him of her womanhood by borrowing one of Mrs. Paterson's dresses and combing her hair in the style she used to wear back on the Thomas farm. In fact, dressed as a member of her true gender, Sampson was quite beautiful. Finally, the general could accept the truth. Robert Shurtliff was Deborah Sampson, the first woman to enlist and fight in the American army.

Honorably discharged. On October 25, 1783, Sampson was honorably discharged from the Continental Army of the United States of America. Her story appeared in all the newspapers, and she became quite popular because of her daring adventure.

Sampson traveled to the house of a favorite aunt and uncle, Alice and Zebulon Waters, who lived on the border of Sharon, Massachusetts. There she met and fell in love with a friend of her aunt and uncle's, a man six years older than she, Benjamin Gannett, Jr. He proposed, and she accepted. They were married on April 7, 1785, at the Gannett family home. The couple had three children, two girls and a boy, in addition to raising a young orphan girl. In regards to Sampson's stint as a soldier, her husband is said to have respected her bravery and independence in going to war. Money was scarce, and despite her leg injury, which troubled her all her life, Sampson grew restless for activity. She decided to try her hand at lecturing others about her war experience.

She was well received by the townspeople she lectured to, becoming not only America's first enlisted woman soldier but also its first paid woman lecturer. She traveled, giving lectures for about a year and earning just enough money to help support her family. Then she tired of lecturing, however, and decided to return home.

By this time pensions were being paid by the government to soldiers who had served in the armed forces. With the help of a letter of recommendation from her new friend Paul Revere, Sampson began receiving a much-needed pension of four dollars a month. This sum soon increased, and she was paid until her death on April 29, 1827, at age sixty-seven. She was also the first woman in American history to receive pension funds from the government.

After her death, Sampson continued to gain recognition for her bravery and independence. In Sharon, Massachusetts, a street was named after her. A warship, the *Deborah Gannett,* also took her name, a symbol that it was as ready to do battle as America's first enlisted woman soldier had been.

For More Information

Cheney, Cora. *The Incredible Deborah: A Story Based on the Life of Deborah Sampson.* New York: Charles Scribner's Sons, 1967.

Felton, Harold W. *Deborah Sampson: Soldier of the Revolution.* New York: Dodd, Mead & Company, 1976.

Freeman, Lucy, and Alma Bond. *America's First Woman Warrior: The Courage of Deborah Sampson.* New York: Paragon House, 1992.

Bibliography

Bailyn, Bernard. *Faces of Revolution.* New York: Alfred A. Knopf, 1990.

Boorstin, Daniel J. *The Americans: The National Experience.* New York: Random House, 1966.

Boorstin, Daniel J. *The Discoverers: A History of Man's Search to Know His World and Himself.* New York: Random House, 1983.

Foner, Eric. *Tom Paine and Revolutionary America.* New York: Oxford University Press, 1976.

Friede, Juan, and Benjamin Keen, eds. *Bartolomé de Las Casas in History: Toward an Understanding of the Man and His Work.* Dekalb, Illinois: Northern Illinois University Press, 1971.

Galvin, John. *Three Men of Boston.* New York: Thomas Y. Crowell Co., 1976.

Hanke, Lewis. *The Spanish Struggle for Justice in the Conquest of America.* Philadelphia: University of Pennsylvania Press, 1949.

Hatch, Charles E., Jr. *Jamestown, Virginia.* National Park Service Historical Handbook Series No. 2. Washington, D.C.: U.S. Government Printing Office, 1957.

Johnson, Curt. *Battles of the American Revolution.* London, England: Roxbury Press, 1975.

Konig, Hans. *Columbus: His Enterprise; Exploding the Myth.* New York: Monthly Review Press, 1976, 1990.

Malone, Dumas. *Jefferson the Virginian.* Volume 1 of *Jefferson and His Time.* Boston: Little, Brown and Co., 1948.

Meade, Robert Douthat. *Patrick Henry: Patriot in the Making.* Philadelphia: J. B. Lippincott Co., 1957.

Morison, Samuel Eliot. *Admiral of the Ocean Sea: A Life of Christopher Columbus.* New York: Time Inc., 1942.

Peterson, Merrill, D., ed. *The Portable Thomas Jefferson.* New York: Viking Press, 1975.

Pohl, Frederick J. *The Viking Explorers.* New York: Thomas Y. Crowell Co., 1966.

Powe, Lucas A., Jr. *The Fourth Estate and the Constitution.* Los Angeles: University of California Press, 1991.

Raup, Henry, with Helen Rand-Parish. *The Life and Writings of Bartolomé de Las Casas.* Albuquerque: The University of New Mexico Press, 1967.

Smith, Anthony. *The Newspaper.* London, England: Thames and Hudson Ltd., 1979.

Stein, M. L. *Freedom of the Press: A Continuing Struggle.* New York: Julian Messner, 1966.

Williamson, Audrey. *Thomas Paine: His Life, Work and Times.* New York: St. Martin's Press, 1973.

Youings, Joyce, ed. *Privateering and Colonisation in the Reign of Elizabeth I.* Exeter, England: University of Exeter, 1985.

Index

Boldface indicates profiles.